SIXTH EDITION
GRAMMAR 3
IN CONTEXT

SANDRA N. ELBAUM

Australia • Brazil • Mexico • Singapore • United Kingdom • United States

Grammar in Context 3, Sixth Edition

Student Book

Sandra N. Elbaum

Publisher: Sherrise Roehr

Executive Editor: Laura Le Dréan

Development Editor: Claudi Mimó

Executive Marketing Manager: Ben Rivera

Senior Director, Production: Michael Burggren

Content Project Manager: Mark Rzeszutek

Manufacturing Planner: Mary Beth Hennebury

Interior Design: Brenda Carmichael

Compositor: SPi Global

Cover Design: Brenda Carmichael

ISBN 13: 978-1-305-07539-9

National Geographic Learning

20 Channel Center Street

Boston, Massachusetts 02210

USA

Cengage Learning is a leading provider of customized learning solutions with office locations around the globe, including Singapore, the United Kingdom, Australia, Mexico, Brazil, and Japan. Locate our local office at international.cengage.com/region

Cengage Learning products are represented in Canada by Nelson Education, Ltd.

Visit National Geographic Learning online at **ngl.cengage.com**

Visit our corporate website at **www.cengage.com**

Printed in the United States of America

Print Number: 01   Print Year: 2015

3

GRAMMAR **Passive and Active Voice**
CONTEXT **The Movies**

4

GRAMMAR **The Past Continuous**
                  The Past Perfect
                  The Past Perfect Continuous
CONTEXT **Travel by Land, Sea, and Air**

GRAMMAR **Modals and Related Expressions**
CONTEXT **Technology**

GRAMMAR **Modals in the Past**
CONTEXT **U.S. Presidents and Elections**

GRAMMAR **Adjective Clauses**
                  Descriptive Phrases
CONTEXT **Online Interactions**

8

GRAMMAR **Infinitives and Gerunds**
CONTEXT **Helping Others**

9

GRAMMAR **Adverbial Clauses and Phrases**
Sentence Connectors (Conjunctive Adverbs)
So/Such That **for Result**
CONTEXT **Coming to America**

10

GRAMMAR Noun Clauses
CONTEXT Children

11

GRAMMAR Unreal Conditionals
Wishes
CONTEXT Science or Science Fiction?

APPENDICES

GLOSSARY OF GRAMMATICAL TERMS

INDEX

ACKNOWLEDGMENTS

I am grateful to the team at National Geographic Learning/Cengage Learning for showing their faith in the *Grammar in Context* series by putting their best resources and talent into it. I would especially like to thank Laura Le Dréan for driving this series into an exciting, new direction. Her overall vision of this new edition has been a guiding light. I would also like to thank my development editor, Claudi Mimó, for managing the difficult day-to-day task of polishing and refining the manuscript toward its finished product. I would like to thank Dennis Hogan, Sherrise Roehr, and John McHugh for their ongoing support of *Grammar in Context* through its many editions.

I wish to acknowledge the immigrants, refugees, and international students I have known, both as a teacher and as a volunteer with refugee agencies. These people have increased my understanding of my own language and taught me to see life from another point of view. By sharing their observations, questions, and life stories, they have enriched my life enormously.

This new edition is dedicated to the millions of displaced people in the world. The United States is the new home of many refugees, who survived unspeakable hardships in Burundi, Rwanda, Iraq, Sudan, Burma, Bhutan, and other countries. Their resiliency in starting a new life and learning a new language is a tribute to the human spirit.
—*Sandra N. Elbaum*

Heinle would like to thank the following people for their contributions:

Dorothy S. Avondstondt, Miami Dade College—Wolfson Campus;

Pamela Ardizzone, Rhode Island College;

Patricia Bennett, Grossmont College;

Mariusz Bojarczuk, Bunker Hill Community College;

Rodney Borr, Glendale Community College;

Nancy Boyer, Golden West College;

Charles Brooks, Norwalk Community College;

Gabriela Cambiasso, Harold Washington College;

Julie Condon, St. Cloud State University;

Anne Damiecka, Lone Star College — CyFair;

Mohammed Debbagh, Virginia Commonwealth University;

Frank DeLeo, Broward College;

Jeffrey DiIuglio, Boston University Center for English Language and Orientation Programs;

Monique Dobbertin Cleveland, Los Angeles Pierce College;

Lindsey Donigan, Fullerton College;

Jennifer J. Evans, University of Washington;

Norm Evans, Brigham Young University—Hawaii;

David Gillham, Moraine Valley Community College;

Martin Guerra, Mountain View College;

Eric Herrera, Universidad Técnica Nacional;

Cora Higgins, Bunker Hill Community College;

Barbara Inerfeld, Rutgers University;

Barbara Jonckheere, California State University, Long Beach;

Gursharan Kandola, University of Houston;

Roni Lebrauer, Saddleback College;

Dr. Miriam Moore, Lord Fairfax Community College;

Karen Newbrun Einstein, Santa Rosa Junior College;

Stephanie Ngom, Boston University Center for English Language and Orientation Programs;

Charl Norloff, International English Center, University of Colorado Boulder;

Gabriella Nuttall, Sacramento City College;

Fernanda Ortiz, University of Arizona;

Dilcia Perez, Los Angeles City College;

Stephen Peridore, College of Southern Nevada;

Tiffany Probasco, Bunker Hill Community College;

Elizabeth Seabury, Bunker Hill Community College;

Natalia Schroeder, Long Beach City College;

Maria Spelleri, State College of Florida, Manatee-Sarasota;

Susan Stern, Irvine Valley College;

Vincent Tran, University of Houston;

Karen Vlaskamp, Northern Virginia Community College—Annandale;

Christie Ward, Intensive English Language Program, Central Connecticut State University;

Colin Ward, Lone Star College—North Harris;

Laurie A. Weinberg, J. Sargeant Reynolds Community College

My parents immigrated to the United States from Poland and learned English as a second language as adults. My sisters and I were born in the United States. My parents spoke Yiddish to us; we answered in English. In that process, my parents' English improved immeasurably. Such is the case with many immigrant parents whose children are fluent in English. They usually learn English much faster than others; they hear the language in natural ways, in the context of daily life.

Learning a language in context, whether it be from the home, from work, or from a textbook, cannot be overestimated. The challenge for me has been to find a variety of high-interest topics to engage the adult language learner. I was thrilled to work on this new edition of *Grammar in Context* for National Geographic Learning. In so doing, I have been able to combine exciting new readings with captivating photos to exemplify the grammar.

I have given more than 100 workshops at ESL programs and professional conferences around the United States, where I have gotten feedback from users of previous editions of *Grammar in Context*. Some teachers have expressed concern about trying to cover long grammar lessons within a limited time. While ESL is not taught in a uniform number of hours per week, I have heeded my audiences and streamlined the series so that the grammar and practice covered is more manageable. And in response to the needs of most ESL programs, I have expanded and enriched the writing component.

Whether you are a new user of *Grammar in Context* or have used this series before, I welcome you to this new edition.

Sandra N. Elbaum

For my loves
Gentille, Chimene, Joseph, and Joy

Grammar in Context presents grammar in interesting contexts that are relevant to students' lives and then recycles the language and context throughout every activity. Learners gain knowledge and skills in both grammar structures and topic areas.

New To This Edition

NATIONAL GEOGRAPHIC PHOTOGRAPHS
introduce lesson themes and draw learners into the context.

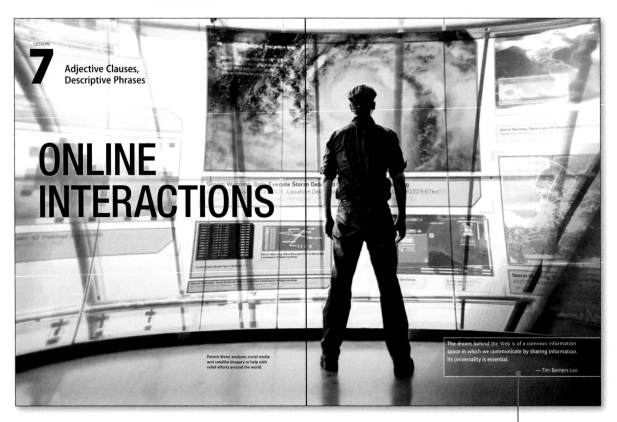

LESSON

7

Adjective Clauses, Descriptive Phrases

ONLINE INTERACTIONS

Patrick Meier analyzes social media and satellite imagery to help with relief efforts around the world.

The dream behind the Web is of a common information space in which we communicate by sharing information. Its universality is essential.

— Tim Berners-Lee

New To This Edition

EVERY LESSON OPENER
includes a quote from an artist, scientist, author, or thinker that helps students connect to the theme.

NEW AND UPDATED READINGS, many with National Geographic content, introduce the target grammar in context and provide the springboard for practice.

NEW LISTENING EXERCISES reinforce the grammar through natural spoken English.

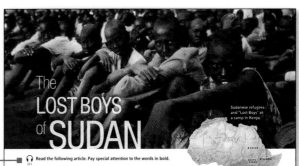

The
LOST BOYS
of SUDAN

Sudanese refugees and "Lost Boys" at a camp in Kenya.

🎧 Read the following article. Pay special attention to the words in bold.

Besides immigrants, the United States takes in thousands of refugees a year. The Lost Boys of Sudan were children, living in southern Sudan in the late 1980s, their long and difficult journey to the United States began. **While** these young boys were in the field taking care of their cattle,[3] their villages were attacked. These children, mostly boys between the ages of 4 and 12, ran for their lives. **For** three months, they walked hundreds of miles **until** they reached Ethiopia. They survived by eating leaves, roots, and wild fruit.

During that time, many died of starvation[4] and disease or were eaten by wild animals. Those who reached Ethiopia stayed in refugee camps **until** 1991, when a war started in Ethiopia and the camps were closed. They ran again, back to Sudan and then to Kenya, where they stayed in refugee camps **for** almost ten years. Of the approximately 27,000 boys who fled Sudan, only 11,000 survived.

During their time in the refugee camp, they got some schooling and learned basic English. In 1999, the United Nations and the U.S. government agreed to resettle 3,800 Lost Boys in the United States.

When they arrived in the United States, many challenges awaited them. They had to learn a completely new way of life. Many things were new

for them: apartment living in a big city, strange foods, new technologies, and much more. **When** they saw an American supermarket for the first time, they were amazed by the amount of food. One boy was so surprised by the quantity of food in a supermarket that he asked if it was the palace of the king.

Agencies helped the Lost Boys with money for food and rent for a short time **until** they found jobs. **While** they were working, most of them enrolled in ESL classes. Now men, many have graduated from college and have started projects to help their villages back home. Peter Magai Bul, of Chicago, helped establish a school in his hometown. **While** he was studying for his college degree, Peter helped to raise funds for this school, which is currently educating over five hundred South Sudan students.

Although their future in the United States looks bright, **whenever** they think about their homeland, they are sad because so many of their family members and friends have died.

---
[3] *cattle:* cows, bulls, and oxen as a group
[4] *starvation:* the state of having no food, being extremely hungry

Connecting Ideas **257**

COMPREHENSION CHECK Based on the reading, tell if the statement is true (**T**) or false (**F**).

1. The Lost Boys were in a refugee camp in Ethiopia until they came to the U.S.
2. When their villages were attacked, the Lost Boys ran back home.
3. Some of the Lost Boys are helping their people in South Sudan.

9.3 Time Clauses and Phrases

Examples	Explanation
When their villages were attacked, the Lost Boys ran. Some young men will help their people back home **when** they finish college.	*When* means "at that time" or "immediately after that time." In a future sentence, we use the present in the time clause.
Whenever they think about their country, they are sad. **Whenever** they tell their story, Americans are amazed.	*Whenever* means "any time" or "every time."
They walked **until** they reached Ethiopia. They received money for a short time **until** they got jobs.	*Until* means "up to that time."
Peter has been a student **since** he came to the U.S. He has been working **(ever) since** he arrived in the U.S.	*Since* or *ever since* means "from that time in the past to the present." We use the present perfect or present perfect continuous in the main clause.
While they were taking care of their cattle, their villages were bombed. **As** they were coming to the U.S., they were thinking about their new life ahead.	We use *while* or *as* with a continuous action.
They walked **for** three months. They stayed in a refugee camp **for** many years.	We use *for* with an amount of time.
During the day, they walked. **During** their time in the refugee camp, they studied English.	We use *during* with a time such as *the day* or *summer*, or with a specific time period (*their time in Ethiopia, the month of August*) or an event (*the flight to the U.S.*).

EXERCISE 6 Fill in the blanks with *since, until, while, when, as, during, for,* or *whenever*. In some cases, more than one answer is possible.

1. The Lost Boys were very young _____when_____ they left Sudan.
2. The Lost Boys walked _____ many months.
3. _____ their march to Ethiopia, many of them died.
4. They lived in Ethiopia _____ about four years.

258 Lesson 9

NEW REDESIGNED GRAMMAR CHARTS offer straightforward explanations and provide contextualized clear examples of the structure.

TEST/REVIEW

Use the sentence under each blank to form a noun clause. Answers may vary.

Two years ago, when I was eighteen, I didn't know ___what to do___ with my life. I had just
　　　　　　　　　　　　　　　　　　　　　　　1. What should I do?

graduated from high school, and I couldn't decide _____
　　　　　　　　　　　　　　　　　　　　　2. Should I go to college or not?

A neighbor of mine told me _____ and decided to
　　　　　　　　　　　　　3. I had the same problem when I was your age.

go to the U.S. for a year to work as an au pair. She asked me

_____. I told her _____. She told me
4. Have you ever heard of this program?　　　　5. I haven't.

_____ and _____
6. I lived with an American family for a year.　　7. My English has improved a lot.

I asked her _____. I was surprised to find out
　　　　　8. How much will this program cost me?

_____. I asked her _____, and
9. You'll earn about $200 a week.　　　　　10. Is the work very hard?

she said _____ but _____.
　　　　11. It is.　　　12. It is very rewarding.

When I told my parents _____, they told me
　　　　　　　　　　　13. I am thinking about going to the U.S. for a year.

SUMMARY OF LESSON 10

Direct Statement or Question	Sentence with an Included Statement or Question	Explanation
She loves kids. She is patient.	I know **that she loves kids.** I'm sure **that she is patient.**	A noun clause is used as an included statement.
Is the baby sick? What does the baby need?	I don't know **if the baby is sick.** I'm not sure **what the baby needs.**	A noun clause is used as an included question.
What should I do with a crying baby? Where can I find a babysitter?	I don't know **what to do with a crying baby.** Can you tell me **where to find a babysitter?**	An infinitive can replace *should* or *can.*
You know more than you think you do. Do you have children?	Dr. Spock said, **"You know more than you think you do."** **"Do you have children?"** asked the doctor.	An exact quote is used to report what someone has said or asked.
Do your kids watch Sesame Street? I will teach my son to drive.	She asked me **if my kids watched** Sesame Street. She said **that she would teach her son to drive.**	A noun clause is used in reported
Trust yourself. Don't give the baby candy.	He told us **to trust ourselve** He told me **not to give the** candy.	

Punctuation with Noun Clauses	
I know where he lives.	Period at
Do you know where he lives?	Question noun clau
He said, "I like you."	Comma a Period be
"I like you," he said.	Quotation the final
He asked, "What do you want?"	Comma a quote. Qu
"What do you want?" he asked.	Quotation before the

PART 2 Editing Practice

Some of the shaded words and phrases have mistakes. Find the mistakes and correct them. If the shaded words are correct, write *C*.

　　　　　　　　　　　　　　　　　　　　　that
When I was fourteen years old, I told my parents ~~what~~ I wanted to work as a babysitter, but they
　　　　　　　　　　　　　　　　　　　　　　1.
　C
told me that I was too young. At that time, they told me that they will pay me $1 an hour to help
2.　3.　　　　　　　　　　　　　　　　　　　　　　　4.
with my little brother. A few times they asked me could I watch him when they went out. They
　　　　　　　　　　　　　　　　　5.
always told me call them immediately in case of a problem. They told me don't watch TV or text my
　　　　6.　　　　　　　　　　　　　　　　　　　　　7.
friends while I was working as a babysitter. They always told me that I have done a good job.
　　　　　　　　　　　　　　　　　　　　　　　　8.
When I was fifteen, I got a few more responsibilities, like preparing small meals. They always
told that I should teach my brother about good nutrition. I asked them whether I could get more
9.　10.　　　　　　　　　　　　　　　　　　　　　11.
money because I had more responsibilities, and they agreed. I asked them if I can buy something
　　　　　　　　　　　　　　　　　　　　　　　12.
new with my earnings. My parents said, "Of course."
　　　　　　　　　　　　13.
When I turned eighteen, I started working for my neighbors, who have three children. The
neighbors asked me had I gotten my driver's license yet. When I said yes, they were pleased because
　　　　　　14.　　　　　　　　　　　　　　15.
I could drive the kids to different places. I never realized how hard was it to take care of so many
　　　　　　　　　　　　　　　　　　　　　　　16.
kids. As soon as we get in the car, they ask, "Are we there yet?" They said so we should arrive
　　　　　　　　　　　　17.　　　　　　　18.
immediately. When they're thirsty, they ask me to buy them soda, but I tell them what it is healthier
　　　　　　　　　　　19.　　　　20.　　21.
to drink water. They always tell, "In our house we drink soda." I don't understand why do their
　　　　　　　　　22.　　　　　　　　　　　　　　　23.
w whether to follow the rules of my house or
24.
arents told me not to say anything about their
26.
lthy habits by example.

hildren. I hope that I will be as good a mom to
28.

when you were a child. Explain what the

ou or encouraged you when you were a child.

. Edit your writing from Part 3.

Noun Clauses　**313**

WRITING

PART 1 Editing Advice

1. Use *that* or nothing to introduce an included statement. Don't use *what.*
　　that
   I know ~~what~~ she is a good driver.

2. Use statement word order in an included question.
　　　　　　　　　　he is
   I don't know how fast ~~is he~~ driving.

3. We *say* something. We *tell* someone something.
　　told
   He ~~said~~ me that he wanted to go home.
　　said
   He ~~told~~, "I want to go home."

4. Use *tell* or *ask*, not *say*, to report an imperative. Follow *tell* and *ask* with an object.
　　　told
   Dr. Spock ~~said~~ parents to trust themselves.
　　　　　me
   My son asked ⌃ to give him the car keys.

5. Don't use *to* after *tell.*

   She told ~~to~~ me that she wanted to be a teacher.

6. Use *if* or *whether* to introduce an included yes/no question. Use statement word order.
　　　　　whether
   I don't know ⌃ teenagers understand the risks while driving.
　　　　　　　　if I should
   I can't decide ~~should~~ I let my daughter get her driver's license.

7. Follow the rule of sequence of tenses when the main verb is in the past.
　　　　　　　　　　　　　　would
   Last year my father said that he ~~will~~ teach me how to drive, but he didn't.

8. Don't use *so* before a noun clause.

   I think ~~so~~ raising children is the best job.

9. Use an infinitive to report an imperative.
　　　　　　　　　　　to
   My parents told me ⌃ drive carefully.
　　　　　　　　　　　not to
   My parents told me ~~don't~~ text while driving.

312 Lesson 10

Updated For This Edition!

ONLINE WORKBOOK

powered by MyELT provides students with additional practice of the target grammar and greater flexibility for independent study.

- Engages students and supports classroom materials by providing a variety of interactive grammar activities.

- Tracks course completion through student progress bars, giving learners a sense of personal achievement.

- Supports instructors by maximizing valuable learning time through course management resources, including scheduling and grade reporting tools.

Go to NGL.Cengage.com/MyELT

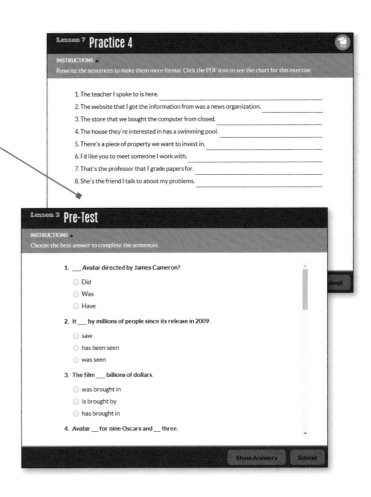

Lesson 7 Practice 4

INSTRUCTIONS
Rewrite the sentences to make them more formal. Click the PDF icon to see the chart for this exercise.

1. The teacher I spoke to is here. _____
2. The website that I got the information from was a news organization. _____
3. The store that we bought the computer from closed. _____
4. The house they're interested in has a swimming pool. _____
5. There's a piece of property we want to invest in. _____
6. I'd like you to meet someone I work with. _____
7. That's the professor that I grade papers for. _____
8. She's the friend I talk to about my problems. _____

Lesson 3 Pre-Test

INSTRUCTIONS
Choose the best answer to complete the sentences.

1. ___ *Avatar* directed by James Cameron?
   - Did
   - Was
   - Have

2. It ___ by millions of people since its release in 2009.
   - saw
   - has been seen
   - was seen

3. The film ___ billions of dollars.
   - was brought in
   - is brought by
   - has brought in

4. *Avatar* ___ for nine Oscars and ___ three.

Show Answers   Submit

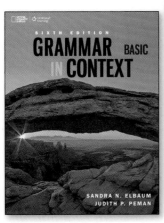

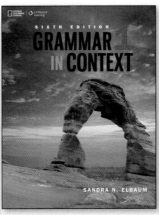

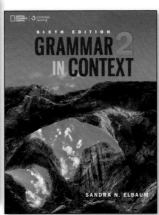

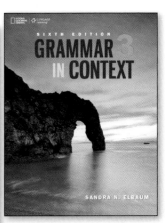

Verb Review

LANGUAGE

Ute petroglyph on Walnut
Knob, east of Blanding, Utah

The limits of my language means the limits of my world.

— Ludwig Wittgenstein

The AMAZING TIMOTHY DONER

Timothy Doner

🎧 Read the following article. Pay special attention to the words in bold.

CD 1
TR 2

Timothy Doner **looks** like an average student in his T-shirt and jeans. But there **is** something very special about him. He **speaks** 20 languages. He **doesn't speak** all of them equally well, but he **is** very comfortable in many of them. He **feels** most comfortable with Hebrew,[1] Farsi,[2] French, and Arabic. At any one time, he **is studying** three to four languages.

Videos of him **are going** around the Internet. In one video, he **is riding** in a taxi and **talking** to a Haitian taxi driver in French. **In it, he is telling** the driver that he **wants** to learn Creole, a language of Haiti. In another he **is speaking** Russian with the owners of a video store in New York, where he **lives**. In another, he **is speaking** Farsi with the owner of a bookstore. He **is asking** the Farsi speaker for more information about that language. In other videos, he **is studying** Mandarin or **discussing** the similarities between Hebrew and Arabic with native speakers of these languages. He also **speaks** Urdu,[3] Indonesian, Swahili,[4] and Ojibwe, an American Indian language.

Doner **spends** almost all his time trying to learn languages. To learn some languages, he **takes** classes. To learn others, he **studies** on his own. He always **looks** for opportunities to practice with native speakers. Sometimes he **uses** video chats to practice with native speakers in other countries. He **uses** other methods to improve his language ability: He **memorizes** the lyrics[5] of songs or **watches** movies in other languages. He really **enjoys** himself. He **thinks** that language **helps** you connect to other people. When he **speaks** another language, he **feels like** a different person.

Interestingly, he **doesn't study** Spanish. For him, Spanish **isn't** challenging enough.

---

[1] *Hebrew:* an official language spoken in the State of Israel
[2] *Farsi:* the official language of Iran
[3] *Urdu:* an official language spoken in Pakistan
[4] *Swahili:* a language spoken in Kenya and other countries of the African Great Lakes region
[5] *lyrics:* the words of a song

COMPREHENSION CHECK Based on the reading, tell if the statement is true (**T**) or false (**F**).

1. Timothy Doner always takes classes to learn foreign languages.

2. He prefers to learn challenging languages.

3. It's impossible for him to practice with native speakers in other countries.

1.1 The Present of *Be*

Examples			Explanation
I	**am**		*Be* has three forms in the present: *am, is, are.*
He She It	**is**	from New York.	
You We They	**are**		
I**'m** surprised about Timothy's abilities. Timothy**'s** an amazing person. He**'s** very intelligent.			Subject pronouns and most singular nouns can contract with a present form of *be*. *I'm, He's, She's, It's, You're, We're, They're, Timothy's*
Timothy **is** smart. Mandarin and Cantonese **are** languages of China. Haiti **is** southeast of Florida. It **is** warm in Haiti all year. I **am** hot. Let's turn on the air-conditioning. Timothy Doner **is** from New York. How old **is** Timothy now? I **am** hungry. What time **is** it in New York now? There **are** many languages in India.			We use a form of *be* with: • a description • a classification • a location • weather • reaction to weather • place of origin • age • physical states • time • *there*

Observe these seven patterns with the verb *be*:

AFFIRMATIVE STATEMENT:	Spanish **is** the official language of Colombia.
NEGATIVE STATEMENT:	It **isn't** the language of Brazil.
YES/NO QUESTION:	**Is** Spanish easy for Italians?
SHORT ANSWER:	Yes, it **is**.
WH- QUESTION:	Why **is** Spanish easy for Italians?
NEGATIVE *WH-* QUESTION:	Why **isn't** Spanish a challenge for Timothy?
SUBJECT QUESTION:	What **is** the official language of Brazil?

Language Note:

We don't make a contraction with *is* if the noun ends in *s, se, ce, ge, ze, sh, ch,* or *x*.

    French is one of Timothy's languages. (NOT: French's)

EXERCISE 1 Listen to the first part of a conversation between two students. Fill in the blanks with the words you hear.

A: What _'s your native language?_
_____
1.

B: My native _____ French.
2.

A: _____ France?
3.

B: No. _____ from France. _____ from Cameroon.
4.   5.

A: _____ Cameroon?
6.

B: _____ in Africa.
7.

A: What part of Africa _____?
8.

B: It's in West Africa.

A: _____ the only language in Cameroon?
9.

B: No, _____. _____ many languages in Cameroon, but the two official
10.   11.

languages _____ French and English.
12.

EXERCISE 2 Complete the rest of the conversation from Exercise 1 on your own. Use contractions wherever possible.

A: How many languages _____ are there _____ in Cameroon?
1.

B: There _____ about 250 languages. French _____ my official language,
2.   3.

but my home language _____ Beti.
4.

A: _____ similar to French?
5.

B: No, it _____. Not at all. They _____ completely different.
6.   7.

A: How many speakers of Beti _____ there?
8.

B: _____ about 2 million.
9.

A: Then _____ an important language in your country.
10.

B: Yes, it definitely _____.
11.

A: My roommate _____ from Nigeria. _____ near Nigeria?
12.   13.

B: Yes. Cameroon and Nigeria _____ neighbors. Nigeria _____ north of Cameroon.
14.   15.

A: I _____ interested in your country, but I _____ hungry.
16.   17.

_____ hungry?
18.

B: Yes, I _____. Let's go get something to eat. We can finish our conversation over lunch.
19.

1.2 The Simple Present

FORM

Examples	Explanation
I **like** English. You **know** Mandarin. We **come** from China. The people of Iran **speak** Farsi.	We use the base form of the verb with *I, you, we, they,* and plural subjects. Note: *People* is a plural word.
Timothy **lives** in New York. He **studies** languages. Every language **shows** something about the culture. No one in this class **speaks** Ojibwe. Timothy's family **lives** in New York.	We use the –s form with *he, she, it,* and singular subjects. We use the –s form with subjects beginning with *every* and *no.* Note: *Family* is a singular word.
Timothy **likes to learn** languages.	We can follow the main verb with an infinitive.

Observe these seven patterns with the base form:	
AFFIRMATIVE STATEMENT:	You **speak** Urdu.
NEGATIVE STATEMENT:	You **don't speak** Hindi.
YES/NO QUESTION:	**Do** you **speak** Farsi?
SHORT ANSWER:	Yes, I **do**.
WH- QUESTION:	Where **do** you **speak** Urdu?
NEGATIVE *WH-* QUESTION:	Why **don't** you **speak** Hindi?
SUBJECT QUESTION:	How many people **speak** Hindi?

Observe these seven patterns with the -s form:	
AFFIRMATIVE STATEMENT:	Timothy **studies** Farsi.
NEGATIVE STATEMENT:	He **doesn't study** Spanish.
YES/NO QUESTION:	**Does** he **study** French?
SHORT ANSWER:	Yes, he **does**.
WH- QUESTION:	Where **does** he **study** French?
NEGATIVE *WH-* QUESTION:	Why **doesn't** he **study** Spanish?
SUBJECT QUESTION:	Who **studies** Spanish?

Language Notes:

1. *Have* has an irregular –s form:

    I **have** a language dictionary. Timothy **has** many language dictionaries.

2. The –s form of *go* is *goes.*

    We **go** to college. My sister **goes** to high school.

3. The –s form of *do* is *does.* The pronunciation is /dʌs/.

    You **do** your homework at home. She **does** her homework at the library.

4. When we ask questions about *meaning, spelling, cost,* and *take* + time, we use normal question word order.

    What **does** "challenge" **mean**?
    How **do** you **say** "challenge" in your language?
    How **do** you **spell** "challenge"?
    How much **does** a dictionary app **cost**?
    How long **does** it **take** to learn another language?

USE

Examples	Explanation
Timothy **speaks** 20 languages. He **loves** languages, but he **doesn't like** math.	We use the simple present with facts, general truths, habits, and customs.
Timothy **often** practices with native speakers. He **always** tries to learn new things. Does he **ever** use videos? **How often** does he use a dictionary?	We use the simple present with regular activities and repeated actions.

Language Notes:

1. The frequency adverbs are *always, almost always, usually, generally, frequently, sometimes, occasionally, seldom, rarely, hardly ever, almost never, not ever,* and *never.* Frequency adverbs usually come after the verb *be* and before other verbs.

    Timothy is **always** interested in languages.

    He **sometimes** finds native speakers to talk to.

2. We can put *sometimes* at the beginning of the sentence too.

    Sometimes he finds native speakers to talk to.

3. *Seldom, rarely, hardly ever,* and *almost never* have the same meaning. *Seldom* and *rarely* are more formal. Generally, we use *hardly ever* and *almost never* in conversational English and informal writing.

    Do you **ever** speak English with your parents?

    No, I **almost never** do. OR I **hardly ever** do.

EXERCISE 3 Use the underlined verbs to help you complete the sentences.

1. Timothy <u>lives</u> in New York. ___Does he live___ with his parents?

2. He <u>speaks</u> French. He ___doesn't speak___ Spanish.

3. Timothy <u>speaks</u> a lot of languages. _____ Urdu? Yes, he _____.

4. He <u>memorizes</u> songs. _____ poems too?

5. He _____ video chat. Does he <u>use</u> other methods too? Yes, he _____.

6. He <u>takes</u> classes. _____ Farsi classes?

7. New York _____ people from all over the world. _____ New York <u>have</u> people

    from Indonesia? Yes it _____.

8. Some languages _____ accent marks. _____ Hebrew <u>have</u> accent marks?

9. Timothy <u>feels</u> different when he speaks another language. Why _____ different?

10. He's interested in Creole, but he _____ interested in Spanish. Why _____

    interested in Spanish?

11. Farsi <u>challenges</u> him. Spanish _____ him.

12. He _____ comfortable in Arabic. _____ <u>feel</u> comfortable in Hebrew?

    Yes, he _____ .

13. His parents <u>speak</u> English. _____ Hebrew?

14. He <u>is</u> very good at languages. He _____ so good at math.

15. He <u>studies</u> languages every day. _____ from books?

    Yes, he _____ .

16. He <u>practices</u> with native speakers. How _____ with native speakers?

17. Not many people <u>speak</u> Ojibwe. How many people in the U.S. _____ Ojibwe?

EXERCISE 4 Fill in the blanks to complete the conversation. Use the words given.

A: Hi. My name's Bai. I'm from China.

B: Hi Bai. My name's Khalid. ___<u>Do you speak</u>___ Chinese?
    1. you/speak

A: Well, a lot of people _____ our language is Chinese. But there are several dialects, or
    2. say

    forms, of Chinese. I _____ Mandarin. China _____ over 1 billion people,
    3. speak   4. have

    and most people _____ Mandarin, but not everyone does. Mandarin
    5. speak

    _____ over 800 million speakers. What about you?
    6. have

B: I speak Farsi. _____ anything about my language?
    7. you/know

A: No, I _____ . Who _____ Farsi?
    8.   9. speak

B: People in Iran do. We sometimes _____ the language "Persian."
    10. call

A: What alphabet _____ ?
    11. you/use

B: We _____ the Arabic alphabet, with some differences. We _____ from
    12.   13. write

    right to left. _____ my writing?
    14. you/want/see

A: Yes, I _____ .
    15.

B: تصویر، I want to see your writing too.

A: Here's an example of my writing. 書

B: How many letters _____ ?
    16. Chinese/have

continued

A: Chinese _____ letters. It _____ characters. Each character

_____ a word or a syllable.

19. represent

B: Wow. It _____ like a hard language.

20. seem

A: Well, it isn't hard to speak it. But it _____ a long time to learn to read and write well.

21. take

B: It _____ so beautiful.

22. look

A: Your writing _____ beautiful too. And interesting.

23. look

EXERCISE 5 About You Tell if the statement is true or false for you. If the statement is not true for you, correct it. Then work with a partner and ask him or her about these statements.

1. I'm from Mexico. F

    A: I'm not from Mexico. I'm from Ecuador. Are you from Mexico?

    B: No, I'm not.

    A: Where are you from?

    B: I'm from the Philippines.

2. I speak English with my friends from my country.

3. I speak English with my family.

4. I want to learn another language (besides English).

5. I am interested in seeing Timothy Doner's videos.

6. My favorite songs are in my language.

7. Most people in my country study English.

8. Spanish is my native language.

9. I'm interested in linguistics.

10. I use video chat to communicate with my friends and family.

11. I know more than two languages.

EXERCISE 6 Read the conversation between two new students. Fill in the blanks by using the words given and context clues.

A: Hi. My name's Marco. I come from Brazil. What _'s_ your name and where _are you from_ ?

1.   2. you

B: My name's Ly. I'm from Vietnam.

A: How _____ Ly?

3. spell

B: It's very simple: L-Y. _____ Spanish?

4.

A: No. I don't speak Spanish. Spanish _____ the official language of most countries in
5.

South America. But Brazilians _____ Portuguese. What about you?
6.

B: Vietnamese _____ my native language.
7.

A: I _____ anything about Vietnamese. _____ the same
8. not/know   9. Vietnamese/use

alphabet as English?

B: Yes, it _____ . But we use many accent marks on our words. Look. Here's a text message I
10.

have in Vietnamese from my sister. Bạn đang ở đâu? _____ all the extra marks we use on
11. you/see

our letters?

A: Yes, I _____ . Wow! It _____ very complicated. _____
12.   13. look   14.

similar to Chinese?

B: Not at all. But there's one similarity: both Chinese and Vietnamese are tonal languages.

A: What _____ ?
15. mean/"tonal"

B: It _____ the tone affects the meaning. There _____ six tones in
16. mean   17.

Vietnamese. For example, "ma" _____ six different things, depending on the tone.
18. mean

continued

Terraced rice fields in Vietnam

EXERCISE 8 Listen to the first part of a conversation between two students. Fill in the blanks with the words you hear.

A: Look at those people over there. It looks like _they're talking_ with their hands.
1.

Why _____ that?
2.

B: Oh. That's American Sign Language, or ASL.

A: What's that?

B: It's the language of deaf people or people who can't hear well.

A: _____ each word?
3.

B: No. They _____ symbols. Each symbol is a whole word. But sometimes they have to spell
4.

a word, such as a name.

A: How do you know so much about it?

B: I have a nephew who's deaf. _____ to learn ASL because I want to communicate
5.

with him.

A: Where _____ it?
6.

B: At a community college near my house.

EXERCISE 9 Complete the rest of the conversation from Exercise 8 using the present continuous form of one of the verbs from the box below. Use contractions wherever possible.

learn	get	take✓	knit	wear

B: I <u>'m taking</u> sign language classes with my sister and her husband. Like any new language, it takes
        1.

time and practice. We _____ better every day.
               2.

A: How old is your nephew?

B: He's three years old.

A: That's pretty young to learn sign language.

B: No, it isn't. He _____ it very quickly, more quickly than we are! Do you want to see a
             3.

picture of him?

A: He's so cute. He _____ an adorable hat.
               4.

B: It's from me. I knit. In fact, I _____ a sweater for him now.
             5.

EXERCISE 10 About You Tell if the statement is true or false for you. If the statement is not true for you, correct it. Then work with a partner and ask your partner about these statements.

1. I'm forgetting words in my first language. F
   A: I'm not forgetting words in my first language. Are you forgetting words in your first language?
   B: No, I'm not. But my younger sister is.
   A: Why is she forgetting words?
   B: She's in first grade and all her friends speak English.

2. I'm studying another language (besides English).

3. I'm beginning to mix English with my native language.

4. I'm living with my family.

EXERCISE 11 About You Write sentences to tell about something you are learning at this time in your life.

1. <u>I'm learning to budget my time better.</u>

2. _____

3. _____

4. _____

1.4 The Present Continuous vs. The Simple Present—Action and Nonaction Verbs

Examples	Explanation
You don't have to speak so loud. I **hear** you. Mandarin now **has** more than 800 million speakers. I **know** something about Farsi.	Some verbs are nonaction verbs. They describe a state, condition, or feeling, not an action. These verbs don't use the present continuous form even when we talk about now. NOT: Mandarin *is now having* more than 800 million speakers.
I **am listening** to a language video. I **hear** some unusual sounds.	*Listen* is an action verb. *Hear* is a nonaction verb.
We **are looking** at a video. We **see** Timothy in a taxi.	*Look* is an action verb. *See* is a nonaction verb.
I'**m thinking about** a major in linguistics. I **think (that)** linguistics is interesting.	*Think about* or *of* is an action verb. *Think (that)* is a nonaction verb.
My mom **is having** a hard time with English. English **has** many irregular verbs in the past. Marco isn't in class today. He **has** a cold.	*Have*, when it means *experience*, is an action verb. *Have* for possession, relationship, or illness is a nonaction verb.
You **are looking** at the video online.	Some verbs can describe either a sense perception or an action: *look, smell, taste, sound, feel.*
You **look** very interested in that video. Timothy Doner **looks like** an average student.	When these verbs describe a sense perception, an adjective or the word *like* usually follows.

Language Notes:

1. Some common nonaction verbs are:
   - Sense perception verbs: *smell, taste, feel, look, sound, appear*
   - Feelings and desires: *like, dislike, love, hate, hope, want, need, prefer, agree, disagree, care (about), expect, matter*
   - Mental states: *believe, know, hear, see, notice, understand, remember, think (that), suppose, recognize*
   - Others: *mean, cost, spell, weigh*

2. When *see* means *have a relationship with* (personal or professional), it can be an action verb.
   I'**m seeing** someone new. (I'm dating someone new.)
   I'**m seeing** an ASL specialist for lessons on signing.

3. Native speakers sometimes use *hope, understand,* and *think* as action verbs.
   I'**m hoping** to become an English major.
   If I'**m understanding** you correctly, you're afraid of making a mistake.
   I'**m thinking** that I need to practice English more. (This use of the present continuous often means *I'm beginning to think . . .*)

EXERCISE 12 Fill in the blanks with the present simple or present continuous to complete the conversation. In some cases, the verb is provided for you. In other cases, use context clues to find the verb.

A: What ___are you looking___ at?
   ___1.___

B: I'm looking at a video of Timothy Doner. Listen!

A: What language _____? I _____ it.
   ___2.___   ___3. not/recognize___

_____ it?
___4. you/understand___

B: Of course. He's speaking my language, Russian! I _____ this for the second time
   ___5. watch___

now. I _____ very carefully now and I _____ a few small
   ___6. listen___   ___7. hear___

mistakes, but he _____ almost like a native Russian. And he _____ so
   ___8. sound___   ___9. know___

much slang. He even _____ like a Russian using Russian gestures.
   ___10. look___

A: Who _____ to? And what _____ about?
   ___11. he/talk___   ___12. they/talk___

B: He _____ to the owners of a Russian video store. They _____
   ___13.___   ___14. introduce___

themselves. The Russians _____ surprised to hear an American speak their language so well.
   ___15. look___

A: Learning so many languages _____ time. I wonder if he has any fun in his life.
   ___16. take___

B: He _____ languages, and he _____ a great time. Listen.
   ___17. love___   ___18. have___

He _____ and _____ with the Russians.
   ___19. laugh___   ___20. joke___

A: I _____ that he's amazing. Is he good in other subjects too?
   ___21. think___

B: He says he _____ math.
   ___22. not/like___

A: What _____ to do with so many languages?
   ___23. he/plan___

B: He _____ of becoming a linguist.
   ___24. think___

A: I _____ that's a perfect profession for him.
   ___25. think___

EXERCISE 13 About You Write statements about language and culture.

1. I think that ___it's important to be bilingual._____

2. I think that _____

3. I now know that _____

Abamu Degio (left) watches a recording of herself singing a traditional Koro song with Anthony Degio (center) and K. David Harrison (right), who works for the Living Tongues Institute.

The ENDURING⁶ VOICES PROJECT

 Read the following article. Pay special attention to the words in bold.

CD 1
TR 5

You probably know that there are endangered animals and plants. These are living things that are disappearing. Some animals, like dinosaurs, are already extinct.⁷ And many more living things **are going to become** extinct. But do you know that many languages are also disappearing? Every year, several languages go extinct. Today there are more than 7,000 languages. By the year 2100, more than half of these languages **will** probably **disappear**. When the last speaker of a language dies, the world loses the knowledge contained in that language.

Some languages have a lot of speakers. Mandarin, for example, now has 845 million speakers. English has 360 million first-language speakers. The Ojibwe language of Native Americans has about 5,000 speakers. Most of them are older than 65. Other languages have only 1 or 2 speakers. If nothing changes, these languages **will die** when the last speaker dies. The disappearance of languages is happening all over the world.

Why do some languages disappear? Languages like English, Mandarin, Russian, Arabic, Hindi, and Spanish dominate world communication and business. In a part of Russia where the Tofa language exists, parents want their children to learn Russian because it **will permit** greater education and success. Right now there are very few speakers of Tofa. How **will** this language **survive? Is** it **going to be** completely lost?

In the project Enduring Voices, linguists visit areas around the world to record native speakers of endangered languages. They are helping many communities preserve their languages online. If you visit the Enduring Voices project online, you **will be able to** hear the sounds of these endangered languages. Even when the last speaker dies, these languages **won't be** lost.

Why are linguists doing this project? Language tells us a lot about a culture. You probably have words in your native language that have no exact translation in English. These special words say something about your culture. When a language dies, an entire culture disappears with it. Seri is a language of Mexico. According to a Seri elder, if one child learns to speak Seri and another child learns to speak Spanish, they **will be** different people.

---

⁶ *enduring:* long lasting
⁷ *extinct:* no longer in existence

COMPREHENSION CHECK Based on the reading, tell if the statement is true (**T**) or false (**F**).

1. One language dies each day.

2. Hindi is an important language in business.

3. Technology is helping to preserve dying languages.

1.5 The Future—Form

Examples	Explanation
Many languages **will disappear**. English **will not disappear**. Some languages **won't survive**.	We can use *will* + the base form for the future. The contraction for *will not* is *won't*.
Some living things **are going to become** extinct. The Tofa language **is** probably **going to disappear**.	We can use *be going to* + the base form for the future.
You **are going to hear** some strange sounds if you **visit** the Enduring Voices website. When the last speaker of Tofa **dies**, the language **will die**.	Some future sentences have two clauses: a main clause and an *if* or time clause. We use the future only in the main clause. It doesn't matter which clause comes first.

Observe these seven patterns with *will*:

AFFIRMATIVE STATEMENT:	Some languages **will disappear**.
NEGATIVE STATEMENT:	My language **won't disappear**.
YES/NO QUESTION:	**Will** English **disappear** soon?
SHORT ANSWER:	No, it **won't**.
WH- QUESTION:	Why **will** some languages **disappear**?
NEGATIVE *WH-* QUESTION:	Why **won't** English **disappear** soon?
SUBJECT QUESTION:	Which languages **will disappear** soon?

Observe these seven patterns with *be going to*:

AFFIRMATIVE STATEMENT:	We **are going to study** English.
NEGATIVE STATEMENT:	We **aren't going to study** Mandarin.
YES/NO QUESTION:	**Are** we **going to study** French?
SHORT ANSWER:	No, we **aren't**.
WH- QUESTION:	Why **are** we **going to study** English?
NEGATIVE *WH-* QUESTION:	Why **aren't** we **going to study** French?
SUBJECT QUESTION:	Who **is going to study** French?

Language Notes:

1. You can contract pronouns with *will: I'll, you'll, he'll, she'll, it'll, we'll, they'll*. In conversation, you also hear contractions with some question words: *who'll, where'll*, etc.

2. In conversational English and informal writing, such as texting, *going to* for future is often pronounced and written "gonna."

2 The Present Perfect and the Present Perfect Continuous

RISK

A man stands at the edge of Victoria Falls, in Africa.

Risks must be taken because the greatest hazard in life is to risk nothing.

— Leo Buscaglia

EXERCISE 3 Listen to the story and fill in the blanks with the missing words.

CD 1
TR 10

I _'ve never thought_ of myself as a risk taker. I _____ (2.) to make safe

decisions in my life. I _____ (3.) out of an airplane.

I _____ (4.) a mountain. These things _____ (5.) to

me. But then a new friend told me, "I really admire you. You _____ (6.) a lot of risks in

your life." "No, I _____ (7.) ," I replied. "What _____ (8.) that

involves risk?" I _____ (9.) that risk meant doing something dangerous. My

friend answered, "Risk means facing an unknown future. You _____ (10.) up your past

life to enter a completely different world."

EXERCISE 4 Below is a continuation of the story from Exercise 3. Use the words given to form the present perfect. Use contractions wherever possible. Add the adverb given.

My friend asked, "How long ___ have you been ___ in this country? Less than a year, right?
                                          1. you/be

_____ about how many risks you _____ since you left your
        2. you/ever/think   **3.** take

country?"

I started to think about my friend's comments, and I realized that maybe she's right. First, of course,

I _____ learn another language. Even though I studied English in my country, I never had to
        4. have to

communicate with native speakers. My English _____ a lot. But talking
                                                        5. already/improve

with strangers _____ scary for me, especially by telephone.
                      6. always/be

I _____ what Americans _____ to me,
        7. not/always/understand   **8.** say

but most people _____ very patient with me.
                      9. usually/be

Back home, I lived with my mother. She always cooked for my family and me. But here I _____
                                                                                              10. have to

be independent. I _____ to pay bills, rent an apartment, and make my own decisions. I
                        11. learn

_____ to cook for myself.
        12. even/learn

In my hometown I walked or took the bus. But here the bus system isn't very good, and almost everyone

drives. So I took driving lessons, got my license, and bought a used car. I used to be afraid of driving, but

little by little I _____ experience and driving _____ easier for me.
                        13. gain   **14.** get

Since my friend pointed these things out to me, I realized that I _____ a
                                                                          15. already/make

lot of changes, and each change _____ some risk.
                                        16. involve

2.4 The Present Perfect — Overview of Uses

Examples	Explanation
Paul Nicklen **has been** a photojournalist since 1995. He **has photographed** underwater animals for a long time.	The action started in the past and **continues** to the present.
Paul Nicklen **has gone** to the Arctic many times. He **has received** many awards for his photographs.	The action **repeats** during a period of time from the past to the present.
Recently scientists **have begun** to study brain chemicals. **Have** you ever **done** anything dangerous?	The action occurred at an **indefinite time** in the past. It still has importance to a present situation or discussion.

EXERCISE 5 Fill in the blanks with the present perfect form of the verb given to complete this paragraph.

Nik Wallenda comes from a long line of risk takers. He doesn't take risks for science or nature. He's a

circus performer; he walks a tightrope. His family, known as the Flying Wallendas, ___has been___ in this
1. be

business for seven generations. Nik started walking on a tightrope when he was two years old. Over time,

he _____ famous for some amazing acts of danger. He _____
2. become   3. walk

across Niagara Falls and over a deep canyon near the Grand Canyon on a tightrope. So far, he

_____ a serious accident.
4. never/have

Nik Wallenda walks the tightrope across the Grand Canyon.

Two climbers on their way to the summit of Mount Everest

Climbing
MOUNT EVEREST

🎧 Read the following article. Pay special attention to the words in bold.

CD 1
TR 11

Have you **ever thought** about taking a risk for the fun or excitement of it? Mount Everest, the tallest mountain in the world, **has always been** a symbol of man's greatest challenge. Located between China and Nepal, Mount Everest **has attracted** mountain climbers from all over the world. In 1953, Edmund Hillary, from New Zealand, and his Nepalese guide, Sherpa Tenzing Norgay, were the first to reach the top. Since then, about 4,000 people **have reached** the summit.[5] But more than 200 climbers **have died** while trying.

Between 1953 and 1963, only 6 people successfully climbed to the top. But things **have changed** a lot in recent years. In 2012 alone, 500 people made it to the top.

What **has changed**? Why **has** the number of climbers **increased** so much **recently**? One reason is that there are more companies leading expeditions.[6] Now 90% of climbers use expedition companies. A climber pays about $100,000 to go up the mountain with a guide. But these guided expeditions **have attracted** a lot of inexperienced climbers. And the

continued

---

5 *summit:* the top of a mountain
6 *expedition:* a group journey organized for a specific purpose

crowds[7] **have made** it even more dangerous to make the climb. Danuru Sherpa, who **has lead** 14 expeditions, **has dragged** at least five people off the mountain to save their lives. Some clients don't respect the knowledge and experience of the guides and die as a result.

Has technology **come** to Everest **yet**? Yes, it **has**. As a result, more accurate[8] information about weather conditions at the summit **has made** it easier for expeditions to choose the safest time to make it to the top.

How **has** all of this traffic **affected** Mt. Everest? Lately the mountain **has become** dirty as climbers leave behind garbage and equipment they no longer need. There is now a pollution control committee and lately conditions **have improved** at the Base Camp,[9] but higher on the mountain, the garbage accumulates. One organization, Eco Everest Expedition, **has tried** to clean up the garbage. They started in 2008 and so far they've **collected** over 13 tons of garbage.

According to one climber, Mark Jenkins, "It's not simply about reaching the summit but about showing respect for the mountain and enjoying the journey."

---

[7] *crowd:* a large group of people close together
[8] *accurate:* exact, correct
[9] *base camp:* the main place from which expeditions set out

COMPREHENSION CHECK   Based on the reading, tell if the statement is true (**T**) or false (**F**).

1. Most climbers on Mt. Everest have successfully reached the summit.

2. Today, most climbers use a guide.

3. The number of climbers has gone down over the years.

2.5 The Present Perfect with Indefinite Past Time —Overview

We use the present perfect for an action that occurred at an indefinite time in the past. This action still has importance to a present situation or discussion.

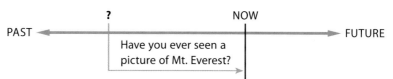

Examples	Explanation
Have you *ever* **taken** a big risk? No, I *never* **have**.	We can use *ever* and *never* to show any time in the past. The time is indefinite.
I've *always* **wanted** to climb a mountain. I've *never* **heard** of Edmund Hillary.	We use *always* and *never* to connect the past to the present.
Has technology **come** to Everest *yet*? Yes, it *already* **has**.	We use *yet* to ask about an expected action. We use *already* with affirmative statements to show that an expected action happened.
Scientists **have** *recently* **begun** to study risk. *Lately* Mt. Everest **has become** dirty. The expedition **has** *just* **reached** the top.	We use *recently, lately,* and *just* with recent past actions.
Everest **has attracted** climbers from all over the world. Over 4,000 people **have** successfully **climbed** Everest.	Some present perfect sentences have no mention of time. The use of the present perfect indicates that the time is indefinite past.

Two climbers ascend this sea cliff in
Maine's Acadia National Park

EXERCISE 6 Fill in the blanks with the words that you hear.

CD 1
TR 12

A: I _'ve thought_____ about mountain climbing. I'd love to climb Mt. Everest. It sounds so exciting.
          1.

B: I _____ that it's very dangerous. Many people _____ while trying
          2.   **3.**

to reach the top. _____ any experience in mountain climbing?
                                    4.

A: No. I _____ a course in rock climbing at my gym.
                      5.

B: I _____ interested in risky activities. But I'm happy reading adventure books and
              6.

seeing exciting movies. In fact, I _____ a book about an expedition
                                                              7.

on Mt. Everest. It's called *Into Thin Air*. _____ of it?
                                                                    8.

A: No, I _____ . Is it new?
                    9.

B: No. It came out in the 1990s. But it's very exciting. I think you'd like it.

A: Does it have a good ending?

B: I _____ it yet. But I know that a lot of people died on this
                              10.

expedition. Do you want to borrow it when I'm finished?

A: Lately I _____ much time to read because of school. But thanks for the offer.
                      11.

EXERCISE 7 Use the words given to fill in the blanks.

A: I <u>'ve just seen</u> an amazing video of Nik Wallenda. _____ him?
      1. just/see   **2.** you/ever/hear of

B: No, I _____. Who is he?
             3. never

A: He's a tightrope walker. He's from a famous family of circus performers. Take a look at this video online.

   You can see what he does.

B: Wow! That looks terrific. I'd love to see a circus.

A: There's a circus in town. Do you want to go? I _____ two tickets for
                                                      4. already/buy

   my girlfriend and me. But I think I can get another one.

B: I'd love to go. I _____ to the circus before. Have you?
                       5. never/be

A: Yes. But not since I was a child. I _____ one recently.
                                          6. not/see

B: What kind of circus is it? Is one of the Wallendas going to be there?

A: No. It's a circus from China.

2.6 The Present Perfect with *Ever* and *Never*

Examples	Explanation
A: Has a climber *ever* **died** on Mt. Everest? **B:** Yes. Many climbers **have died** on Mt. Everest.	We use *ever* to ask a question about any time in the past.
A: Have you *ever* **seen** a movie about Mt. Everest? **B:** No, I never **have**.	We use *never* in a negative answer. For example: No, I never **have**. OR No, he never **has**.
A: Has Nick Wallenda **ever gone** across Niagara Falls on a tightrope? **B:** Yes, he **has**.	We can answer an *ever* question with the present perfect. The present perfect shows no reference to time. The time is indefinite.
A: Has anyone from the Wallenda family **ever had** an accident? **B:** Yes. Nik Wallenda's great-grandfather **fell** to his death in 1978 at the age of 73.	We can answer an *ever* question with the simple past. The simple past shows a definite time (*in 1978, last week, last summer, last Friday, two weeks ago,* etc.).

EXERCISE 8 Fill in the first blank with *Have you ever* and the correct form of the verb given. Then complete the rest of the conversation with the correct form of the verb given and any other words you see.

1. **A:** ___Have you ever done___ anything dangerous?

a. do

   B: Yes, I ___have___.

b.

   A: What was it?

   B: Last year I ___went___ bungee jumping over a canyon.

c. go

   A: Wow! I ___'ve never done___ anything like that in my life. And I never will!

d. never/do

2. **A:** _____ in a helicopter?

a. fly

   B: No, I _____. Have you?

b. never

   A: No, I _____. But I'd like to.

c.

3. **A:** _____ a dangerous sport?

a. play

   B: Yes, I _____.

b.

   A: Oh, really? What sport is that?

   B: When I lived in Spain, I _____ with the bulls. It's very popular in Spain.

c. run

   A: Oh, yes. I think I _____ of that.

d. hear

Bungee jumping

4. A: _____ money in business?
a. risk

B: Yes, I _____ . Ten years ago, I _____ a business.
b. c. start

A: How did that work out for you?

B: Unfortunately, I _____ a lot of money.
d. lose

5. A: _____ someone from a dangerous situation?
a. save

B: No, I _____ . But my brother _____ .
b. c.

A: Really? What did he do?

B: A few years ago, he was passing a burning building. He _____ in to save a child.
d. run

6. A: _____ money to a friend?
a. lend

B: No, I haven't. _____ you?
b.

A: Yes. One time I _____ $100 to my best friend.
c. lend

B: Did he pay you back?

A: Yes. He _____ me back two months later.
d. pay

7. A: _____ a mountain?
a. climb

B: No, I _____ . _____ you?
b. never c.

A: No. But my sister _____ Mt. McKinley last year.
d. climb

B: I _____ Mt. McKinley. Where is it?
e. never/hear of

A: It's in Alaska. It's the highest mountain in North America.

8. A: _____ a big mistake in your life?
a. make

B: Of course, I _____ . I _____ many mistakes in my life.
b. c. make

9. A: _____ a serious accident?
a. have

B: Yes, unfortunately. Three years ago, I _____ skiing. I _____
b. go c. fall

and _____ my leg.
d. break

10. A: _____ in a marathon?
a. run

B: Yes. I _____ in the New York marathon five years ago.
b. run

EXERCISE 9 [About You] Find a partner. Ask each other questions starting with *Have you ever . . .?* and the past participle of the verb given. If your partner answers *Yes, I have,* ask for more specific information.

1. *swim* across a lake

    A: Have you ever swum across a lake?

    B: Yes, I have.

    A: When did you do it?

    B: I swam across a lake when I was in high school.

2. *go* bungee jumping

3. *win* a contest or a prize

4. *be* in a car accident

5. *fly* in a helicopter

6. *break* a bone

7. *make* a big change in your life

8. *climb* a mountain

9. *lose* money in an investment

10. *risk* your safety to help someone

11. *run* a long distance

12. *play* a dangerous sport

2.7 The Present Perfect with *Yet* and *Already*

Examples	Explanation
Over 4,000 people **have *already* climbed** Mt. Everest. We **have read** about several risk takers *already*.	We use *already* in affirmative statements for an indefinite time in the past. We can put *already* at the end of the verb phrase or between the auxiliary verb and the main verb.
A: I'm planning to climb a mountain next year. **B: Have** you **begun** to train for it *yet*? **A:** Yes, I **have**. But I **haven't trained** at a high altitude *yet*.	We use *yet* or *already* to ask about an expected action.
B: Have you **bought** your equipment *already*? **A:** No, not *yet*.	We use *yet* with a negative verb. We use *not yet* for a short answer.
A: Have you **seen** the new movie *Risking it All* yet? **B:** Yes. I **saw** it last week.	If we answer a present perfect question with a definite time, we use the simple past.

Language Note:

1. Using *already* in a question shows a greater expectation that something has happened than using *yet*.

2. We often hear the simple past in questions and negatives with *yet* and in affirmative statements with *already*. There is no difference in meaning between the present perfect and the simple past.

    Have you **bought** the equipment *yet*? = **Did** you **buy** the equipment *yet*?

    No, I **haven't bought** the equipment *yet*. = No, I **didn't buy** the equipment *yet*.

    I **have bought** the equipment *already*. = I **bought** the equipment *already*.

EXERCISE 10 Fill in the blanks to complete each conversation using the correct verb form and *yet* or *already*.

1. **A:** _____Has_____ your brother come back from his skiing trip _____yet_____?

             a.   **b.**

   B: Yes. He _____came_____ back last week.

                c.

   A: Did he have a good time?

   B: He _____hasn't had_____ time to call me _____yet_____.

                d.   **e.**

2. **A:** Is that a good book?

   B: Yes, it is. It's about an expedition in South America. I haven't _____

                                                                         a.

   it _____. But when I finish it, you can have it.

     b.

   A: Wait a minute. I think I've read it _____.

                                         c.

3. **A:** I want to see the movie *Trapped on Mt. Everest* this weekend. Have you _____ it

                                                                                           a.

   _____?

     b.

   B: No, not _____.

                     c.

   A: Then let's go. I'm planning to go Friday night.

   B: Sorry. I've _____ _____ other plans for Friday. Maybe we can

                                     d.   **e.**

   make plans for the following week.

4. **A:** What are you going to do during summer vacation?

   B: I haven't _____ about it _____. It's only February. I'll think about it

                            a.   **b.**

   in April or May. What about you?

   A: I've _____ decided to go to Alaska.

                     c.

   B: You're going to love it. We _____ there a few years ago.

                                    d.

5. **A:** Let's have an adventure this summer.

   B: I _____ told you _____, I'm not interested in an adventure.

              a.   **b.**

   A: How do you know? You've never had one.

EXERCISE 11 Circle the correct words to complete this conversation between a grandmother (A) and granddaughter (B). In some cases, both answers are possible. If both answers are correct, circle both.

A: I'm planning to take a vacation next summer.

B: I see you have some information on the kitchen table. Have you (*look*/(*looked*)) at these brochures yet?
1.

A: No, not (*already/yet*). I've been so busy. I (*haven't/didn't*) had time (*already/yet*). But I've (*already/yet*)
2.   3.   4.   5.

decided that I want to have some kind of adventure.

B: Wow, Grandma. These look like exciting trips. How about this one? A kayak trip on the Mississippi River?

A: Oh. (*I've done that one already./I've already done that one.*)
6.

B: I don't remember.

A: (*I've done/I did*) it two years ago with my friend Betty.
7.

B: How about skydiving? Have you tried that (*yet/already*)?
8.

A: No. I (*never have/never had*). But it's not for me. It's a bit too risky.
9.

B: How about this one: white water rafting. It's so much fun. (*Have ever you tried/Have you ever tried*) it?
10.

A: No. I (*haven't/didn't*). (*Have/Did*) you?
11.   12.

B: Yes, I (*did/have*). Many times, in fact.
13.

A: It looks dangerous.

B: It really isn't. You wear a life jacket. And the rafting trips are rated according to difficulty. Look.

Here's an easy trip on the Colorado River. (*Have you/Did you*) seen this one yet?
14.

A: No, I (*haven't/didn't.*) It looks interesting.
15.

B: Should we fill out the application?

A: Wait a minute. I haven't made up my mind (*already/yet*).
16.

White water rafting on a river

2.8 The Present Perfect with *Lately, Recently,* and *Just*

Examples	Explanation
Lately Mt. Everest **has become** crowded. The number of climbers on Everest **has increased** *recently*. Companies **have** *recently* **begun** to collect garbage on Everest.	*Lately* and *recently* with the present perfect refer to an indefinite time in the near past. We use these words at the beginning or end of the sentence. More formally, *recently* can come between the auxiliary and the main verb.
A: **Have** you **taken** any risks *lately*? B: No, I **haven't**. A: **Has** your brother **done** anything adventurous *lately*? B: Yes. He **took** skydiving lessons last month.	Questions with *lately* and *recently* ask about an indefinite time in the near past. When the answer is *no*, we usually use the present perfect. When the answer is *yes*, we often give a definite time and use the simple past.
I've *just* **come** back from a rafting trip. I *just* **came** back from a rafting trip.	We use *just* for an action that happened close to the present. We can use either the simple past or the present perfect. The present perfect is more formal.

Language Notes:

1. In affirmative statements, *recently* or *lately* with the present perfect refers to something that happened over time (in recent weeks, in recent months, in recent years). With the simple past, *recently* usually refers to a single event.

    Mt. Everest **has had** problems with garbage *recently*. (over a period of time; in recent years)

    My cousin **climbed** Mt. Everest *recently*. (once)

2. *Lately* refers to a repeated or continuous event.

    We **have read** a lot of stories about risk *lately*.

3. Another way to show recent activity is by using *these days*.

    Everest **has become** crowded and dirty *these days*.

EXERCISE 12   Fill in the blanks with the present perfect or the simple past of the verb given.

1. **A:** ___Have you read___ any good books lately?

       a. you/read

    B: I _____ much time lately. I've been busy with schoolwork. What about you?

       b. not/have

    A: I _____ an exciting book called *The Lost City of Z*.

       c. just/finish

    Lately a lot of people _____ interested in finding this place in South America.

       d. become

2. **A:** I know you love adventure. _____ any exciting trips lately?

       a. you/take

    B: No, I _____ . Lately I _____ busy with my job. What about

       b.   **c.** be

    you? _____ anything adventurous these days?

       d. you/do

    A: No, I _____ . But my sister _____ . Last month she

       e.   **f.**

    _____ rock climbing.

       g. go

continued

3. A: Mt. Everest _____ problems with pollution. Many climbers
                         a. have

       _____ behind garbage.
          b. leave

B: _____ recently?
       c. conditions/improve

A: Yes, they _____. Recently a company _____ to pick up
              d.   **e.** start

the garbage left behind by climbers.

4. A: I _____ an article about unusual climbers on Mt. Everest.
          a. just/read

B: What do you mean?

A: It's about the first woman, the youngest person, the oldest person, etc.

B: How old was the oldest person to climb Mt. Everest?

A: The oldest was 64; the youngest was 16.

5. A: In recent years there _____ a lot of deaths and accidents on Mt. Everest.
                              a. be

B: I wonder why.

A: Lately a lot of inexperienced climbers _____ to climb the mountain.
                                    b. try

EXERCISE 13 About You Work with a partner. Ask and answer *yes/no* questions with the words given. If the answer is *yes,* ask for more specific information.

1. go swimming recently

   A: Have you gone swimming recently?

   B: Yes, I have.

   A: When did you go swimming?

   B: I went swimming yesterday.

2. see any exciting movies lately

3. take a vacation recently

4. read any good books recently

5. do anything exciting lately

6. have any adventures lately

EXERCISE 14 Fill in the blanks with the correct form of the words given. Include other words you see.

A: There's a video online about space tourism. ___Have you seen it yet___ ?

       1. you/see/it/yet

B: Yes, I have. I _____ it a few weeks ago. It was very exciting.

                2. see

_____ about going into space?

    3. you/ever/dream

A: Yes. I _____ about it lately. Maybe I'll do it someday. It sounds very exciting.

              4. think

B: _____ ?

    5. you/hear about/the cost/yet

A: No, not _____ .

                    6.

B: A ticket costs $250,000.

A: I _____ my mind.

          7. just/change

2.9 The Present Perfect with No Time Mentioned

Examples	Explanation
I**'ve made** a decision. I'm going to take skydiving lessons. I admire Paul Nicklen. He**'s worked** very hard so we can connect with the polar and marine environments.	We can use the present perfect to talk about the past without any reference to time. The time is not important or not known or imprecise. Using the present perfect, rather than the simple past, shows that the past is relevant to a present situation or discussion.

EXERCISE 15 Fill in the blanks with the present perfect using one of the words from the box. You can use the same verb more than once.

walk	win	give	entertain	photograph✓
be	attract	save	discover	experience

1. Paul Nicklen ___has photographed___ marine animals. He _____ awards for his

             a.   b.

   photographs. He _____ afraid to take risks. He _____

                    c. not   d.

   us an amazing look at underwater life.

2. Scientists _____ certain chemicals in the brain that affect risk.

              a.

3. Nik Wallenda _____ across the Niagara Falls on a tightrope. He

                a.

   _____ people with his performances.

        b.

4. Mt. Everest _____ inexperienced climbers lately. One guide, Danuru Sherpa,

              a.

   _____ the lives of at least five people.

        b.

Sylvia Earle dives to the ocean floor in one of her underwater explorations.

Exploring THE OCEAN

CD 1
TR 13

Read the following article. Pay special attention to the words in bold.

When she first explored the ocean, Sylvia Earle thought the sea was too large to suffer harm from people. But in just a few decades, many marine animal species **have disappeared** or **become** scarce.[10]

Sylvia Earle is an oceanographer, explorer, author, and lecturer. She **has taken** many risks to explore the ocean. If you put all the time she **has spent** underwater together, it adds up to more than 7,000 hours, or nearly a year of her life. So far, she **has led** over 100 expeditions. In the 1960s, she had to fight to join expeditions. Women weren't welcome. Today she fights to protect marine life.

What **has happened** to the ocean in recent years? Unfortunately, many harmful things **have happened**. For millions of years, sharks, tuna, turtles, whales, and many other large sea animals lived in the Gulf of Mexico without a problem. But by the end of the 20th century, many of these animals were starting to disappear because of overfishing.[11] Drilling[12] for oil and gas on the ocean floor **has** also **harmed** many sea animals.

Earle **has won** many awards for her work. She **has received** 26 honorary degrees from universities and **has been** on hundreds of radio and television shows. In her effort to protect the ocean, she **has lectured** in more than 90 countries and **has written** more than 200 publications. She **has** even **written** several children's books. In 1998, *Time* magazine named Earle its first Hero for the Planet.

Earle said, "As a child, I did not know that people could protect something as big as the ocean or that they could cause harm. But now we know: The ocean is in trouble, and therefore so are we."

She added, "We still have a really good chance to make things better than they are. They won't get better unless we take the action and inspire others to do the same thing. No one is without power. Everybody has the capacity to do something."

---

[10] *scarce:* not plentiful
[11] *to overfish:* fishing so much that the amount of fish available is reduced to very low levels
[12] *to drill:* to open a hole on the earth

COMPREHENSION CHECK   Based on the reading, tell if the statement is true (**T**) or false (**F**).

1. Sylvia Earle has been an oceanographer for more than 50 years.

2. Drilling for oil on the ocean floor has harmed animal life.

3. Earle's ideas about the ocean have changed over the years.

2.10 The Present Perfect with Repetition from Past to Present

We use the present perfect to talk about repetition in a time period that includes the present.

Examples	Explanation
We **have read** several articles about risk this week. Earle **has taken** several risks this year.	When we use *this week, this month, this year,* or *today* to include the present, we use the present perfect. The present perfect shows that the time period is open, and that it is possible for the action to occur again.
Earle **has written** more than 200 publications.	If there is a possibility for a number to increase, we use the present perfect. It's possible that Earle will write more books.
Sylvia Earle **has won** many awards. She **has lectured** in more than 90 countries.	We can use *a lot of, many, several,* or a number to show repetition from past to present.
So far over 4,000 people **have climbed** Mt. Everest. *Up to now,* more than 200 climbers **have died**.	*So far* and *up to now* show repetition from past to present.
How many women **have climbed** Mt. Everest? *How much* time **has** Earle **spent** under water?	To ask a question about repetition, use *how much* or *how many.*
Sylvia Earle **was** the chief scientist of a government organization from 1990 to 1992. Between 1953 and 1963, six people **reached** the top of Mt. Everest.	We use the simple past in a closed time period because the number of repetitions in this time period is final.
Karl Wallenda **performed** on a tightrope many times in his life. He died in 1978. Nik Wallenda **has performed** on a tightrope many times in his life.	If we refer to the experiences of a deceased person (Karl Wallenda), we must use the simple past because nothing more can be added to that person's experience. A living person can repeat an action or experience.

2.11 The Present Perfect with Continuation from Past to Present

Examples	Explanation
Nik Wallenda **has been** a performer *for* many years.	We use *for* to show the duration of time.
Paul Nicklen **has been** interested in sea animals *all his life*.	We can use an expression with *all* (*all his life, all day, all week*) to show duration. We don't use *for* before *all*.
I climbed mountains many years ago, but I **haven't done** it *in* a long time.	In a negative statement, we often use *in* rather than *for*.
Nik **has been** a tightrope performer *since* 1992.	We use *since* to show the starting time.
James Cameron **has been** interested in the ocean *(ever) since* he started work on the movie *Titanic*.	We use *since* or *ever since* to begin a clause that shows the start of a continuous action. The verb in the *since* clause is in the simple past.
I **have** *always* **been** interested in adventure.	*Always* with the present perfect shows the continuation of an action from the past to the present.
How long has Sylvia Earle **been** interested in the ocean?	We use *how long* to ask a question about duration.
Paul Nicklen **takes** many photographs during his expeditions. He **has taken** photographs during his expeditions.	Don't confuse the present perfect with the simple present. The simple present refers only to the present time. The present perfect connects the past to the present.

Language Notes:

1. We can use the simple past with *for* when the event started and ended in the past.

   Sylvia Earle **did** research at the University of California from 1969 to 1981. She worked there *for* 12 years.

2. We can use the simple past with *how long* when the event started and ended in the past. Compare

   How long **have** you **lived** in the U.S.? (continues to the present)

   How long **did** you **live** in your country? (completely in the past)

3. We can put *ever since* at the end of the sentence. It means "from the past time mentioned to the present."

   Paul Nicklen became interested in sea animals when he was a child, and he **has been** interested in them *ever since*.

EXERCISE 19 Fill in the blanks with the present perfect and any missing words.

1. Paul Nicklen _____has worked_____ as a photojournalist _____since_____ 1985.
                  a. work   **b.**

2. The Wallendas _____ circus performers _____
                             a. be   **b.**

   seven generations.

3. Sylvia Earle _____ a good team.
                           a. always/have

4. _____ Earle first started to explore the ocean, it _____ a lot.
           a.   **b.** change

5. In 1953, Edmund Hillary was the first person to reach the top of Mt. Everest. Many people

_____ to reach the top ever _____ .
       a. try   **b.**

6. _____ 1990, Apa Sherpa _____ Mt. Everest over 20 times.
        a.   **b.** climb

7. Ever _____ James Cameron made his first deep sea dive in 1985, he
                a.

_____ many deep sea expeditions.
      b. lead

8. How _____ _____ a movie director?
             a.   **b.** Cameron/be

EXERCISE 20 Fill in the blanks using the correct form of the words given and any missing words. In some cases, no answer is needed in the blank. If that is the case, write Ø.

A: How do you feel about risk?

B: I _'ve been_ interested in risk taking _____Ø_____ all my life.
          1. be   **2.**

A: So you _____ a lot of articles and books about risk takers.
                         3. probably/read

B: Well, yes, I have. But I _____ a lot of risks, too. I _____
                               4. take   **5.** have

three lessons in parachuting so far.

A: How long have you _____ interested in parachuting?
                               6.

B: Ever _____ I graduated from high school.
           7.

continued

A man parachuting smiles as he falls through the air.

3

Passive and Active Voice

An outdoor movie plays in front of the Brooklyn Bridge.

THE MOVIES

> Every great film should seem new every time you see it.
>
> — Roger Ebert

Angelina Jolie and Brad Pitt at the 2014 Academy Awards, in Hollywood, California.

OSCAR NIGHT IN HOLLYWOOD

🎧 **Read the following article. Pay special attention to the words in bold.**

CD 1
TR 16

The movie stars are arriving to walk the red carpet to the Dolby Theater. As they are getting out of their limousines,[1] they **are being photographed** from every angle. The women **are being interviewed** about their choice of gowns,[2] and they **are** always **told** how beautiful they look. People at home are starting to gather around their TVs to see their favorite stars. It's Oscar night in Hollywood. The Dolby Theater will fill up with more than three thousand people from the movie industry and their guests.

If you have seen this show, you know that these awards (also known as the Academy Awards) **are given** out each year in February or March. A few months before the show, the nominees[3] **are announced**. Movie critics[4] often make predictions about who will win in each category.

The awards **are presented** in twenty-four categories: best foreign film, best actor, best music, and best costume, to name a few. But the audience **is** not **given** the results quickly. In fact, the show often lasts more than two hours, with suspense[5] building until the last winner **is announced**—the Best Picture of the year.

This is how it **is done** today. But when the awards ceremony started in 1929, only fifteen awards **were presented** and the ceremony **was attended** by only 250 people. Tickets cost $10 (about $139 in today's dollars), and anyone who could afford a ticket could attend. Until 1941, the winners' names **were** already **known** before the ceremony and **published** in newspapers the night before. So there was not much suspense. But when television **was invented** and came into more and more people's homes, Oscar night started to become the spectacular show that it is today. Since 1953, Oscar night **has been televised** and **broadcast**[6] all over the world. This show **is seen** by millions of people.

---

1 *limousine:* a large, expensive car, usually with a driver
2 *gown:* a long, formal dress for women
3 *nominee:* a person recommended to receive an award
4 *movie critic:* a person who reviews and gives opinions about movies
5 *suspense:* a feeling of anxiety and tension about a future event
6 *to broadcast:* to send over the radio or the TV

COMPREHENSION CHECK Based on the reading, tell if the statement is true (**T**) or false (**F**).

1. Both the actors and the actresses are asked about their choice of clothes.
2. The number of Oscars presented has always been the same.
3. At one time, an invitation was not needed to attend the Oscar presentation.

3.1 Active and Passive Voice — Introduction

Examples	Explanation
subject verb object **Active:** The children **saw** the movie. subject verb agent **Passive:** The movie **was seen** _by_ the children.	Some sentences are in the **active voice**. The subject performs the action of the verb. Some sentences are in the **passive voice**. The subject receives the action of the verb. The passive voice is formed with _be_ + the past participle.
The dress **was designed** by Prada. The next award **will be presented** by Brad Pitt.	Sometimes the agent is used. If so, the agent follows _by_.
The actresses **are photographed** from every angle. The awards **are presented** in 24 categories.	More often, the agent is omitted.
Active: He photographed **her**. **Passive: She** was photographed by **him**.	Notice the difference in pronouns in an active sentence and a passive sentence. After _by_, the object pronoun is used.
In 1929, tickets **were** sold for $10. (simple past) Today tickets **are** not **sold**. (simple present)	The tense of the passive sentence is shown with the verb _be_. The past participle is used with every tense.

Language Notes:

1. If two verbs in the passive voice are connected with _and_, we do not repeat the verb _be_.

   The Oscar ceremony **is televised and seen** by millions of people.

2. An adverb can be placed between _be_ and the main verb.

   Before 1941, the winners' names **were _already_ known** before the ceremony.
   Today the winners **are _never_ announced** ahead of time.

Compare these patterns with the passive voice in the past.

AFFIRMATIVE STATEMENT:	The movie **was filmed** in the United States.
NEGATIVE STATEMENT:	It **wasn't filmed** in Canada.
YES/NO QUESTION:	**Was** it **filmed** in Hollywood?
SHORT ANSWER:	No, it **wasn't**.
WH- QUESTION:	When **was** it **filmed**?
NEGATIVE WH- QUESTION:	Why **wasn't** it **filmed** in Hollywood?
SUBJECT QUESTION:	Which movie **was filmed** in Canada?

WRITING

PART 1 Editing Advice

1. Use *be*, not *do,* to make negatives and questions with the passive voice.

    The movie ~~didn't~~ *wasn't* made in Hollywood.

2. Don't use the passive voice with intransitive verbs.

    The main character ~~was~~ died at the end of the movie.

3. Don't confuse the present participle with the past participle.

    Popcorn is often ~~eating~~ *eaten* during a movie.

4. Don't forget the *–d/–ed* ending for a regular past participle.

    Music was play*ed* during silent movies.   I got bore*d* during the movie and fell asleep.

5. Don't forget to use a form of *be* in a passive sentence.

    The movie *was* seen by everyone in my family.

6. Use *by* to show the agent of the action. Use an object pronoun after *by.*

    Life of Pi was directed ~~for~~ *by* Ang Lee.   *Hulk* was directed by ~~he~~ *him* too.

7. In present and past questions and negatives, use *do* when you use *get* with the passive voice.

    My favorite movie ~~wasn't~~ *didn't* get nominated.

8. Don't forget to include a verb (usually *be*) before a participle used as an adjective.

    The movie theater *is* located on the corner of Main and Elm Streets.

9. Use *be*, not *do*, with past participles used as adjectives.

    ~~Do~~ *Are* you interested in French movies?

10. Make sure you use the correct past participle in the passive voice.

    A new movie theater is being ~~build~~ *built* near my house.

11. Don't confuse participles like *interested/interesting; bored/boring,* etc.

    I fell asleep during the ~~bored~~ *boring* movie.

12. Choose active or passive carefully.

    I ~~was~~ invited friends to watch a movie with me.   Some movies should *be seen* ~~see~~ on a large screen.

PART 2 Editing Practice

Some of the shaded words and phrases have mistakes. Find the mistakes and correct them. If the shaded words are correct, write C.

        One of my favorite movies is *12 Years a Slave*. This is an amazing movie. Everyone ~~should be seen~~ *should see* it.

                                                        1.   **2.**

The first time I saw it, I wasn't very interested in it. The movie shown on my flight from my country to the
           3.   **4.**   **5.**

United States. The screen was small and I was exhaust. I was fell asleep before the movie was ended.
                                  6.   **7.**   **8.**

        A few months ago, a friend of mine invited me to his house to watch a movie. I surprised when
                                       9.   **10.**

he told me that the movie was *12 Years a Slave*. I told him that I saw part of the movie on TV, but I

never saw the ending. I asked my friend, "Was the main character died? Or was he get rescue? Just
                                     11.   **12.**   **13.**   **14.**

tell me what was happened. That's all I need to know."
            15.

        "Let's watch it," my friend said. "I know you'll like it." I was agreed to watch it with him. It's
                                                          16.

based on a true story of a black man, Solomon Northup. He lived in the North and he was free, but he
  17.   **18.**

was kidnap. He was sold into slavery in the South. He was remained a slave for 12 years. I didn't
 19.   **20.**   **21.**

know much about slavery in the U.S. and I was amazed at how horrible life was for the slaves.
                                  22.

        When I came home, I looked for more information about the movie. I looked for information on

the Internet. A lot of information can found on the film and the real person. The movie directed by
                              23.   **24.**

Steve McQueen. I wanted to find other movies directed by he too, so I googled his name. I found that
                                        25.   **26.**

he directed *Shame* and *Hunger*. He also wrote the script for these movies. However, *12 Years a Slave*
   27.   **28.**

was writing by someone else.
    29.

        12 Years a Slave was nominate for several Oscars. It won for best picture of 2013. The star did a
                        30.   **31.**

great job as Solomon, but he didn't chosen as Best Actor that year. I was disappointing.
                    32.   **33.**

        Do you interested in American history? Then this movie should be seeing.
    34.   **35.**

PART 3 Write About It

1. How are American films different from films made in your country or another country you know about? Give several examples.

2. How have movies changed over the years? Give several examples.

PART 4 Edit Your Writing

Reread the Summary of Lesson 3 and the editing advice. Edit your writing from Part 3.

4

The Past Continuous
The Past Perfect
The Past Perfect Continuous

TRAVEL BY
LAND
SEA and
AIR

Interior and exterior
perspective from a streetcar
traveling on St. Charles Avenue,
New Orleans, Louisiana.

The real voyage of discovery consists not in seeking new landscapes, but in having new eyes.

— Marcel Proust

TRAVEL BY LAND: The **LEWIS** and **CLARK** EXPEDITION

 Read the following article. Pay special attention to the words in bold.

CD 1
TR 20

Imagine a time when most people in the eastern part of the United States had no idea what was on the other side of the Mississippi River. That was the case at the beginning of the nineteenth century, when Thomas Jefferson was the third president of the United States. The nation was only eighteen years old then and had about five million people. They **were living** between the Atlantic Ocean and the Mississippi River.

President Jefferson wanted control over the Indian tribes, who were living throughout the continent. In addition, he wanted to find a land passage to the Pacific Ocean. He **was hoping** to create a country that went from sea to sea.

Meriwether Lewis **was working** as an aide to the president. Jefferson appointed[1] Lewis and his friend William Clark to lead a dangerous, 33-man expedition[2] to the Northwest, through rivers and over the Rocky Mountains.

The expedition left St. Louis in May, 1804. As the men **were going** down the Missouri River, Clark stayed on the boat and drew maps and planned the course. Lewis often stayed on land to study animals and plants. While they **were crossing** the continent, they met some Indian tribes who were helpful. But they also met some who were hostile.[3]

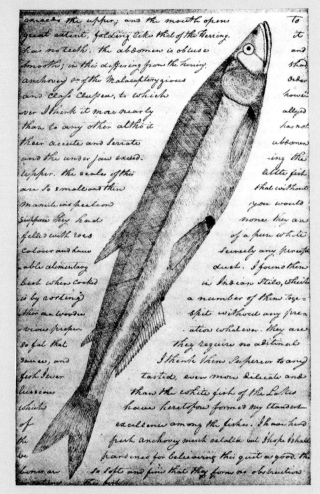

A page from Clark's journal shows his drawing of a white salmon trout.

By the time the expedition reached North Dakota, winter **was** fast **approaching**. They needed to wait until spring to cross the Rocky Mountains. As they **were waiting** out the winter, they met a Shoshone[4] woman, Sacagawea, and her Canadian husband. With their help, the expedition started the most dangerous part of the journey: crossing the Rocky Mountains. They were going to need horses. Sacagawea helped them get horses from her tribe.

While they **were traveling**, they faced many hardships: hunger, danger from bears, bad weather, and uncertainty about their future. Several times, while they **were sleeping**, their horses were stolen. They had no communication with anyone back east. No one even knew if they were still alive.

In November, 1805, tired but successful, they finally made it to the Pacific. When they returned to St. Louis, almost two and a half years later, the people of St. Louis **were waiting** to greet them. They were heroes.

---

1 *to appoint:* to choose somebody to do something
2 *expedition:* a journey made by a group of people organized and equipped for a special purpose
3 *hostile:* hateful, angry
4 *Shoshone:* member of the Shoshone Indians, an American Indian tribe

COMPREHENSION CHECK   Based on the reading, tell if the statement is true (**T**) or false (**F**).

1. President Jefferson's main goal was to learn about Indian life.

2. Lewis and Clark couldn't cross the mountains in the winter.

3. While traveling, they communicated with Jefferson about their location.

4.1 The Past Continuous — Form

PART A   The past continuous is formed with *was* or *were* + the present participle (*-ing* form of the verb).

Subject	Was/Were (+ not)	Present Participle	Complement
I	was	reading	about Lewis and Clark.
Clark	was	making	maps.
You	were	looking	at the map of the U.S.
Lewis and Clark	were not	traveling	fast.

Language Note:

> An adverb can be placed between *was/were* and the present participle.
>> Winter **was** *fast* **approaching**.
>> They **were** *probably* **getting** worried.
>> Clark **wasn't** *always* **riding** in the boat.

PART B   Compare statements, *yes/no* questions, short answers, and *wh-* questions.

Statements	Yes/No Questions & Short Answers	Wh- Questions
They **were traveling** to the West.	**Were** they **traveling** far? Yes, they **were**.	How far **were** they **traveling**?
Lewis **wasn't making** maps.	**Was** Clark **making** maps? Yes, he **was**.	Why **wasn't** Lewis **making** maps?
Lewis **was working** for the President.	**Was** Lewis **working** in St. Louis? No, he **wasn't**.	Who else **was working** for the President?

Language Note:

> The past continuous of the passive voice is *was/were* + *being* + past participle.
>> In 1803, preparations **were being made** for the expedition.

EXERCISE 1 Listen to each conversation. Fill in the blanks with the words you hear.

CD 1
TR 21

1. **A:** Where _were most Americans living_ at the beginning of the 1800s?

a.

   B: They _____ _were living_ _____ east of the Mississippi River.

b.

2. **A:** Lewis _____ for the president. _____ for President Jefferson at that time too?

a.   b.

   B: No, he _____ .

c.

3. **A:** While _____ the continent, did they meet a lot of American Indians?

a.

   B: Yes, they did. They met a lot of American Indians while they _____ .

b.

4. **A:** Why _____ during the winter?

a.

   B: It was too cold. They had to wait until spring to cross the mountains.

5. **A:** Did they have any problems while _____ the mountains?

a.

   B: Yes, they did. Sometimes at night while they _____ , their horses were stolen.

b.

6. **A:** A Shoshone woman _____ them. How _____ them?

a.   b.

   B: The expedition needed horses. She got horses from her tribe.

7. **A:** How many people _____ to greet them when they returned to St. Louis?

a.

   B: Almost all of the people of St. Louis were there. They _____ to see Lewis and Clark.

b.

4.2 The Past Continuous — Use

Examples	Explanation
In 1803, Lewis **was working** as an aide to the president. working NOW PAST ←————————→ FUTURE 1803	The past continuous is used to show that an action was in progress at a specific past time. It didn't begin at that time.
When they **arrived** in St. Louis, many people **were waiting** for them. **As** they **were going** down the river, Clark drew maps. **While** they **were crossing** the **continent**, they **met** many Indian tribes. crossing the continent NOW PAST ←————————→ FUTURE met Indians	We often use the simple past in one clause and the past continuous in another clause to show the relationship of a longer past action to a shorter past action. The simple past is used to express the shorter action. The past continuous is used with the longer action. **When** is used with the shorter action. **While** or **as** is used with the longer action.

Punctuation Note:

If the time clause (starting with *when, while,* or *as)* precedes the main clause, we separate the two clauses with a comma.

As they were traveling**,** Clark drew maps. (comma between clauses)

Clark drew maps *as* they were traveling. (no comma)

EXERCISE 2 Read this article about a space mission that took place in 2003. Pay attention to the verb forms in **bold**. If the verb form describes a longer past action, write *L* over it; if it describes a shorter past action, write *S*. Then discuss your choice with a partner.

NASA is the United States National Aeronautics and Space Administration. On January 16, 2003,

NASA sent the space shuttle *Columbia* into space with seven crew members. While the *Columbia* **was going**
                                                       L
1.

around the Earth, the crew **conducted** science experiments. On February 1, 2003, it **was traveling** back to.
      2.   3.

Earth after completing its mission. As the *Columbia* **was flying** over east Texas just 16 minutes from its
                                           4.

landing in Florida, it **broke** up. While families **were waiting** for the return of their relatives, they **received**
                5.   6.   7.

the tragic news. People were shocked when they **heard** about the accident.
                                                                 8.

The causes of the disaster were studied, and this is what was found: as the *Columbia* **was lifting** off, a
                                                                         9.

piece of the fuel tank **broke** off and **hit** the wing.
                      10.   11.

The *Columbia* was the second major disaster in space. The first one was in January 1986, when the

space shuttle *Challenger* **exploded** while it **was lifting** off. All seven crew members were killed in that
                            12.   13.

tragedy as well.

EXERCISE 3 About You Think of an important event that happened during your lifetime. Write what you were doing when you heard the news. Share your answers with a partner.

When the Soviet government fell, I was living in Kiev.

When Hurricane Sandy hit the United States, I was going to school in New York.

_____

_____

_____

_____

4.3 The Past Continuous vs. the Simple Past

Examples	Explanation
What **were** you **doing** *when* you heard the news about the *Columbia*? I **was eating** breakfast.	*When* can mean "at that time" or "after that time," depending on whether the past continuous or the simple past is used. The past continuous shows what was in progress *at* the time a specific action occurred.
NOW ← were doing → PAST ←———◉———✖———◉———→ FUTURE heard	
What **did** you **do** *when* you heard the news about the *Columbia*? I **called** my friend.	The simple past shows what happened *after* a specific action occurred.
NOW heard PAST ←——————✖——✖——→ FUTURE called	
On February 1, 2003, relatives **were waiting** in Florida for the astronauts. They **were getting** ready to celebrate. Camera crews **were preparing** to take pictures of the landing.	The past continuous shows the **events leading up to** the main event **of the story**.
Suddenly, just 16 minutes before landing, the *Columbia* **broke** up.	The simple past tense shows the **main event**.

EXERCISE 4 Fill in the blanks using the words given. Use the simple past or the past continuous.

1. **A:** I remember the *Columbia* accident well. I _____was living_____ in Texas at that time.
       a. live

   B: What _____ the morning of the accident?
       b. you/do

   A: I _____ ready for work. I _____ breakfast and _____ to the
       c. get   d. eat   e. listen
   radio. Then suddenly I _____ a loud noise.
       f. heard

   B: What _____ when you heard the loud noise?
       g. you/do

   A: I _____ outside. I saw pieces of metal on my property.
       h. run

   B: What _____ when you found these pieces?
       i. you/do

   A: I _____ the police.
       j. call

2. A: Where _____ when the accident _____?
           a. the *Columbia*/go   **b.** happen

  B: It _____ to Florida.
           c. travel

  A: What _____ when the accident happened?
           d. you/do

  B: I _____ ready for school. Then my sister called me. When she _____ me about
           e. get   **f.** tell

    the accident, I _____ on the TV. When they _____ the sad faces of the relatives,
           g. turn   **h.** show

    I _____ to cry.
           i. start

3. A: As I _____ an article on my tablet about Lewis and Clark, I _____ a word I
           a. read   **b.** find

    didn't know: "tribe."

  B: What _____ to find out the meaning?
           c. you/do

  A: I _____ my finger on the word and the definition popped up.
           d. put

EXERCISE 5 Choose the correct tense (simple past or past continuous) to complete the following conversations.

  1. A: While I (*looked*/*was looking*) for a movie at the library yesterday, I (*found*/*was finding*) a DVD about
           a.   **b.**

    Lewis and Clark.

    B: What (*did you do*/*were you doing*) with it?
           c.

    A: I (*took*/*was taking*) it out of the library.
           d.

  2. A: While Lewis and Clark (*crossed*/*were crossing*) the country with their team of 33 men, one of their men
           a.

    (*died*/*was dying*).
      b.

    B: What (*did they do*/*were they doing*) when he died?
           c.

    A: They (*buried*/*were burying*) him and continued their expedition.
           d.

  3. A: While the teacher (*explained*/*was explaining*) the lesson, I (*fell*/*was falling*) asleep.
           a.   **b.**

    B: What (*did the teacher talk about*/*was the teacher talking about*) when you fell asleep?
           c.

    A: I think he (*talked*/*was talking*) about Lewis and Clark.
           d.

    B: I can't believe you fell asleep. The story was so exciting.

    A: I thought so too. But the night before, while I (*slept*/*was sleeping*), the phone rang and (*woke*/*was waking*) me
           e.   **f.**

    up. When I finished talking on the phone, I (*tried*/*was trying*) to go back to sleep but couldn't.
           g.

continued

4. **A:** I haven't seen you for a while.

B: I (*visited/was visiting*) my cousin in Washington, DC, all week.
     a.

A: Did you have a good time?

B: Yes. We were planning to visit the Air and Space Museum, but it was closed for repair.

A: So what (*did you do/were you doing*) instead?
       b.

B: We (*went/were going*) to the National Museum of the American Indian instead.
       c.

5. **A:** What (*did you do/were you doing*) at around eight o'clock last night? I called you and texted you,
       a.

but you didn't reply.

B: I (*watched/was watching*) a documentary about American history.
       b.

A: But I called you again around midnight. What (*did you do/were you doing*) around midnight?
                                                   c.

B: I'm sure I (*slept/was sleeping*). When I got in bed, I (*turned/was turning*) off the phone.
       d.   e.

TRAVEL BY SEA:
The First and Last
VOYAGE of
the *TITANIC*

A remotely operated vehicle explores the anchor of the *Titanic*.

Ken Marschall '87 ©

 Read the following article. Pay special attention to the words in bold.

CD 1
TR 22

The year was 1912. The railroad across the United States **had** already **been built**. The Wright brothers **had** already **made** their first successful flight. Henry Ford **had** already **produced** his first car. The *Titanic*—the ship of dreams— **had** just **been built** and was ready to make its first voyage from England to America, with over two thousand people aboard.[5]

The *Titanic* was the most magnificent[6] ship that **had** ever **been built**. It had luxuries that ships **had** never **had** before: electric light, elevators, a swimming pool, libraries, and more. It was built to give its first-class passengers all the comforts of the best hotels. Some of the wealthiest people in the world were on the *Titanic*. But not everyone on the *Titanic* was rich. Most of the passengers in third class were emigrants who **had left** behind a complete way of life and were going to America with hopes of a better future.

The *Titanic* began its voyage on April 10. The previous winter **had been** unusually mild, and by spring large blocks of ice **had broken** away from the Arctic region. The captain **had been receiving** warnings about ice, but he was not very worried; he did not realize how much danger the ship was in. On April 14, at 11:40 p.m., an iceberg was spotted right ahead. The captain tried to reverse the direction of his ship, but he couldn't, because it **had been traveling** too fast. It hit the iceberg and started to sink. The *Titanic* **had** originally **had** 32 lifeboats, but 12 of them **had been removed** before sailing to make the ship look more elegant.[7] There were only enough lifeboats for about half of the people aboard.

While the ship was sinking, passengers were being put on lifeboats, women and children before men. First-class passengers boarded[8] the lifeboats before second- and third-class passengers. By the time the third-class passengers came up from their cabins, most of the lifeboats **had** already **left**, some of them half empty. Within two hours and forty-five minutes, the ship **had gone** completely down.

Cold and afraid, people in the lifeboats **had been waiting** all night, not knowing if they would be saved or if their loved ones were dead or alive. In the early morning, the *Carpathia*, a ship that responded to the *Titanic*'s call for help, arrived to rescue the survivors. Only one-third of the passengers survived.

---

[5] *aboard:* on a ship
[6] *magnificent:* very beautiful or impressive
[7] *elegant:* stylish in appearance
[8] *to board:* to enter a ship, airplane, train, etc.

4.5 The Past Perfect — Use (Part 1)

When showing the time relationship between past events, the past perfect is used to show the event that took place first.

Examples	Explanation
By April, 1912, large blocks of ice **had broken** away from the Arctic region. **By the age of fifty**, Jack Thayer **had lost** several loved ones.	The past perfect can be used with *by* + a time reference. The past perfect shows that something occurred before that time. NOW lost loved ones PAST ← ✖ ✖ → FUTURE 50 years old
Time Clause **By the time** the rescue ship **arrived**, *Main Clause* most passengers **had** already **died**. *Main Clause* I **had** never **heard** of the *Titanic* *Time Clause* **until** I **read** the article about it today.	The past perfect can be used in a sentence with a time clause. The time clause shows the later past event and uses the simple past. The main clause shows the earlier past event and uses the past perfect. NOW rescue ship arrived PAST ← ✖ ✖ → FUTURE passengers died
When Jack's family got on the *Titanic*, they **had *never* been** on such a luxurious trip **before**. When Jack was rescued in the morning, he **hadn't *yet* learned** of his father's death.	*Never … before* or *not … yet* can be used in the main clause to emphasize the earlier time.
The ship **had been** at sea ***for five days*** when it hit an iceberg.	The past perfect can be used in the main clause with *for* + a time period to show the duration of the earlier past action.
Before he **jumped** in the water, he **(had) put** on his lifejacket. Many years ***before*** he **died**, he **had written** his personal story and **had given** copies to family and friends.	In sentences with a time clause that begins with *before* or *after*, the past perfect is optional in the main clause. Often the simple past is used in both clauses. The past perfect is more common if the earlier event does not immediately precede the later one.
It **was** 1912. The railroad **had** already **been** built.	We can start with a past sentence and follow it with a past perfect sentence to go further back in time.

Language Note:

Time clauses begin with *by the time, when, until,* etc.

EXERCISE 7 Fill in the blanks with the simple past or the past perfect of the verb given.

1. By 1912, the airplane <u>had already been invented</u>.
   passive: already/invent

2. By the time the *Titanic* _____ England, some of the lifeboats _____
   a. leave   **b.** passive: remove
   to make the ship look more elegant.

3. By the spring of 1912, pieces of ice _____ away from the Arctic region.
   _____
   break

4. The captain _____ several warnings by the time the ship _____
   a. receive   **b.** hit

   the iceberg.

5. Jack _____ in his cabin for a short time when he _____ that there was
   a. be   **b.** realize

   a problem.

6. When Jack _____ a bump, many passengers _____ to bed.
   a. feel   **b.** already/go

7. By the time Jack Thayer _____ into the water, he _____ separated from
   a. jump   **b.** get

   his parents.

8. He _____ the night in a lifeboat by the time he _____ .
   a. spend   **b.** passive: rescue

9. When the rescue ship _____ , most of the passengers _____ .
   a. arrive   **b.** already/die

10. When the *Titanic* _____ in 1985, it _____ on the ocean floor for 73 years.
    a. passive: find   **b.** be

EXERCISE 8 Read the sentences below. Decide which time or event took place first. Write *1* above
the first action or event and *2* above the second.

1. When the Lewis and Clark expedition traveled to the west, no one had done it before.
   (2 above "traveled"; 1 above "done")

2. They finally entered a territory that no white man had ever entered before.
   (2 above "entered"; 1 above "entered")

3. It was 1803. For almost 20 years, President Jefferson had thought about sending an expedition to the west.

4. The expedition had traveled more than six hundred miles by the end of July.

5. Up to this time, most of the trip had been done by boat.

6. Lewis and Clark were the first white Americans to go west of the Rocky Mountains. But these lands had

   been occupied by native people for a long time.

7. Many American Indians had never seen a white man before they met Lewis and Clark.

8. Only one man had died by the end of the expedition.

9. He had died long before the expedition ended.

10. They returned to St. Louis, almost two and one-half years after they had left.

4.6 *When* with the Simple Past or the Past Perfect

Sometimes *when* means *after*. Sometimes *when* means *before*.

Examples	Explanation
When Jack Thayer was rescued, he **found** his mother.	If the simple past is used in the main clause, *when* means **after**.
When Jack Thayer was rescued, he **had been** in a lifeboat all night.	If the past perfect is used in the main clause, *when* means **before**.

EXERCISE 9 Fill in the blanks with the correct form of the verb given. Use the simple past to show that *when* means *after*. Use the past perfect to show that *when* means *before*.

1. When people saw the *Titanic* for the first time, they _____ had never seen _____ such a magnificent ship before.

never/see

2. When the ship was built, people _____ were _____ amazed at how beautiful it was.

be

3. When the ship left England, twelve lifeboats _____ .

passive: remove

4. When the weather got warmer, pieces of ice _____ to break away.

start

5. When the ship hit an iceberg, the captain _____ several warnings.

receive

6. When Jack Thayer felt a bump, he _____ to investigate.

go

7. When the passengers heard a loud noise, they _____ to get on the lifeboats.

run

8. When the *Titanic* sank, a rescue ship _____ to pick up the survivors.

come

9. When Thayer died, he _____ several tragedies in his life.

have

10. When he died, his notebooks _____ .

passive: not/yet/ publish

11. When his notebooks were published, people _____ more about what had happened that night.

learn

12. When I saw the movie *Titanic*, I _____ my friends about it.

tell

13. When I saw the movie *Titanic*, I _____ of this ship before.

never/hear

4.7 The Past Perfect — Use (Part 2)

Examples	Explanation
Many people **died** *because* the lifeboats **had left** half empty. Jack **survived** *because* he **had jumped** into the water and **swum** to a lifeboat.	The past perfect is often used in a *because* clause to show that something happened before the verb in the main clause.
The captain **didn't realize** that his ship **had come** so close to an iceberg. Until he was rescued, Jack **didn't know** that his mother **had survived**.	The past perfect can be used in a noun clause when the main verb is past. (A noun clause begins with *know that, think that, realize that,* etc.)*
The *Titanic* **was the most** magnificent ship that **had** *ever* **been** built. The sinking of the *Titanic* **was** one of ***the worst*** transportation tragedies that **had** *ever* **happened**.	In a past sentence with the superlative form, the past perfect is used with *ever*.
One of the ship's designers, ***whom*** the Thayer family **had met**, **told** them that the ship would not last an hour.	The past perfect can be used in an adjective clause. (An adjective clause begins with *who, that, which, whom,* or *whose.*)**

*For more about noun clauses, see Lesson 10.

**For more about adjective clauses, see Lesson 7.

EXERCISE 10 Complete each sentence by circling the correct verb form. Use both the simple past and the past perfect in the same sentence.

1. Jack Thayer and his father (*went*/had gone) to investigate because they (felt/*had felt*) a bump.
  a.   b.

2. Jack, who (*got/had gotten*) separated from his parents, (*jumped/had jumped*) into the water and was
  a.   b.

  picked up by a lifeboat.

3. Some people in the lifeboats (*reported/had reported*) that they (*heard/had heard*) music as the ship
  a.   b.

  was going down.

4. Jack was seventeen years old. Losing his father (*was/had been*) the worst thing that
  a.

  (*ever happened/had ever happened*) to him at that time.
  b.

5. Later, Jack (*became/had become*) very depressed because his son and his mother (*died/had died*)
  a.   b.

  in one year.

6. People (*didn't know/hadn't known*) Jack Thayer's story because he (*didn't publish/hadn't published*) it.
  a.   b.

7. Jack's family (*knew/had known*) about his story because he (*gave/had given*) them copies of it.
  a.   b.

8. His story, which he (*wrote/had written*) in the 1940s, (*wasn't/hadn't been*) published until after his death.
  a.   b.

EXERCISE 11 Fill in the blanks with the simple past or the past perfect of the verbs given and any other words you see. Use both tenses in each item.

1. Lewis and Clark _____*entered*_____ a land that no
   a. enter

   white man _had ever entered_.
   b. ever/enter

2. The expedition to the west _____ one of
   a. be

   the most dangerous journeys that men

   _____ at that time.
   b. ever/do

3. During the winter, they _____ busy
   a. keep

   writing reports about what they _____.
   b. see

4. During the winter, they _____ equipment
   a. repair

   that _____ damaged.
   b. become

5. They _____ grizzly bear territory. The
   a. enter

   American Indians _____ them
   b. warn

   about these dangerous animals, but they thought it

   wouldn't be a problem because they had rifles. They were wrong. The grizzly bear _____
   c. be

   one of the most frightening animals they _____.
   d. ever/see

6. On November 7, 1805, they saw a body of water. They _____ that they
   a. think

   _____ the Pacific Ocean. They were disappointed to learn that what they saw was just
   b. reach

   a river.

7. Lewis and Clark _____ the first white men to travel to the west, but these lands
   a. be

   _____ by American Indians.
   b. passive: already/occupy

EXERCISE 12 About You Fill in the blanks and discuss your answers with a partner. Talk about travel or transportation.

1. Until I was _____, I had never _____ before.

2. By the time I was _____ years old, I _____ already

   _____.

4.8 The Past Perfect Continuous—Form

PART A The past perfect continuous is formed with *had been* + the present participle.

Subject	Had (+ not)	Been	Present Participle	Complement
The *Titanic*	**had**	**been**	**crossing**	the Atlantic Ocean.
Jack Thayer	**had**	**been**	**waiting**	all night.
The captain	**had not**	**been**	**paying**	close attention.

Language Note:

An adverb can be placed between *had* and *been*.

Jack **had *probably* been thinking** of his parents all night.

PART B Compare statements, *yes/no* questions, short answers, and *wh-* questions.

Statements	Yes/No Questions & Short Answers	Wh- Questions
The *Titanic* **had been crossing** the Atlantic.	**Had** the ship **been crossing** in the winter? No, it **hadn't**.	How long **had** it been **traveling**?
The captain **hadn't been listening** to the warnings.	**Had** he **been traveling** too fast? Yes, he **had**.	Why **hadn't** the captain **been listening** to the warnings?
Lewis and Clark **had been traveling** for several years.	**Had** American Indians **been traveling** with Lewis and Clark? Yes, they **had**.	Which American Indians **had been traveling** with them?

🎧 **EXERCISE 13** Fill in the blanks with the verb forms you hear.

CD 1
TR 23

Millvina Dean was only a nine-month-old baby when her family took her on the *Titanic*. Mr. and Mrs.

Dean _____ in third class with Millvina and her two-year-old brother.
　　　　　　　　　　1.

Millvina's father _____ a business in London for several years when an
　　　　　　　　　　　　　　　　2.

American cousin invited him to help run his business in the U.S. But, unfortunately, that wasn't going to

happen. Millvina, her mother, and brother were rescued, but Mr. Dean _____. A week after
　　　　　　　　　　　　　　　　　　　　　　　　　　　　　　　　3.

arriving in the United States, Millvina, her mother, and brother returned to England. For many years,

Millvina _____ about her experience because, of course, she couldn't remember
　　　　　　4.

anything. What she knew she _____ from her mother. Millvina
　　　　　　　　　　　　　　　5.

_____ a quiet life for many years until 1985, when the *Titanic* was found. For the
　　　6.

next twenty years she was invited to *Titanic*-related events in the United States, England, and other

countries. When she died in 2009 at the age of ninety-seven, she had been the oldest and last survivor.

5

Modals and Related Expressions

Scientists study computer-generated
3-D simulations of nuclear reactions.

TECHNOLOGY

The real danger is not that computers will begin to think like men, but that men will begin to think like computers.

— Sydney J. Harris

EXERCISE 11 About You Write sentences about computers, passwords, online shopping, online banking, or online music using the words given. Discuss your sentences with a partner.

1. have to _____ When I order something online, I have to pay for shipping. _____

2. should _____

3. have got to _____

4. must _____

5. ought to _____

6. had better _____

7. be supposed to _____

5.6 Suggestion: *Can/Could*

Examples	Explanation
To remember passwords, you **can** create a hint for each password. You **could** keep the hint in a notebook.	We use *can* and *could* to give suggestions.
You **can** open a bank account online, or you **could** go into the bank and do it in person. You **should** change your password frequently.	We use *can* or *could* when several options are possible. We use *should* when you feel that there is only one right way.

EXERCISE 12 Offer two suggestions to answer each of the following questions. You may work with a partner. Use *can* or *could*.

1. How can I make my password more secure?

   You can mix uppercase and lowercase letters. You could include a number or symbol.

2. How can I open a new bank account?

   _____

3. How can I remember all my passwords?

   _____

4. How can I pay for something online?

   _____

5. How can I compare prices on a new TV?

   _____

Taking a Break from Technology

CD 1
TR 28

Read the following article. Pay special attention to the words in bold.

Levi Felix has started a new kind of summer camp in California called Camp Grounded. Even though it's only three days long, campers can get away from their daily routine and swim, hike, take yoga classes, and enjoy nature. Most of all, campers can interact with each other. So what's so special about this camp? It's only for adults. And there's one important rule: Campers **must not** be connected to technology while there.

Many adults report that when they are on vacation, they **aren't able to** stay away from their devices and often check their work-related e-mails. Even when out in nature, they **may not** take the time to admire a spectacular mountain before pulling out their smartphone to take a picture.

Levi Felix wants people to interact with each other, not with their tech devices. At Camp Grounded, campers **are not allowed to** talk about their jobs. They **are not** even **permitted to** use their real names.

They have to pick a nickname. They are supposed to get to know each other as people, not through their professional lives. Felix hopes that campers can get to know themselves better as well.

Why do people have to go to camp to do this? Why not just unplug for the weekend? Many people say that they **can't** control themselves when they have a device nearby. They know they **don't have to** respond every time they hear a beep from their phone, but they do.

Felix is not against technology, but he thinks technology **shouldn't** control us. We **don't have to** give up our devices, but we need more balance in our lives.

A young woman practices yoga at a mountain lake.

COMPREHENSION CHECK Based on the reading, tell if the statement is true (**T**) or false (**F**).

1. Levi Felix has created a technology camp for adults.

2. At Felix's camp, people talk about their professions.

3. Felix wants adults to interact with each other at his camp.

5.7 Negative Modals

Examples	Explanation
Campers **must not** be connected to technology while there.	*Must not* shows that something is prohibited. It has an official tone.
Campers **cannot** use technology at this camp. They **may not** talk about work. They **are not allowed to** use a cell phone. They **are not permitted to** use their real names.	*Cannot* and *may not* show that something is not permitted. The meaning is similar to *must not* but is less formal. Other expressions that show prohibition are *be not allowed to* and *be not permitted to*.
Campers **are not supposed to** talk about their jobs. I **wasn't supposed to** use my cell phone at camp, but I did.	*Be not supposed to* is also used to show that something is not permitted. It is often used when a rule has already been broken.
Technology **shouldn't** control you. You should control technology.	*Should not* shows that something is not advisable.
If your phone beeps, you **don't have to** respond to it immediately. You can wait.	*Not have to* shows that something is not necessary or required.

Language Notes:

1. In the affirmative, *have to* and *must* have the same meaning, although *must* sounds more official.

    You **must** give up your cell phone for three days. = You **have to** give up your cell phone for three days.

2. In the negative, the meanings are completely different. *Must not* shows prohibition. *Not have to* shows that something is not necessary or required.

    One camp rule is that you **must not** use a cell phone for three days.

    When my cell phone rings, I **don't have to** answer it. I can wait.

EXERCISE 13 Circle the correct words in each item. In some cases, both answers are possible. In those cases, circle both choices.

1. At Camp Grounded, you (*may not*/*don't have to*) use a cell phone.

2. When your phone rings, you (*cannot*/*don't have to*) answer it if it's not an emergency.

3. According to Levi Felix, technology (*shouldn't*/*can't*) control you.

4. At Camp Grounded, you (*don't have to*/*are not allowed to*) use technology.

5. Campers (*aren't supposed to*/*don't have to*) bring their devices to camp, but some of them do.

6. According to the camp rules, you (*must not*/*may not*) use a tech device for three days.

7. If you don't want to take a yoga class at camp, you (*must not*/*don't have to*). It's your choice.

8. I want a break from technology. I (*don't have to/shouldn't*) go to camp. I can just turn off my phone.

9. You (*may not/don't have to*) use a computer at Camp Grounded.

EXERCISE 14 Circle the correct words to complete the conversation. In some cases, both answers are possible. In those cases, circle both choices.

A: Every time I get a credit card or bank statement, I just throw it in the garbage.

B: You (*shouldn't/don't have to*) do that. Someone (*can/should*) steal your identity. I read that thieves go
   1.   **2.**
   through the garbage looking for personal information.

A: But they (*don't have to/can't*) use my number without my credit card.
   3.

B: They can and they do. They make purchases by phone and charge it to your credit card. You

   (*may not/might not*) realize your information has been stolen till you review your bill a month later.
   4.
   You (*must not/shouldn't*) just throw away papers with personal information. You (*must/should*) shred
   5.   **6.**
   them. You (*could/can*) buy a shredder at an office supply store or online. Look. On this shopping site,
   7.
   if you spend over $25, you (*are not supposed to/don't have to*) pay for shipping.
   8.

A: OK. I'll buy one.

B: I do all my bill payments online. This way I (*don't have to/must not*) write any checks.
   9.

A: I don't know how to set up an online account. Can you help me?

B: Sure. Let's find your bank's website. OK. Now choose a password. You (*shouldn't/don't have to*) use
   10.
   your birthday. It's too easy for a thief to figure out.

A: OK. Let me try my mother's maiden name. Oh. It rejected this.

B: You used all letters. You (*couldn't/can't*) use just letters. You (*have to/can*) include at least one number.
   11.   **12.**
   Now try to memorize it.

A: I (*'m not supposed to/can't*) memorize so many passwords. It's impossible.
   13.

B: You (*have to/'ve got to*) find a way to keep track of your passwords.
   14.

EXERCISE 15 About You Write about a rule, law, or custom from your country or culture that other people may find strange.

1. In Rwanda, children are supposed to greet older people.

2. _____

USING TECHNOLOGY to ENFORCE the LAW

 Read the following article. Pay special attention to the words in bold.

CD 1
TR 29

Michelle O'Brien of Chicago opened her mail one day and found a surprise—but not a pleasant surprise. It was a traffic ticket for going through a red light two weeks earlier. Ms. O'Brien had always thought of herself as a careful driver and thought, "This **must** be a mistake. I always stop at a red light." But the evidence was unmistakable: the city sent her a link to a website, where she **could** clearly see her car in the intersection after the light had turned red.

Welcome to the world of photo-enforced intersections. Many cities in the United States and Canada have been using photo-enforced red lights at busy intersections for several years. Chicago now has about two hundred of them. We all know we're not supposed to go through a red light. But sometimes we don't even realize that we're doing it.

How do cities choose where to put a camera? City officials study the intersections that have the most serious accidents. While the number of serious side collisions goes down at these places, often there are more rear-end collisions. When a driver stops suddenly for a red light, the driver behind him sometimes **can't** stop in time.

Many drivers think that this kind of technology is a nuisance.[4] They say this is just a way for the city or state to collect more money. Others say the government **shouldn't** have so much information about us. But photo-enforced red lights **could** save lives.

---

[4] *nuisance:* a bother; something that causes irritation or frustration

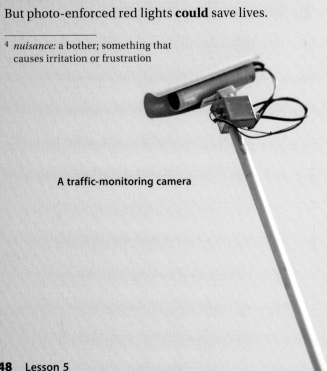

A traffic-monitoring camera

COMPREHENSION CHECK Based on the reading, tell if the statement is true (**T**) or false (**F**).

1. The United States is the only country that has photo-enforced red lights.

2. You can get a ticket in the mail.

3. Photo-enforced red lights reduce the number of rear-end collisions.

5.8 Ability/Possibility: *Can, Be Able To*

Examples	Explanation
The light is turning yellow. I think you **can** stop. If the street is wet, you **can't** stop quickly.	*Can* shows ability or possibility.
Are you **able to** see the camera at the red light?	*Be able to* is another way to express ability/possibility.
Could you stop? = **Were** you **able to** stop? I **couldn't** stop. = I **wasn't able to** stop.	We use *could* or *was/were able to* for past questions and negative statements.
I **was able to** stop when the light turned yellow. I **could** drive for many hours without stopping when I was younger.	In affirmative past statements, we use *was/were able to* for a single past action. We use *could* to express *used to be able to*.

Pronunciation Note:

Can is not usually stressed in affirmative statements. In negative statements, *can't* is stressed, but it is hard to hear the final **t**. We must pay attention to the stress to hear the difference between *can* and *can't*.

     I can gó. /kɪn/   I cán't go. /kænt/

EXERCISE 16 There are many ways drivers can be distracted. Fill in the blanks with one of the phrases from the box to complete the statements about driver distraction.

can eat	can't do	are you able to keep	are able to read	can do ✓
can change	are able to reach	can look at	can talk	couldn't answer

1. Some drivers think they _____ *can do* _____ other things safely while driving. But driver distraction is dangerous.

2. _____ your eyes on the road and text at the same time? Absolutely not.

3. Most drivers know that it's dangerous to send a text message while driving. But some drivers think they

   _____ a text message while driving.

4. You probably think you _____ the station on your radio without being distracted, but even this can be dangerous.

5. Some drivers think they _____ a sandwich or drink a cup of coffee while driving.

continued

Modals and Related Expressions **149**

WRITING

PART 1 Editing Advice

1. Don't use *to* after a modal (exception: *ought to*).

    You should ~~to~~ drive more carefully.

2. Don't forget the **d** in *supposed to*.

    You are suppose $\overset{d}{\wedge}$ to stop at a red light.

3. Don't forget the **d** to express *had* in *had better*.

    You $\overset{'d}{\wedge}$ better not talk on your cell phone while driving.

4. Use *have/has* before *got to*.

    You $\overset{'ve}{\wedge}$ got to have a password for each account.

5. Don't forget *be* or *to* in these expressions: *be supposed to, be able to, be permitted to, be allowed to*.

    You $\overset{are}{\wedge}$ supposed to have license plates on your car.

    I'm not able $\overset{to}{\wedge}$ remember so many passwords.

6. Use correct word order in a question with a modal.

    How ~~I can~~ $\overset{can\ I}{}$ get a vanity license plate?

7. Don't put *can* after another modal. Change to *be able to*.

    You must ~~can~~ $\overset{be\ able\ to}{}$ drive well if you want to pass the driver's test.

PART 2 Editing Practice

Some of the shaded words and phrases have mistakes. Find the mistakes and correct them. If the shaded words are correct, write C.

I think technology isn't good for small children. Kids should ~~to~~ play with other kids, not just
                                                                    1.

devices. How $\underset{C}{can}$ they develop social skills if they always play with devices? I have a five-year-old
         2.

nephew. He must to spend at least four hours a day on his tablet. He doesn't even like to watch
        3.

TV anymore. He should spend more time outdoors with other kids. I often tell my brother, "You
                  4.

better put some limits on how much time Kyle can play with his tablet." My brother always tells me,
  5.

"What we can do? We're too busy to take him to the park to play." I think my brother and his wife
    6.

supposed to set a good example for their son. Instead, Kyle sees his parents always texting, tweeting,
    7.

checking e-mail, etc. They think he should be able have good technology skills before he goes to
                          8.

school. I can't convince my brother and sister-in-law to change their habits.
$\underset{9.}{}$

My sister is raising her daughter differently. Maya is four years old, and she not permitted use
$\underset{10.}{}$

technology at all. My sister thinks that Maya got to learn social skills first. She's not allow to watch
$\underset{11.}{}$ $\underset{12.}{}$

more than one TV program a day. In nice weather, she's got to play outside and get some exercise.
$\underset{13.}{}$

Sometimes she sees her friends playing with a tablet. She asks my sister, "Why I can't have a tablet?"
$\underset{14.}{}$

My sister has to explain to her that people are more important than electronic devices. It's not easy
$\underset{15.}{}$

raising children today. But we got to set a good example for them.
$\underset{16.}{}$

PART 3 Write About It

1. Write about some advantages and disadvantages of technology in our daily lives.

2. Do you think it's important to take a break from technology from time to time? Why or why not?

PART 4 Edit Your Writing

Reread the Summary of Lesson 5 and the editing advice. Edit your writing from Part 3.

The faces of U.S. presidents George Washington, Thomas Jefferson, Theodore Roosevelt, and Abraham Lincoln are carved into this granite mountain, Mount Rushmore, South Dakota.

U.S. PRESIDENTS
and ELECTIONS

Those who deny freedom
to others deserve it not for
themselves.

— Abraham Lincoln

LINCOLN and the GETTYSBURG ADDRESS

Read the following article. Pay special attention to the words in bold.

CD 1
TR 30

From the time of the first English colonies[1] in America, Africans were brought to America as slaves. Most of them were taken to the South, where they worked on farms in the production of sugar, cotton, and other crops.[2] White farmers in the South **couldn't have been** prosperous without slaves. But many Northerners were against slavery. One of those was Abraham Lincoln, the president who finally brought an end to slavery in the United States.

Today many people consider Abraham Lincoln to be one of the greatest presidents of the United States. But before he became president, many had doubts about his abilities. Lincoln's parents were poor and uneducated, and Lincoln had only eighteen months of schooling. But he loved to read, and he educated himself. Because Lincoln had so little schooling, journalists thought he **must not have been** very smart.

Much to his opponents' surprise, Lincoln won the presidential election in 1860. At that time, southern slave owners wanted to continue slavery, but Lincoln wanted to stop the spread of slavery. What followed was the worst internal crisis in American history: the Civil War. Over half a million soldiers died in the conflict, the most of any war that the United States fought in.

On November 19, 1863, President Lincoln was invited to say a few words at Gettysburg, Pennsylvania, where a terrible battle had taken place. There **must have been** about 20,000 people there. Edward Everett, the main speaker, spoke first. His speech lasted two hours. Lincoln followed Everett with a two-minute speech. When he finished, everyone was silent. The audience **may have been surprised** by the brevity[3] of the speech. Some people thought he **must not have been** finished. Seeing the reaction of the crowd, Lincoln turned to Everett and said he was afraid his speech had been a failure. He said he **should have prepared** it more carefully. Everett disagreed. He said the speech was perfect. He said the president had said more in two minutes than he, Everett, had said in two hours. This speech, known as the Gettysburg Address, is one of the greatest speeches in American history. Lincoln said that the country was dedicated to freedom and that "government of the people, by the people, for the people" had to continue.

The Civil War continued until April 9, 1865, when the North finally won. Less than a week later, Lincoln was assassinated.[4]

---

[1] *colony:* a group of people who have moved to another area of land, but are still governed by their home country

[2] *crop:* plant grown as food, especially grains, vegetables, or fruit

[3] *brevity:* shortness

[4] *to assassinate:* to murder or kill

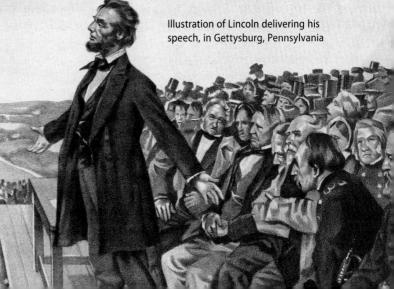

Illustration of Lincoln delivering his speech, in Gettysburg, Pennsylvania

COMPREHENSION CHECK Based on the reading, tell if the statement is true (**T**) or false (**F**).

1. Lincoln didn't have much formal education.

2. Lincoln's short speech surprised the audience.

3. Lincoln was assassinated before the Civil War ended.

6.1 Modals in the Past — Form

Examples	Explanation
"I **should have prepared** the speech more carefully," thought Lincoln. Southern farmers **could not have become** rich without slaves.	To form the past of a modal, we use modal + (*not*) + *have* + past participle.
Lincoln probably **could have been elected** again, but he was assassinated. Africans **should not have been brought** to the U.S. to work as slaves.	To form the passive of a modal, we use modal + (*not*) + *have been* + past participle.

Pronunciation Note:

In informal speech, *have* is often pronounced like *of* or /ə/.

EXERCISE 1 Fill in the blanks with the words you hear to complete the conversations.

CD 1
TR 31

1. **A:** Did you read the story about Lincoln before class?

   B: No. I didn't have time.

   A: You _should have read_ it. Our lesson depends on it.

a.

   B: I studied American history in high school.

   A: Then you _____ about Lincoln and the Civil War.

b.

   B: Yes, I did.

2. **A:** Lincoln was a wonderful president.

   B: I agree. Without him, slavery _____ much longer.

a.

   A: Farmers _____ slaves. That was terrible!

b.

   B: They wanted to make money. They _____ rich without slaves.

c.

continued

3. **A:** Do you remember the story we read about Lewis and Clark?

   B: No. I _____ absent that day.

a.

   A: You weren't absent. And we talked about it for almost a week.

   B: Oh. Then I _____ much attention.

b.

   A: You _____ more attention in class. It was an interesting topic.

c.

4. **A:** Lincoln's speech was very short.

   B: He _____ it very fast.

a.

   A: I don't think he wrote it fast. I think he chose his words very carefully.

   B: Edward Everett's speech was two hours long. The audience _____ bored.

b.

   A: Maybe. I wouldn't like to listen to a two-hour speech.

5. **A:** I rented the movie *Lincoln*, but it was very hard for me to understand.

   B: You _____ subtitles.

a.

   A: I don't know how to do that.

   B: You _____ me. I do it all the time.

b.

6.2 Past Regrets or Mistakes — *Should Have*

Examples	Explanation
"I **should have given** a longer speech," thought Lincoln.	We use *should have* + past participle to comment on mistakes or regrets, or to rethink the advisability of a past decision.
I think Everett's speech was too long. He **shouldn't have talked** for such a long time.	We use *should not have* + past participle to say that a past action was not advisable.

EXERCISE 2 Fill in the blanks to express past advisability. Use context clues to help you.

1. **A:** There was a great documentary on TV about Lincoln last night. You should ___*have seen*___ it.

a.

   B: I didn't know about it. You should _____ me about it.

b.

   A: I did tell you. You sometimes write things in your calendar. You should

   _____ it down.

c.

2. A: I rented the movie *Lincoln*, and I thought it was boring. I only watched about twenty minutes of it.

    B: You should _____ the whole thing. It was very good.
                         a.

    A: I don't know much about American history. I never paid much attention to it in school.

    B: History's very important. You should _____ more attention.
                                                              b.

3. A: Did you vote in the last election? I know you're a U.S. citizen now.

    B: I forgot about it. But I really don't like what some politicians are doing now.

    A: Then you should _____ . You're giving me your opinion now. You should
                                      a.

    _____ your opinion on election day too.
                     b.

4. A: I gave a long speech in my English class and everyone started to yawn. I should

    _____ it.
                 a.

    B: You're right. It's best to shorten a speech as much as possible.

    A: You should _____ me. You're good at giving speeches.
                               b.

    B: I didn't have time to help you. I had to prepare my own speech.

5. A: Slavery was a terrible thing. Farmers shouldn't _____ slaves to do their work.
                                                                            a.

    B: I agree. It's an awful thing to use people that way.

    A: They should _____ workers to do the work.
                                     b.

    B: They didn't want to pay workers. They wanted to make a lot of money for themselves.

6.3 Past Possibility — *May / Might / Could + Have*

Examples	Explanation

Why didn't the audience react after Lincoln's speech?
   They **could have been** surprised.
   They **may have expected** him to speak longer than two minutes.
   They **might have thought** that he wasn't finished.
	We use *may/might/could + have + past* participle to express a possibility about the past.
	 They could have been surprised. = *Maybe they were surprised.*
	 They may have expected him to say more. = *Maybe they expected* him to say more.

Everett's speech **may not have been** so interesting. Lincoln **might not have realized** how good his speech was.	To show negative possibility, we use *may not have* and *might not have*. We don't use *could not have*, because it has a different meaning. (See Chart 6.8)

EXERCISE 3 Read the words under the blank. Then fill in the blanks to express the same idea with the modal given.

You may ___have learned___ about Abraham Lincoln in school, but here's something you might
1. maybe you learned

_____. John Wilkes Booth, the man who assassinated Abraham Lincoln, was a
2. maybe you didn't hear

famous actor. His brother, Edwin, was also an actor. John may _____ as good an
3. maybe John was not

actor as his brother, but he was very popular, especially with women. This could

_____ because he was very handsome. John Booth hated the president and was in
4. maybe this was

favor of slavery. Edwin was on Lincoln's side. John and Edwin argued so much about Lincoln and slavery

that Edwin finally refused to have John in his house. John was planning to harm the president. At first, he

might _____ to kill the president, but later he decided to assassinate him.
5. maybe he didn't plan

In a hotel in Pennsylvania, where John Booth often stayed, someone had written these words near a

window: "Abe Lincoln Departed This Life August 13th, 1864 By The Effects of Poison."

After the death of Lincoln, people thought that John Booth may _____ these
6. maybe John Booth wrote

words. But this is not certain. There were many people who hated Lincoln, and someone else could

_____ that sentence.
7. maybe someone else wrote

In 1865, Lincoln was attending a play at the Ford Theater in Washington, DC. Booth was not an actor in

that play, but because he had acted there before, no one thought anything of his presence at the theater.

While Lincoln was sitting with his wife watching the play, Booth entered the president's box and shot him

in the head. At first, it was thought that he may _____ Lincoln, but it was soon
8. maybe he stabbed Lincoln

evident that Booth had shot him. The next morning, Lincoln died.

There's another interesting story about the Booth brothers. A few months before the assassination,

Robert, Lincoln's son, was standing on a train platform. Just as the train was arriving, Robert fell on the

tracks. It could _____ because of the crowds pushing. A stranger reached out and
9. maybe it was

pulled Robert to safety just before the train arrived. This stranger was Edwin Booth, John Wilkes Booth's

brother.

6.4 Logical Conclusion about the Past — *Must Have*

Examples	Explanation
Lincoln had very little schooling. He **must have been** very intelligent to learn so much on his own. I've seen pictures of Lincoln with other people. He looks so tall. He **must have been** over six feet tall.	We use *must have* + past participle to make a logical conclusion, deduction, or estimate about the past. We are saying that something was probably true. *He must have been very intelligent. = He probably was very intelligent.* *He must have been over six feet tall. = I estimate that he was over six feet tall.*
When Lincoln finished his speech after two minutes, some people thought that he **must not have been finished**. Lincoln thought, "They **must not have liked** my speech."	For the negative, we use *must not have* + past participle. We don't use a contraction for *must not*.

EXERCISE 4 Fill in the blanks to express past probability or logical conclusion. Use the underlined verbs and context clues to help you. Answers may vary.

1. **A:** It sounds like Edwin Booth <u>was</u> a kind man.

    B: He risked his life to save Lincoln's son. He must ____have been____ a very kind man.

                                      a.

    A: But Edwin's brother, John, was a terrible person.

    B: The brothers must not _____ each other.

                                  b.

    A: It's obvious that they <u>didn't like</u> each other. Edwin didn't even want John in his house.

2. **A:** How did John Booth <u>enter</u> the theater to kill Lincoln?

    B: He must _____ like everyone else. He was a well-known actor, so people didn't think

                      a.

 anything of it.

    A: It's not easy to <u>plan</u> an assassination.

    B: He must _____ the assassination for a long time.

                      b.

    A: Today, presidents <u>have</u> a lot of security. They must not _____ so much security in

                                                      c.

 Lincoln's time.

3. **A:** Many people loved Lincoln. They must _____ very sad when he died. I <u>felt</u> very sad

                                               a.

 when I read the story.

    B: But some people hated him. People who wanted to continue slavery must _____

                                                              b.

 happy when he died.

continued

4. **A:** Slaves worked so hard. They must _____ a very hard life.
   a.

   B: Yes. They <u>had</u> a very hard life.

   A: The slaves must _____ happy because Lincoln wanted to end slavery.
   b.

   B: I'm sure they <u>were</u> very happy.

5. **A:** Kennedy's death was such a tragedy.

   B: Who's Kennedy?

   A: You never <u>heard</u> of Kennedy? He was so famous. You must _____ of him. There's a
   a.

   picture of him in this book on page 169.

   B: Wow. He <u>was</u> so handsome. He must _____ a movie star.
   b.

   A: No. He <u>was</u> an American president. He was assassinated in 1963 when he was only 46 years old.

   B: That's terrible. It must _____ a hard time for Americans.
   c.

   A: Yes, it <u>was</u>. I remember my grandparents telling me about it.

   B: How old were they at the time?

   A: They <u>were</u> in high school when it happened. They must _____ about fifteen or
   d.

   sixteen years old.

6. **A:** We read about Thomas Jefferson. Wasn't he the president who said "All men are created equal"?

   He must _____ against slavery.
   a.

   B: He <u>wasn't</u> against slavery. Even though he said that, he had a lot of slaves.

7. **A:** Have you ever seen the movie *Lincoln*?

   B: Is it a new movie? Did it just <u>come</u> out?

   A: It's not new. It must _____ out over 10 years ago.
   a.

   B: Was it good? Did you like it?

   A: I thought it was a little boring. I think I missed some of it because I must _____
   b.

   asleep in parts.

   B: I don't think I've ever <u>fallen</u> asleep during a movie.

The CUBAN MISSILE CRISIS

President Kennedy signs the order to block Soviet ships from delivering weapons to Cuba.

Read the following article. Pay special attention to the words in bold.

CD 1
TR 32

It was October and people around the world were terrified. It seemed almost certain that World War III was about to begin, and the planet was in danger of complete destruction. The whole planet? Was this a science fiction story? Unfortunately, no. The danger of worldwide destruction was possible; some thought even probable. "October 27 is a day I'll never forget. The planet **could have been destroyed**," said a former CIA[5] agent. He was referring to October 27, 1962. "It **could have been** the end of the world, but here we are." Forty years later, many of the surviving leaders in this terrifying crisis met to reflect back on the time when their actions **could have resulted** in the end of the world.

Since the 1940s, the United States and the Soviet Union[6] were enemies. The United States discovered that the Soviet Union was beginning to send nuclear missiles to Cuba, which is only about ninety miles from Florida. The American President, John Kennedy, saw this as a direct threat to national security; these weapons **could have been** used to destroy major cities and military bases in the United States. Spy photos showed that missiles in Cuba **could have reached** almost every part of the continental[7] United States in a very short time. On October 22, President Kennedy announced on TV that any attack from Cuba would be considered an attack from the Soviet Union, and he would respond with a full attack on the Soviets. He sent out the U.S. Navy to block Soviet ships from delivering weapons to Cuba. An attack on a U.S. ship **could have grown** into a full nuclear war. This crisis **could have changed** the world as we know it.

Fortunately, diplomacy[8] won over war. The Soviets agreed to send their missiles back and promised to stop building military bases in Cuba. In exchange, the United States promised to remove its missiles from Turkey. What **could have been** a tragic event is now only a chapter in history.

---

[5] *CIA:* Central Intelligence Agency. It gathers information about other countries' secrets.
[6] The Soviet Union was a country that included Russia, Ukraine, and 13 other republics. In 1991, the government collapsed and the Soviet Union broke up into 15 different countries, the largest of which is Russia.
[7] *continental United States:* all U.S. states except Hawaii and Alaska, which are not part of the U.S. mainland
[8] *diplomacy:* skillful negotiation between countries to try to work out problems without fighting

COMPREHENSION CHECK Based on the reading, tell if the statement is true (**T**) or false (**F**).

1. Cuba was helping the Soviet Union in 1962.

2. President Kennedy sent ships to attack the Soviet ships.

3. In 2002, leaders met to discuss the decisions they had made in 1962.

6.5 Past Direction Not Taken — *Could Have*

Examples	Explanation
This crisis **could have changed** the world. The planet **could have been destroyed**.	We use *could have* + past participle to show that it was possible for something to happen, but it didn't.
The U.S. **could have attacked** the Soviet ships. The U.S. **could have invaded** Cuba. But the president didn't do these things.	We use *could have* + past participle to show that a past opportunity was not taken.
A: Before we got to class, I didn't know much about Lincoln. B: You **could have read** the article before class. Or you **could have googled** his name.	We use *could have* + past participle to show suggestions that were not followed.

Language Notes:

1. We often use *could have* + past participle in an expression like this: *I was so… I could have…*
   We use this expression to exaggerate a result.

   > When the missiles were removed, I was so happy **I could have jumped** for joy.

2. Remember, *could have* + past participle can mean *may have/might have* (maybe). (See Chart 6.3)

EXERCISE 5 Fill in the blanks with *have* + one of the verbs from the box.

sent	started✓	ended	continued
tried	bombed	made	been killed

1. World War III could _____have started_____ in 1962.

2. In 1962, the world as we know it could _____.

3. Everyone could _____.

4. The world leaders could _____ a wrong decision, but they made a sensible decision.

5. The Soviets could _____ to send ships to Cuba, but they stopped.

6. The Soviets could _____ missiles to all the major cities of the U.S. from Cuba.

7. The U.S. could _____ the missile sites in Cuba, but Kennedy decided against that.

8. As the Soviet ships came close to the American naval ships, they could _____ to

   cross, but they stopped.

EXERCISE 6 Fill in the blanks with *have* + the past participle of one of the verbs from the box.

| marry | kill | be | give | dress✓ | break |

1. Lincoln wasn't interested in nice clothes. He could _____ have dressed _____ well, but he usually dressed poorly.

2. Lincoln could _____ a farmer like his father, but he wanted to become a lawyer.

3. Mary Todd, Lincoln's wife, was from a wealthy, educated family. Her family thought she could _____ a better man than Lincoln. She had other marriage opportunities.

4. The South could _____ away from the North over the issue of slavery, but Lincoln saved the nation and kept it together.

5. Lincoln could _____ a long speech, but he decided to give a very short speech.

6. A train could _____ Lincoln's son, but Edwin Booth saved him.

EXERCISE 7 About You Write about a direction you could have taken in your life, but didn't. Discuss your response with a partner.

EXAMPLE: I could have gotten married when I was 18, but I decided to finish college first.

_____

_____

_____

_____

EXERCISE 8 Write about something that almost happened in your country or another country you know about. Use *could have*. Discuss your response with a partner.

EXAMPLE: In Chile, 33 miners were trapped in a mine in 2010. They were there for over two months. They could have died, but they were saved.

_____

_____

_____

_____

_____

_____

The Media
and PRESIDENTIAL ELECTIONS

🎧 **Read the following article. Pay special attention to the words in bold.**

CD 1
TR 33

There's no doubt about it—the media influence elections. First newspapers, then radio, then television, and now social media—all of these have played an important part in getting out information and shaping public opinion.

One example of how the media **could influence** election results took place in the 1960 presidential race between John Kennedy and Richard Nixon. For the first time in history, two candidates debated[9] each other on TV. John Kennedy was the first candidate who understood the influence that television had on the result of an election. Both candidates **had to answer** difficult questions. Many people who heard the Nixon-Kennedy debate on the radio thought that Nixon was the stronger candidate. But people who saw the debate on TV thought that the young, handsome Kennedy was the better candidate. Also, Nixon was sweating under the hot lights, and people thought that he **must have been** nervous and uncomfortable with the questions. It was a close election, but Kennedy won. Many people think Kennedy **couldn't have won** without TV.

If Kennedy was the first presidential candidate to understand the influence of TV, Barack Obama was the first candidate who understood the influence of social media. For the 2008 election, he reached out to the Internet generation; his opponent, John McCain, didn't even know how to use a computer. He **had to depend** on his wife to read and send e-mail. By the time of the 2012 election between Barack Obama and Mitt Romney, both parties understood the power of social media, but Obama's team **was able to collect** data online and use it more effectively.

When people started to use social media, they no longer **had to get** their information from TV or newspapers or even the Internet. With social media sites, people **could influence** each other. According to a media blog: "In the 2012 election, 30% of online users report that they were urged to vote via social media by family, friends or other social network connections, 20% actively encouraged others, and 22% posted their decision when they voted."

It is clear that political candidates now need social media to get their images and messages across.

John F. Kennedy (left) and Richard Nixon (far right) during their televised presidential debate.

---

[9] *debate:* to answer questions (before an audience) so that the public can judge who is the best candidate

COMPREHENSION CHECK Based on the reading, tell if the statement is true (**T**) or false (**F**).

1. Some of the people who saw Kennedy on TV were influenced by his good looks.

2. Candidates first started getting their message across with TV.

3. People who use social media often influence their friends and family in elections.

6.6 *Must Have* + Past Participle vs. *Had to* + Base Form

Examples	Explanation
Kennedy and Nixon **had to** answer difficult questions. John McCain **had to** depend on his wife to use e-mail.	To show past necessity or obligation, we use *had to* + base form. *Must*, for necessity or obligation, has no past form.
TV viewers thought that Nixon **must have been** nervous and uncomfortable during the debate. John McCain **must not have understood** the importance of social media.	To show a logical conclusion or deduction in the past, we use *must have* + past participle.

EXERCISE 9 Write *had to* + base form for a past necessity. Write *must have* + past participle for a past deduction or logical conclusion.

A: The 2000 election between Al Gore, the Democratic candidate, and George Bush, the Republican candidate, was so strange.

B: It was?

A: Don't you remember? The election was very close, so they ___had to count___ the votes again to see
    1. count
who won. It took them five weeks to figure out who won the election.

B: Bush and Gore _____ nervous the whole time. They _____
                          2. be   3. wait
a long time to find out the results.

A: This had never happened before. Everyone _____ surprised and confused at that
                                               4. be
time. There were so many problems counting the votes that the decision _____
                                                                        5. *passive*: make
by the Supreme Court.

B: Did you vote in that election?

A: Of course. I always vote.

B: You usually vote for a Democrat, so you _____ for Gore.
                                               6. vote

A: Yes, I did.

continued

B: You _____ very disappointed when they finally announced that Gore lost.
7. be

A: Yes, I was. What about you? Who did you vote for?

B: I _____ overtime that day, so I didn't vote. Anyway, one person's vote doesn't
8. work

matter much.

A: It mattered in 2000.

6.7 Ability and Possibility in the Past

Examples	Explanation
President Lincoln **could give** good speeches. He also had a good sense of humor and **was able to make** people laugh.	In affirmative statements, *could* + base form means *used to be able to*. It shows ability or knowledge over a period of time. *Was/were able to* can also be used for ability over a period of time.
In October 1962, President Kennedy **was able to prevent** war. He **was able to convince** the Soviets to send back their missiles.	In affirmative statements, we use *was/were able to* for success in doing a single action. We don't use *could* for a single action.
I **couldn't understand** Lincoln's speech. **Were** you **able to** understand it?	In negative statements and questions, *could* and *was/were able to* are used interchangeably.
The Cuban Missile Crisis **could have destroyed** the world (but it didn't). Lincoln **could have given** a longer speech, but he chose to give a two-minute speech.	We use *could have* + past participle for an action that was possible but didn't happen.
Some people thought that Kennedy **couldn't have won** the election without TV. And maybe Barack Obama **couldn't have won** without social media.	We use *couldn't have* + past participle to show that something was impossible in the past.
A: My grandparents liked to watch President Roosevelt on TV. **B:** They **couldn't have watched** him on TV. They didn't have TV back then. You probably mean radio.	*Couldn't have* + past participle is used to show disbelief or to disprove a previous statement.

EXERCISE 10 Circle the correct words to complete each sentence. In some cases, both choices are possible, so circle both options.

1. I (*couldn't use*/*couldn't have used*) social media last night because I didn't have an Internet connection.

2. We listened to the Gettysburg Address online, but we (*couldn't understand*/*couldn't have understood*) it. The vocabulary was difficult for us.

3. Do you mean you listened to Lincoln's voice? You (*couldn't listen*/*couldn't have listened*) to Lincoln's voice. There was no recording of his voice. You must have listened to someone else reciting the Gettysburg Address.

4. (*Were you able to/Could you*) vote in the last election?

5. My mother has been a U.S. citizen for the last five years. She (*could vote/could have voted*) in the last election, but she's not interested in politics.

6. Around the time of the 2008 election in the United States, many people (*were able to use/could have used*) social media to get information.

7. You say President Kennedy was killed in a plane crash in 1999. That (*couldn't happen/couldn't have happened*). He was assassinated in 1963. You're probably thinking of his son.

8. John McCain (*couldn't/wasn't able to*) use social media in 2008.

9. I (*couldn't/wasn't able to*) vote in the last election because I was out of the country.

10. My mother uses social media now. But she (*couldn't use/couldn't have used*) it five years ago. I had to show her how.

11. Lincoln (*could be/could have been*) a farmer like his father, but he was more interested in politics.

12. Lincoln's father (*couldn't read/couldn't have read*).

13. Lincoln (*was able to teach/could have taught*) himself law.

6.8 Modals in the Past: Continuous Forms

Example	Explanation
John Wilkes Booth **must have been** planning the assassination for a long time.	To give a continuous meaning to a past modal, we use modal + *have* + *been* + present participle.

EXERCISE 11 Fill in the blanks with one of the verbs from the box. Use the continuous form.

prepare	think	have	use✓	plan	protect

1. Farmers shouldn't _____have been using_____ people as slaves.

2. What was Lincoln thinking after his speech? He might _____ about the audience reaction.

3. Lincoln must _____ doubts about his speech.

4. Everett might _____ his speech for several weeks.

5. Lincoln didn't have good protection. Someone should _____ him better.

6. John Booth must _____ the assassination for months.

SUMMARY OF LESSON 6

Examples	Explanation
Lincoln **should have had** better protection. You **should have voted** in the last election. Every vote is important.	We use *should have* + past participle to comment on mistakes or regrets, or to rethink the advisability of a past decision.
In 1962, a nuclear attack was avoided. It **may have been** because of good diplomacy. It **might have been** because the Soviets feared a world war. When John Booth entered the theater, people **could have thought** he was an actor in the play that night.	*May/might/could have* + past participle shows possibility about a past action or event.
People thought Nixon **must have been** nervous because he was sweating. The whole world **must have been** afraid in October 1962.	*Must have* + past participle shows a logical conclusion or deduction about the past.
President Kennedy **could have attacked** the ships, but he didn't. In 1962, a world war **could have started**, but it didn't. You **could have watched** the movie *Lincoln*, but you weren't interested.	*Could have* + past participle shows a past direction not taken, a past possibility that didn't happen, or a past suggestion that wasn't followed.
A: I voted in the last presidential election. B: You **couldn't have voted**. You weren't even 18 at that time.	*Couldn't have* + past participle can show disbelief or an attempt to disprove a previous statement.
When I was younger, I **could name** all the presidents in my country, but now I've forgotten. I **was able to read** Lincolns' speech without using a dictionary.	To express past ability, we use *could* + base form or *was/were able to* + base form. In affirmative statements, *could* means *used to be able to*. To show success in doing a single action, we use *was/were able to* for affirmative statements.
McCain didn't know how to use a computer. He **had to depend** on his wife.	*Had to* + base form shows an obligation or necessity in the past.
Booth **must have been planning** the assassination for some time.	For a continuous meaning of a past modal, we use modal + *have* + *been* + present participle.

TEST/REVIEW

Circle the correct words to complete each conversation. If both choices are possible, circle both.

1. **A:** Our grandparents (*had to rely*/*should have relied*) on TV or newspapers to get the news.
   a.

   B: I can't imagine a time without social media. Getting the news (*must*/*should*) have been so slow.
   b.

2. **A:** Did you read the article about Lincoln last night?

   B: I (*couldn't read*/*couldn't have read*) it. I didn't have time. What about you?
   a.

   A: I (*was able to*/*could*) read it, but I (*wasn't able to*/*couldn't*) understand every word.
   b.   **c.**

3. **A:** Without Lincoln, slavery (*should*/*could*) have lasted much longer.
   a.

   B: Lincoln (*was able to end*/*could have ended*) slavery and keep the country together.
   b.

4. **A:** Lincoln's bodyguard (*couldn't*/*shouldn't*) have left the president alone. Where was he?
   a.

   B: I'm not sure. He (*might not*/*should not*) have been in the theater with Lincoln.
   b.

5. **A:** After Booth shot Lincoln, he jumped onto the stage.

   B: The audience (*had to think*/*must have thought*) this was part of the play.
   a.

6. **A:** Did they take Lincoln back to the White House?

   B: It was too far. They (*had to take*/*must have taken*) him to a house across the street. He died there the
   a.

   next morning.

7. **A:** When Lincoln died, the Secretary of War said something interesting, but people

   (*couldn't have agreed*/*weren't able to agree*) on what he said.
   a.

   B: Yes. He (*may*/*might*) have said, "Now he belongs to the ages" or he (*could*/*may*) have said, "Now he
   b.   **c.**

   belongs to the angels."

8. **A:** When John Kennedy was president, a world war (*could happen*/*could have happened*), but it didn't.
   a.

   He had to make some difficult decisions.

   B: He (*could*/*must*) have made the right decision back then. He prevented a war.
   b.

9. **A:** Kennedy was another president who was assassinated. Who killed him?

   B: We don't know for sure. It (*may*/*might*) have been the Soviets. The assassination (*must*/*could*) have
   a.   **b.**

   been prevented. He was in an open car. He (*should*/*must*) have had better protection.
   c.

WRITING

PART 1 Editing Advice

1. After a modal, always use a base form.

   Lincoln should ~~has~~ *have* had more protection.

2. To express the past with some modals, use modal + *have* + past participle.

   The bodyguard shouldn't ∧*have* left the theater.

3. Don't use *of* after a modal to express past. Use the auxiliary verb *have*.

   The Cuban Missile Crisis could ~~of~~ *have* caused a third world war.

4. Use the correct form for the past participle.

   Lincoln shouldn't have ~~went~~ *gone* to the theater that night.

5. *Can* is never used for the past.

   I ~~can't voted~~ *couldn't vote* in the last election.

6. Don't confuse *couldn't have* + past participle with *couldn't* + base form.

   When we read the article about Lincoln, I couldn't ~~have understood~~ *understand* a few words.

   If you didn't understand the article, you could ∧*have* use ∧*d* a dictionary.

PART 2 Editing Practice

Some of the shaded words and phrases have mistakes. Find the mistakes and correct them. If the shaded words are correct, write C.

You probably know about the assassination of President Kennedy. But do you know about the

tragic death of his son in 1999?

John Junior was less than three years old when his father was killed. Because he was so young,

he can't remembered [*couldn't remember*] much about father. But of course he must have known [*C*] a lot about his father
    1.   **2.**

from his family and from history. And he must remembered his uncle Robert, who was assassinated
                                    3.

when John was eight years old.

John Junior could be a politician like his dad and uncles. He might have been discouraged from
              4.   **5.**

going into politics because both his father and uncle Robert were assassinated. Instead he became a

lawyer. After a few years as a lawyer, he decided to publish a political magazine. So he must of been
                                                                                    6.

interested in politics.

Because he was so famous, he couldn't go out in public without being followed by photographers.
7.
When he flew on commercial airlines, other passengers asked him questions, took his picture, and wanted his autograph. He can't got any privacy at all. So he decided to get his pilot's license and fly
8.
his own airplane.

Only fifteen months after getting his license, he planned to fly with his wife to his cousin's wedding in Massachusetts. They were supposed to be there after a short flight. Family members waited and waited. They couldn't have understood why John didn't arrive on time. After waiting all
9.
night with no word from John, they must knew that something terrible had happened.
10.

The following morning, searchers found their suitcases on the shore. They concluded that the plane must has crashed. Families members couldn't go on with the wedding. Six days later, the
11.   12.
bodies were found.

Experts tried to understand the reason for the crash. John didn't have a lot of experience as a pilot and flew over water, which is difficult for new pilots. Experts say he should have flew over land.
13.
Also, the weather wasn't good that evening. So he should have waited. He had broken his ankle a few
14.
months before. Some people think he may not been able to handle the foot pedals of the airplane.
15.
This tragedy could be prevented. He could of used a commercial airline. Or he could have hired
16.   17.   18.
a professional pilot to take him there in his own airplane.

John Kennedy, Jr. was only 38 years old. This was just one more tragedy for the Kennedy family.

PART 3 Write About It

1. Write about an event that had a big impact on the U.S., your country, or the world. Or write about a tragedy that was avoided. Provide the sources you used to write your essay.

2. Write about the tragic death of a famous person. Provide the sources you used to write your essay.

PART 4 Edit Your Writing

Reread the Summary of Lesson 6 and the editing advice. Edit your writing from Part 3.

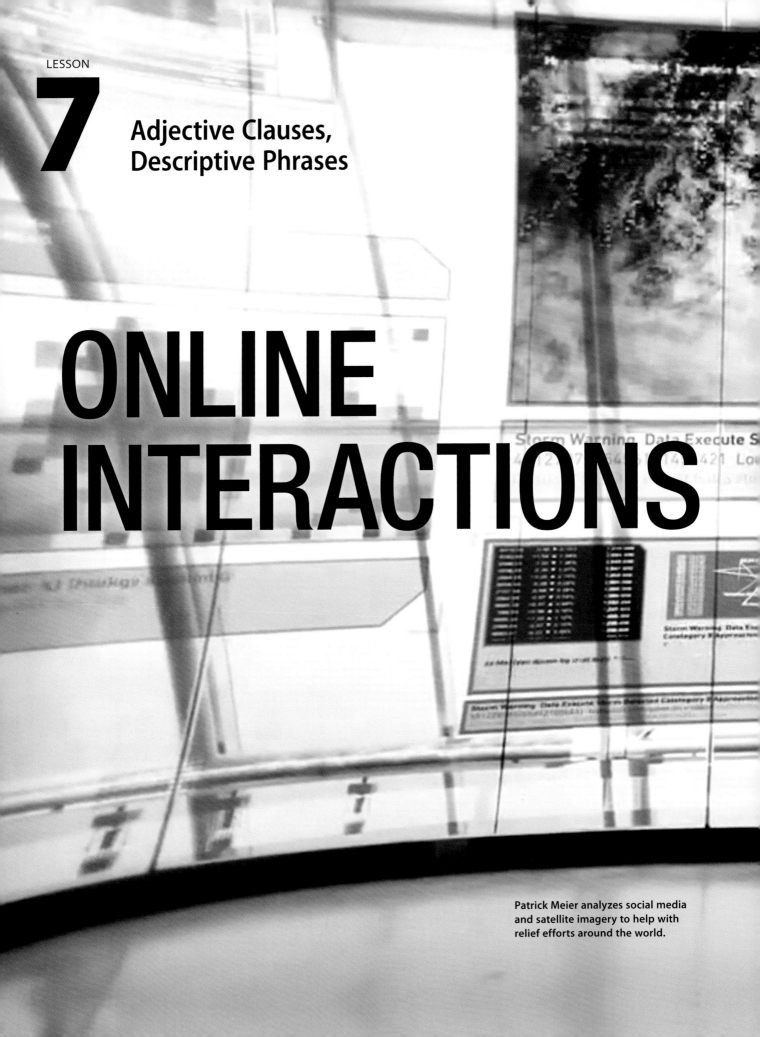

ONLINE INTERACTIONS

Patrick Meier analyzes social media and satellite imagery to help with relief efforts around the world.

The dream behind the Web is of a common information space in which we communicate by sharing information. Its universality is essential.

—Tim Berners-Lee

PIERRE OMIDYAR and eBAY

 Read the following article. Pay special attention to the words in bold.

Did you ever want to sell a birthday present **that you didn't like**? Or an old toy **that is taking up space in your closet**? In the old days, buyers and sellers were limited to newspapers, garage sales, and flea markets[1] in the area **where they lived**. But in the early 1990s, **when people started to use the Internet**, Pierre Omidyar had an idea. Omidyar, **who was working as a computer programmer**, realized that sellers no longer had to be limited to finding buyers **who lived in their local area**. He came up with the idea of eBay, **which he started as a hobby**. He didn't charge money at first because he wasn't sure eBay would work. Buying online requires you to trust sellers **whom you've never met**. But people liked eBay. Soon there was so much activity on eBay that his Internet service provider upgraded his site to a business account, **which was no longer free**. So Omidyar started to charge the sellers a small fee for each sale. Before long, this hobby grew into a big business.

By 1998, eBay had become so big that Omidyar needed a business expert. He brought in Meg Whitman, **whose knowledge of business helped make eBay a success**. She changed eBay from a company **that sold used things in several categories** to a large marketplace of seventy-eight million items, both new and used, in fifty thousand categories.

Many companies **that start out well on the Internet** later fail. When Whitman left the company, it started to decline. In 2008, John Donahoe was brought in as the new CEO.[2] He fired many people **who had been working there for years**. He understood that smartphones and tablets were changing the way **that people shopped**; people no longer had to shop from their home computers. He created an eBay app so that people could shop 24/7 and could pay with one click. eBay, **which was about to follow other Internet businesses into decline**, was brought back to life.

By the time Omidyar was 31, he was worth more than $7 billion. The money **that he has earned** is much more than he needs. He and his wife signed a promise, the Giving Pledge, to give away the majority of their wealth during their lifetime to help others.

---

[1] *flea market:* a market where used items are sold
[2] *CEO:* Chief Executive Officer; the highest executive in charge of a company or organization

COMPREHENSION CHECK Based on the reading, tell if the statement is true (**T**) or false (**F**).

1. Omidyar did not start out with the intention of making money.

2. Because of John Donahoe, eBay was starting to fail.

3. Omidyar believes in sharing his wealth.

7.1 Adjective Clauses — Introduction

Examples	Explanation
I received a birthday present **that I didn't like.** You have to trust sellers **whom you've never met.** Omidyar changed to a business account, **which** was not free.	The adjective clause identifies which present. An adjective clause is a group of words that contains a subject and verb. It describes or identifies the noun before it. It is a dependent clause. In these examples, the adjective clauses describe the nouns: *present*, *sellers*, and *account*.

Language Notes:

1. The following words mark the beginning of an adjective clause: *who, whom, that, which, whose, where, when.*

2. Sometimes an adjective clause begins with no marker.
   I received a birthday present **I didn't like.**

3. Some adjective clauses are set apart from the rest of the sentence by commas.
   John Donahoe saved eBay, **which was declining.**

4. An adjective clause can follow any noun in a sentence.
   The company hired Meg Whitman, **who knew a lot about business.**
   Meg Whitman, **who left the company to go into politics,** helped make eBay a success.

🎧 **EXERCISE 1** Listen to each sentence and fill in the word that marks the beginning of the adjective clause.

CD 2
TR 3

1. Amazon was founded in 1994 by Jeff Bezos, _____ who _____ predicted that the Internet offered an

   opportunity to make money.

2. Amazon, _____ is now the largest online retailer, began by selling books.

3. First Bezos made a list of about 20 products _____ could be sold online. He eventually

   decided on selling books.

4. Bezos wanted a name _____ began with "A." He decided on Amazon, because it is a place

   _____ is "exotic and different."

5. But a good company name is not enough. Bezos needed to hire people _____ talents

   would improve the company.

continued

A: Did you buy your computer online?

B: Oh, no. I'm talking about a time (*when/about which*) no one had even heard of the Internet. There were
                                                                        4.

very few stores (*Ø/where*) you could buy computers. And they were so expensive.
                     5.

A: More than $500?

B: More than $2,000!

A: Wow! It must have had a big memory.

B: Absolutely not. I'm talking about a time (*when/that*) 100 kilobytes was considered a big memory. The
                                                               6.

computer tower was very big. I had to find a place under my desk (*that/where*) I could put the tower.
                                                                                 7.

A: Who taught you to use it?

B: I had to find a time (*which/when*) I could study on my own because I had no one to help me. Later
                             8.

I started taking a class at a community college near my house. Did you know that there was a time

(*Ø/when*) most computer students were guys? I was the only woman in the class.
    9.

A: Grandma. I'm so proud of you. What happened to your first computer?

B: For many years, it was in my garage. Then I decided to put it on a website (*where/that*) people go in
                                                                                    10.

order to buy old computers.

A: Why would anyone want such an old computer?

B: There are collectors who consider my first computer a collector's item.

A: Cool. So, Grandma, you were ahead of your time.

B: I guess I was. But now, when I have a computer question, I have to ask my grandchildren. It's just hard to

find a time (*when/where*) you're not too busy to give your old grandma some help.
             11.

EXERCISE 9 About You Write the name of three websites you use frequently. Tell what a person
can find on these websites. Share your answers with a partner.

1. Weather.com is a site where you can find out the weather in your area.

2. CCC.edu is a site that has a listing of college courses in Chicago.

3. _____

4. _____

5. _____

EXERCISE 10 About You Write three years or time periods. Tell what happened at that time. Share your answers with a partner.

1. _2012 was the year (when) I got married._

2. _December 22 through January 5 were the weeks during which we had our winter break._

3. _____

4. _____

5. _____

7.6 *Whose* in Adjective Clauses

Whose is the possessive form of *who*. It stands for *his, her, its, their*, or the possessive form of the noun.

Whose + noun can be the subject of the adjective clause.

Subject

Freecycle is an online community. *Its* **members** help each other.

Freecycle is an online community *whose* **members help each other**.

Subject

People can offer their kids' old clothes. *Their* **children** are growing.

People *whose* **children are growing** can offer their kids' old clothes.

Whose + noun can be the object of the adjective clause.

Object

You should always thank the person. You received *her* **item**.

You should always thank the person *whose* **item you received**.

Object

You want *a person's* **item**. The person will suggest a way for you to get it.

The person *whose* **item you want** will suggest a way for you to get it.

EXERCISE 15   Decide which of the following sentences contain a nonessential adjective clause. Put commas in those sentences. If the sentence doesn't need commas, write *NC*.

1. People who text use abbreviations. NC
2. My father, who texted me a few minutes ago, is sick.
3. Kids who spend a lot of time on the computer don't get much exercise.
4. The Freecycle Network™ which was created in 2003 helps keep things out of landfills.
5. People usually have a lot of things they don't need.
6. Berners-Lee whose parents were very educated loves learning new things.
7. At first Amazon was a company that only sold books.
8. Meg Whitman who ran eBay for ten years left the company in 2008.
9. Berners-Lee worked in Switzerland where a physics laboratory is located.
10. The Windows operating system which was developed by Microsoft came out in 1985.
11. Did you like the story that we read about Berners-Lee?
12. The computer that I bought three years ago doesn't have enough memory.
13. The Web which is one of the most important inventions of the twentieth century has changed the way people get information.
14. Bill Gates who created Microsoft with his friend became a billionaire.
15. Steve Jobs who died in 2011 helped create the Apple computer.
16. It's hard to remember a time when computers were not part of our everyday lives.
17. Do you remember the year when you bought your first computer?

EXERCISE 16   Combine the two sentences into one. The sentence in parentheses ( ) is not essential to the main idea of the sentence. It adds extra information.

1. eBay is now a large corporation. (It was started in Pierre Omidyar's house.)

   _____ eBay, which was started in Pierre Omidyar's house, is now a large corporation. _____

2. Tim Berners-Lee works at MIT. (He does research on artificial intelligence there.)

   _____

3. Pierre Omidyar started eBay as a hobby. (His wife became part of the company.)

   _____

4. eBay hired Meg Whitman in 1998. (More expert business knowledge was needed at that time to run the company.)

   _____

5. In 2008, eBay hired John Donahoe. (He fired a lot of people.)

   _____

6. E-mail did not become popular until the 1990s. (It was first created in 1972.)

_____

7. Pierre Omidyar had to charge money for each sale. (His idea started to become popular.)

_____

8. Berners-Lee created the Web at a laboratory in Switzerland. (He was working there in the 1980s.)

_____

9. Berners-Lee wrote a book called _Weaving the Web_. (He answers questions about his project in this book.)

_____

7.10 Descriptive Phrases

Examples	Explanation
(a) There are millions of items **that are listed on eBay**. (b) There are millions of items **listed on eBay**.	Compare sentence (a) with an adjective clause to sentence (b) with a descriptive phrase. This descriptive phrase begins with a past participle.
(a) I sold some things **that were taking up space in my closet**. (b) I sold some things **taking up space in my closet**.	Compare sentence (a) with an adjective clause to sentence (b) with a descriptive phrase. This descriptive phrase begins with a present participle (verb _-ing_).
(a) Pierre Omidyar, **who is the founder of eBay**, is one of the richest men in the world. (b) Pierre Omidyar, **the founder of eBay**, is one of the richest men in the world.	Compare sentence (a) with an adjective clause to sentence (b) with a descriptive phrase. This descriptive phrase is a noun (phrase). It gives a definition or more information about the preceding noun. This kind of descriptive phrase is called an appositive.
(a) Pierre Omidyar, **who is from France**, created eBay. (b) Pierre Omidyar, **from France**, created eBay.	Compare sentence (a) with an adjective clause to sentence (b) with a descriptive phrase. This descriptive phrase begins with a preposition (_with, in, from, of,_ etc.).

Language Notes:

1. We can only shorten an adjective clause to a descriptive phrase if the relative pronoun is followed by the verb _be_.

> I often use the computers ~~that are~~ in the library.

2. A descriptive phrase can be essential or nonessential. A nonessential phrase is set off by commas.

> I have two computers. The computer **in my bedroom** is newer. (Essential)
>
> The Amazon office, **in Seattle,** has over 100,000 employees. (Nonessential)

3. An appositive is always nonessential.

> Amazon, **an online store**, is a very popular website.

	Essential Adjective Clauses	Nonessential Adjective Clauses
Pronoun as subject	People **who/that sell on eBay** have to pay a fee. Amazon is a website **that/which sells a lot of different things.**	Berners-Lee, **who created the Web**, didn't make money from it. Pierre Omidyar created eBay, **which helps people buy and sell items online.**
Pronoun as object	The people **(who/whom) Omidyar hired** helped him build his company. The first computer **(that/which) I bought** didn't have much memory.	Pierre Omidyar, **who(m) I admire**, believes in donating money to help others. I'm very happy with my present computer, **which** I bought online.
Pronoun as object of preposition	INFORMAL: The person **(who/that) I sold my computer to** paid me $200. FORMAL: The person **to whom I sold my computer** paid me $200.	INFORMAL: Berners-Lee, **who(m) we read about**, is very creative. FORMAL: Berners-Lee, **about whom we read**, is very creative.
Where	I want to go to a college **where I can study computer science.**	Berners-Lee worked in Switzerland, **where he met other scientists.**
When	My grandparents grew up at a time **when there were no personal computers.**	The Web was created in 1991, **when most people did not have personal computers.**
Whose + noun as subject	Freecycle is a community **whose members help each other.**	Berners-Lee, **whose parents worked on computers**, learned a lot about technology when he was young.
Whose + noun as object	I sent a thank-you e-mail to the person **whose radio I received through Freecycle.**	Meg Whitman, **whose business expertise Omidyar needed**, started to work at eBay in 1998.
Adjective clause after indefinite compound	I don't know anyone **who doesn't have a cell phone.** Everything **(that/which) I've learned about the Internet** is fascinating.	
Descriptive phrase	Computers **made in the 1980s** had a very small memory.	Bill Gates, **the founder of Microsoft**, never finished college.

TEST/REVIEW

PART 1 Circle the correct words to complete the sentences. Ø means no word is necessary. In some cases, more than one answer is possible. If so, circle all possible answers.

1. What is a computer virus? A virus is a computer code (*that*/who/whose/*which*) attaches itself to other programs and causes harm to programs, data, or hardware.

2. Who is Deron Beal? Deron Beal is the man (*who/whom/which/that*) created the Freecycle Network.

3. Tim Berners-Lee was born at a time (*when/that/which/Ø*) personal computers were not even in people's imaginations.

4. Tim Berners-Lee is a name (*which/with which/that/Ø*) people are not familiar.

5. Omidyar needed to bring in someone (*who/whose/that/which*) knowledge of business was greater than his own.

6. The Web is a tool (*Ø/that/about which/which*) most of us use every day.

7. The Web, (*which/that/about which/about that*) we read on page 199, is not the same as the Internet.

8. What is eBay? eBay is a website (*that/where/whom/which*) you can buy and sell items.

9. The people (*Ø/which/whose/where*) I've met in online recycling sites have been very helpful.

10. Do you save all the e-mails (*that/where/whose/Ø*) your friends have sent to you?

11. The computer lab is never open at a time (*which/where/when/during which*) I need it.

12. I always delete the spam (*what/that/when/whose*) I receive.

13. You can create an address book (*when/that/where/in which*) you can keep the e-mail addresses of your contacts.

14. Do you know anyone (*Ø/who/whom/which*) doesn't own a computer?

15. The person (*who/that/whose/Ø*) computer I bought wanted a much more powerful computer.

16. Don't believe everything (*that/who/whom/Ø*) you read on the Internet.

PART 2 Some of the following sentences need commas. If they do, put them in. If the sentence doesn't need commas, write *NC* (no commas).

1. John Donahoe, who replaced Meg Whitman, saved eBay from decline.

2. In 2008 when John Donahoe came to work at eBay many top employees were fired.

3. Many online businesses that do well in the beginning later fail.

4. Amazon an online retailer was created by Jeff Bezos.

5. At first Amazon was a place where you could buy only books.

6. Now Amazon is a retailer that sells almost anything.

7. I can't remember a time when there were no smartphones.

8. Berners-Lee is a name that most people don't recognize.

9. Everything that we read in this lesson is related to the Internet.

10. Many people confuse the Web with the Internet which was created in the 1970s.

11. There are many websites where you can get travel information.

WRITING

PART 1 Editing Advice

1. Never use *what* as a relative pronoun.

   I bought a used computer from a person ~~what~~ *who* lives in another state.

   Everything ~~what~~ *that or Ø* we learned about the Internet is interesting.

2. You can't omit a relative pronoun that is the subject of the adjective clause.

   I have a cousin ∧*who* doesn't have a computer.

3. If the relative pronoun is the object of the adjective clause, don't put an object after the verb.

   The software that I bought ~~it~~ online was very useful.

4. Make sure you use subject-verb agreement in the adjective clause.

   I have a friend who use∧ *s* e-mail a lot.

5. Put a noun before an adjective clause.

   A person who
   ~~Who~~ ∧doesn't know how to use a computer in today's world is lost.

6. Don't confuse *whose* with *who's*.

   The person ~~who's~~ *whose* computer I bought didn't charge for shipping.

7. Put the subject before the verb in an adjective clause.

   my grandfather uses
   The computer that ~~uses my grandfather~~ is very old.

8. Use *whose*, not *his*, *her*, or *their* to show possession in an adjective clause.

   whose
   I have a friend ~~who his~~ knowledge of programming is very advanced.

PART 2 Editing Practice

Some of the shaded words and phrases have mistakes. Find the mistakes and correct them. If the shaded words are correct, write *C*.

Last semester I took a photo editing class that *[C]* has helped me a lot. The teacher ~~what~~ *who* taught the
1. **2.**

class is an expert in photo editing. This teacher, whose name is Mark Ryan, is patient, helpful, and
3.

fun. A lot of the photos I took were too dark. I learned how to lighten the parts needed lightening
4. **5.**

without lightening the whole photo. I also learned to cut out parts I don't want them. For example, I
6.

have a family picture, but it has one person who's not in the family. It's a woman who live next door
7. **8.**

to us. She came right at the time when was taking the picture my friend and she wanted to be in it.
9.

It's a great photo, except for her. I tried scanning it and editing it at home, but I didn't do a good job.

My teacher, who his scanner is much better than mine, scanned the photo and showed me how to
10.

cut the neighbor out. I learned many things in this class. Everything what I learned is very helpful.
11.

I started to take another photo class this semester. The teacher who's class I'm taking now is not
12.

as good as last semester's teacher. Who wants to learn a lot about photo editing should take Mark
13.

Ryan's class.

PART 3 Write About It

1. Write about the ways computers and the Internet have made life simpler.

2. Write about two websites or apps that you like. Explain how they are helpful or enjoyable for you.

PART 4 Edit Your Writing

Reread the Summary of Lesson 7 and the editing advice. Edit your writing from Part 3.

8

Infinitives and Gerunds

Rescue professionals in a mountain air
rescue training exercise

HELPING OTHERS

Remember that the happiest people are not those getting more, but those giving more.

—H. Jackson Brown Jr.

ANDREW CARNEGIE, PHILANTHROPIST

Read the following article. Pay special attention to the words in bold.

CD 2
TR 6

Andrew Carnegie was one of the world's richest men. He made a fortune[2] in the oil and steel industries. Did he enjoy his wealth? Of course, he did. But there is something he enjoyed even more: giving away his money.

Carnegie was born in Scotland in 1835 to a very poor family. When his father lost his job, his mother started **to work** to support the family. When Andrew was thirteen years old, his mother persuaded his father **to leave** Scotland for the "possibilities of America." A year later, Andrew started **to work** in a factory in Pittsburgh. He met a man who let him and other working boys use his small library. Andrew was eager **to read** and **learn** as much as he could. He was intelligent and hardworking, and it didn't take him long **to become** rich.

As Carnegie's fortunes grew, he started **to give** his money away. One of his biggest desires was **to build** free public libraries. He wanted everyone **to have** access to libraries and education. He believed that education was the key to a successful life. In 1881, there were only a few public libraries. Carnegie started **to build** free libraries so that everyone would have access to knowledge. Over the doors of the Carnegie Library of Pittsburgh, carved in stone, are the words, "Free to the People." By the time Carnegie died in 1919, there were more than 2,500 public libraries in the English-speaking world.

But building libraries was not his only contribution. In his book *The Gospel of Wealth,* he tried **to persuade** other wealthy people **to give** away their money. These are some of the ideas he wrote about in his book:

- **To give** away money is the best thing rich people can do.
- It is the moral obligation of the wealthy **to help** others.
- It is important for a rich person **to set** an example for others.
- It is not good **to have** money if your spirit is poor.
- It is a disgrace[3] **to die** rich.

By the time he died, Carnegie had given away more than $350 million.[4]

---

1 *philanthropist:* person who gives away money to help other people
2 *fortune:* a very large quantity of money
3 *disgrace:* something that brings shame or dishonor
4 In today's dollars, this is equivalent to approximately $8 billion.

Elegant staircase inside the Carnegie Library building at Mt. Vernon Square, Washington, DC

COMPREHENSION CHECK Based on the reading, tell if the statement is true (**T**) or false (**F**).

1. The Carnegie family left Scotland because they saw more economic possibilities in the United States.

2. When Carnegie was young, he had no help from anyone.

3. Carnegie encouraged rich people to help others.

8.1 Infinitives—Overview

An infinitive is *to* + the base form of the verb: *to go, to be, to see.*

Examples	Explanation
Carnegie wanted **to help** others.	An infinitive is used after certain verbs.
He wanted rich people **to give** away their money.	An infinitive can be used after the object of the sentence.
I'm happy **to help**.	An infinitive can follow certain adjectives.
It's important **to help** others.	An infinitive follows certain expressions that begin with *it*.
To help others makes a person feel good.	An infinitive can be the subject of a sentence.
Do you volunteer your time in order **to help** others?	An infinitive can be used to show purpose.
He's old enough **to help**. She's too young **to help**.	An infinitive is used after expressions with *too* and *enough*.

Language Notes:

1. In a sentence with two infinitives connected by **and** or **or**, the second *to* is usually omitted.

    I want **to make** money **and** help others.

    You can choose **to volunteer** time **or** donate money.

2. Put *not* before an infinitive to make it negative.

    Carnegie decided **not to die** rich.

3. For a passive infinitive, we use *to be* + past participle.

    Everyone wants **to be given** an opportunity to succeed.

 EXERCISE 1 Fill in the blanks with the words you hear.

CD 2
TR 7

About 25 years ago, Leslie Natzke, an ESL teacher from Chicago, went to Niger _____to work_____ as
                                                                                    1.

a Peace Corps[5] volunteer. She was surprised _____ that so few girls finished high school.
                                                      2.

According to an organization, Save the Children, Niger is the worst place in the world to be a mother. Very

poor parents often marry off their daughters at a very young age in order _____ money from
                                                                            3.

the husband's family. Natzke thought that these girls were too young _____ married and
                                                                          4.

needed _____ their education first.
            5.

[5] *Peace Corps:* an agency of the U.S. government that provides skilled volunteers to assist economic   *continued*
development in underdeveloped countries

When Natzke returned to the United States, she continued _____ about the girls in
6.
Niger. She wanted _____ more for them. In 2008, she started a program called Expanding
7.
Lives. This program brings teenage girls from Niger to Chicago for the summer. At first, Natzke just wanted
them _____ their education and _____ high school. Then she decided
8.   9.
_____ leadership training.
10.

As the program grew, Natzke wanted the girls _____ about finance so that they could
11.
start a business back home. But most of all, she wanted them _____ health education.
12.
It is important for Natzke _____ these girls become leaders. She wants them
13.
_____ their new skills to other girls in Niger and help them expand their lives too.
14.
_____ experience with Americans, Natzke has found volunteer families that give these
15.
girls a place to live during the summer.

8.2 Verbs Followed by an Infinitive

Examples	Explanation
Carnegie **didn't want to die** rich. Natzke **decided to help** girls from Niger. Everyone **deserves to have** an education.	Some verbs can be followed by an infinitive.

Language Notes:

1. The verbs below can be followed by an infinitive:

agree	deserve	learn	prefer*	try*
appear	expect	like*	prepare	want
attempt	forget	love*	pretend	wish
begin*	hate*	manage	promise	
choose	hope	need	refuse	
continue*	intend	offer	seem	
decide	know how	plan	start*	

2. The following modal phrases are also followed by an infinitive: *can afford, can't stand*, would like*.

* These verbs can also be followed by a gerund with little or no change in meaning. See Chart 8.14

EXERCISE 2 Fill in the blanks with the infinitive form of one of the verbs from the box. You may use the same verb more than once.

help	use	make	give	persuade
follow	give away	get	provide	

Bill Gates and Warren Buffet, two of the richest people in the world, know how _____*to make*_____
1.

money. They want _____ the example of Andrew Carnegie; they have also chosen
                    2.

_____ others. They signed a document called the Giving Pledge, where they promise
        3.

_____ more than half of their wealth during their lifetimes. They want
    4.

_____ their money to make life better for others.
    5.

Gates and Buffet have managed _____ over 100 American billionaires to sign the Giving
                               6.

Pledge. Pierre Omidyar, of eBay, has promised _____ at least half of his wealth to charity.
                                              7.

Now Gates and Buffet are attempting _____ billionaires in other countries to sign the Giving
                                     8.

Pledge too. Gates wants _____ all children with a good education and medical care.
                         9.

EXERCISE 3 Fill in the blanks with an infinitive. Use the verbs from the box.

give	build	learn	educate	get
die	work✓	have	start	leave

1. Andrew Carnegie started _____*to work*_____ when he was very young.

2. His parents chose _____ Scotland.

3. They hoped _____ a better life in the U.S.

4. Carnegie wanted _____ free public libraries.

5. He didn't want _____ rich.

6. Children in all countries deserve _____ a good education.

7. Everyone wants _____ a chance to succeed in life. *(passive)*

8. In some countries, poor children can't go to school. Children in all countries need

   _____. *(passive)*

9. Girls in Niger want _____ a better life.

10. They need _____ about computers, health, and finance.

EXERCISE 4 About You Assume you are a billionaire. Fill in the blank with an infinitive phrase to tell how you would like to help others. Share your answers with a partner.

I would like _____

8.3 Object before Infinitive

Some verbs can be followed by an object + an infinitive.

Examples	Explanation
Carnegie wanted **poor people to have** the same opportunities as rich people.	The object can be a noun.
He encouraged **them to use** use libraries.	The object can be a pronoun.

Language Note:

The verbs below can be followed by a noun or object pronoun + an infinitive:

advise	convince	invite	remind	want
allow	encourage	need	teach*	would like
ask	expect	permit	tell	
beg	force	persuade	urge	

* After *teach*, *how* is sometimes used: My parents taught me *how to help* others.

EXERCISE 5 Fill in the blanks with an object pronoun and the infinitive of one of the verbs from the box.

sign	help	buy	use✓	become	think	go
take	volunteer	suffer	save	finish	do	teach

1. **A:** My brother likes to buy a lot of expensive "toys."

   B: You should encourage _____ him to use _____ his money in better ways.

2. **A:** How do Bill and Melinda Gates persuade billionaires to give away their money?

   B: They talk to them. They encourage _____ about helping others. They

                      a.

   ask _____ the Giving Pledge.

        b.

3. **A:** Andrew Carnegie's mother was worried about her children. She didn't want

   _____. She talked to her husband about the possibilities of a better life.

           a.

   B: What did she want _____?

               b.

   A: She wanted _____ the family to America.

            c.

4. **A:** My sister is a very generous person.

   B. Do you mean she gives her children a lot of things?

   A: No. She teaches _____ others.

a.

   B: That's nice to hear. Those words encourage _____ my children to be generous, too.

b.

5. **A:** My parents weren't rich but they always helped other people.

   B: How did they do that?

   A: They donated their time. They taught _____ during my free time. So I tutor

a.

   high school kids after school. I want _____ their education.

b.

6. **A:** My parents always gave me money when I was a child.

   B: Did you buy a lot of toys?

   A: No. They didn't allow _____ a lot of things. They encouraged

a.

   _____ my money.

b.

   B: Save for what?

   A: I saved my money for a charity project.

7. **A:** Why does Leslie Natzke bring African girls to Chicago every summer?

   B: She wants _____ to college. She also wants _____

a.   b.

   leaders and teach other girls.

EXERCISE 6 Change the following imperative statements to statements with an object pronoun plus an infinitive.

1. A woman says to her husband, "Teach the children good values."

   She wants _him to teach the children good values._ _____

2. My parents always said to me, "Help others."

   They expected _____

3. A mother says to her children, "Don't forget about other people."

   She wants _____

4. The father said to his children, "Give to charity."

   He advised _____

continued

5. Parents say to their children, "Be kind to others."

They want _____

6. I said to you, "Work hard."

I would like _____

7. My parents said to us, "Give money to people in need."

They encouraged _____

8. A father says to his daughter, "Be generous."

He wants _____

9. My parents said to me, "Don't be selfish."

They encouraged _____

10. Parents say to their children, "Be polite."

They expect _____

EXERCISE 7 About You Use the verbs given to tell what your family wanted from you when you were growing up. Share your answers with a partner.

1. expect

<u>My parents expected me to be polite.</u>_____

2. advise

_____

3. permit

_____

4. tell

_____

5. expect

_____

6. encourage

_____

8.4 Causative Verbs

Some verbs are called *causative* verbs because one person causes, enables, or allows another to do something.

Examples	Explanation
Gates **has gotten** billionaires **to sign** the Giving Pledge. Carnegie **persuaded** wealthy people **to give** away their money. You **convinced** me **to help** others.	*Get*, *persuade*, and *convince* are followed by an object + infinitive. *Get*, in this case, means persuade.
Carnegie **helped** people **(to) get** an education. Leslie **helps** girls **(to) improve** their lives.	After *help* + object, either the infinitive or the base form can be used. The base form is more common.
When Carnegie was a child, he met a rich man who had a small library. This man **let** children **use** his library. This man **permitted** children **to use** his library. This man **allowed** children **to use** his library.	*Let*, *permit*, and *allow* have the same meaning.
No one can **make** you **give** to charity. Giving to charity **makes** me **feel** good.	*Make* is followed by an object + base form. *Make* can mean *force*. *Make* can mean *cause something to happen*.
Warren Buffet **had** his children **sign** the Giving Pledge. The teacher **had** us **write** a composition about charity.	*Have* means to give a job or task to someone. *Have*, in this case, is followed by an object + base form.

EXERCISE 8 Circle the correct verb form to complete each conversation.

1. **A:** Do you always give to charity?

   B: I know I should. But I don't always do it.

   A: Whenever I get a gift in the mail from a charity, I send a check. I think this is a good way to get people (*give*/*to give*).
   a.

   B: What kind of gifts do you receive in the mail?

   A: I often get address labels. Don't you?

   B: Yes, but that doesn't persuade me (*donate*/*to donate*) money. I just use the labels and throw away
   b.
   the donation envelope.

continued

2. **A:** I volunteered for the public TV station last month.

   B: What did they have you (*do/to do*)?

a.

   A: My job was to address envelopes. It was fun. I met other volunteers. And it made me (*feel/to feel*)

b.

   good about watching the station.

3. **A:** I have a doctor's appointment on Friday, and my car doesn't work.

   B: Let me (*drive/to drive*) you.

a.

   A: I don't want to bother you.

   B: It's not a bother. I love to volunteer my time.

4. **A:** When I was a child, my parents gave me money once a week.

   B: Did they let you (*buy/to buy*) whatever you wanted?

a.

   A: They allowed me (*use/to use*) half of the money. They had me (*save/to save*) the other half.

b.　　　　　　　　　　　　　　　　　　　　　　　　　c.

   They convinced me (*give/to give*) part of my savings to charity.

d.

EXERCISE 9 Fill in the blanks with the base form or the infinitive of the verb given.

There are many ways to help others. Some people donate money. I volunteer for my local public radio

station. The radio station needs money from listeners. Several times a year, the station tries to persuade

listeners _____to give_____ money to the station. Without their support, the radio station could not

1. give

exist. The station managers have us _____ the phones when people call to contribute. We let

2. answer

callers _____ us about their favorite programs. To get people _____,

3. tell　　　　　　　　　　　　　　　　　　　　　　　　　　4. contribute

the station offers some gifts. For example, for a $60 contribution, you can get a coffee mug. For a $100

contribution, you can get a book. Everyone can listen to public radio for free. No one makes you

_____ for it. But listeners should pay for this service, if they can. I'd like to convince my

5. pay

friends _____ or _____ in money.

6. volunteer　　　　　　　　　　7. send

8.5 Adjective plus Infinitive

Examples	Explanation
Some people are **happy to help** others. It makes me **sad to see** so many poor people. I am **proud to be** a volunteer. We are **pleased to help**.	Certain adjectives can be followed by an infinitive. Many of these adjectives describe a person's emotional or mental state.

Language Note:

The following adjectives can be followed by an infinitive:

afraid	eager	pleased	sad
ashamed	glad	prepared	sorry
delighted	happy	proud	surprised
disappointed	lucky	ready	willing

EXERCISE 10 A college student has volunteered her time with an agency that delivers food to poor families. She is discussing her duties with the volunteer coordinator. Fill in the blanks with an appropriate infinitive. Answers may vary.

A: Are you willing ___to donate___ your time on the weekends?

　　　　　　　　　　　　　1.

B: Yes. I'm eager _____ people who need my help. I'm ready _____ whatever

　　　　　　　　　2.　　　　　　　　　　　　　　　　　　　3.

you need me to do.

A: You're going to deliver meals to people in this neighborhood who don't have enough food.

B: I'm surprised _____ that some people don't have enough to eat. This seems like a

　　　　　　　　　4.

middle-class neighborhood.

A: It is. But the economy is bad. Most people are lucky _____ a job. But some people have

　　　　　　　　　　　　　　　　　　　　　　5.

lost their jobs. Often people are ashamed _____ for help.

　　　　　　　　　　　　　　　　　6.

B: I can understand that. But don't worry. I'm willing _____ anyone who needs my help.

　　　　　　　　　　　　　　　　　　　　　7.

A: Don't be afraid _____ into a stranger's home. Someone will always go with you.

　　　　　　　　8.

B: I'm happy _____ food to people who need it.

　　　　　9.

A: I'm glad that you're going to work with us. Your parents must be proud _____ such a

　　　　　　　　　　　　　　　　　　　　　　　　　　　　　10.

generous daughter.

B: And I'm lucky _____ such generous parents. They taught me about giving when I was

　　　　　　　11.

very young.

EXERCISE 11 Fill in the blanks with an infinitive or a base form in this conversation between an uncle and his nephew. Answers may vary.

A: What do you plan _____*to do*_____ this summer?
              1.

B: I wanted _____ a summer job, but I couldn't find one. It's going to be boring. I'm ready
                      2.

_____ , but no one wants _____ me. And my parents expect me
        3.   **4.**

_____ a job. My mom won't let me _____ home all day and watch TV or
        5.   **6.**

hang out with my friends at the swimming pool.

A: Are you trying _____ money for your college education?
                            7.

B: Not really. I haven't even thought about saving for college yet. I want a job because I'm planning

_____ a car.
        8.

A: You need _____ about college too. You're going to graduate next year.
                      9.

B: I'm planning _____ to a community college, so it won't be so expensive. And my parents
                            10.

are willing _____ for my college tuition.
                  11.

A: Have you thought about volunteering your time this summer?

B: Not really. I just want _____ money.
                                  12.

A: Don't just think about money. Try _____ about how you can help other people. You can
                                                13.

help little kids _____ to read. Or you can help _____ the parks by picking
                        14.   **15.**

up garbage.

B: I keep telling you. I just want _____ money. What will I get if I do those things? I won't
                                            16.

get my car.

A: You'll get satisfaction. Helping others will make you _____ good. And you'll learn
                                                                      17.

_____ responsible. After you finish community college and go to a four-year college, it
        18.

will look good on your application if you say you volunteered. It will help you _____ into
                                                                                        19.

a good college.

B: Why are you trying so hard to get me _____ a volunteer?
                                                  20.

A: I volunteered when I was your age, and I found that it was more valuable than money.

B: OK. I'll volunteer if you're willing _____ me the money for the car.
                                                  21.

ONE STEP at a TIME

 Read the following article. Pay special attention to the words in bold.

CD 2
TR 8

Joyce Koenig, an artist, believes that it's important **to help** others. She heard of a summer camp in Wisconsin called One Step at a Time, for children with cancer. Even though these kids are sick, it's important for them **to have** fun too. It costs money for these kids **to go** to camp, so Joyce decided **to see** what she could do to help. It's impossible for her **to donate** a lot of money, so she had to think of another way **to help**.

She wanted **to combine** her love of art and her desire **to help** others. She had an idea: She started making and selling beautiful cards in order **to raise** money for these kids. Because these cards are all handmade, it was taking her a long time **to make** a lot of them. So Joyce had another idea. She started inviting friends to her house **to help** her make the cards. Often, she has card-making parties; the guests go into her studio and make the cards together. At first her friends were hesitant.[6] Many said that they were not artistic and didn't know how **to make** cards. But once they saw the beautiful materials that she had in her studio, her friends felt more comfortable designing, cutting, and pasting in order **to make** an original card.

But the materials are expensive. **To make** money without spending money, Joyce asks for and gets donations of paper, glue, scissors, ribbon, and other supplies from nearby stores. She sells her cards for $2 each at various art fairs during the year. Since she started her project, she has raised more than $40,000—two dollars at a time.

---

[6] *hesitant:* unsure

COMPREHENSION CHECK Based on the reading, tell if the statement is true (**T**) or false (**F**).

1. Joyce uses her love of art to find a way to make money for kids with cancer.

2. To produce a large number of cards, she needed the help of her friends.

3. At first, her friends were eager to help her.

8.6 Infinitives as Subjects

Examples	Explanation
It's important **to help** other people. **It**'s fun **to make** cards. **It**'s possible **to get** materials for free.	An infinitive phrase can be the subject of a sentence. *It* introduces a delayed infinitive subject.
It is important **for Joyce to help** others. It wasn't possible **for her to make** a lot of cards by herself.	*For* + an object gives the infinitive a specific subject.
It costs a lot of money **to send** the kids to camp. **It takes** time and effort **to raise** money.	An infinitive is often used after *cost* + money and *take* + time.
It **took Joyce** three years to raise $30,000. It **costs her** very little to make cards.	An object can follow *take* and *cost*.
To give money away is the best thing rich people can do. **To help** others gives a person satisfaction.	Sometimes we begin a sentence with an infinitive phrase. A sentence that begins with an infinitive is formal.

EXERCISE 12   Fill in the blanks with any missing words.

1. It's enjoyable _____*to*_____ make cards.

2. It doesn't _____ a lot of time to make a card.

3. _____ fun to get together and make cards.

4. It's not hard _____ Joyce's friends to make cards.

5. _____ help sick children is Joyce's goal.

6. It _____ only $2 _____ buy a card.

7. "_____ give away money is the best thing rich people can do," said Carnegie.

EXERCISE 13   Complete each statement with an infinitive phrase to talk about volunteering, donating money, etc. Share your answers with a partner.

1. It's important _to think about the needs of others._

2. It isn't necessary _____

3. It's a good idea _____

4. It's everyone's responsibility _____

5. It costs a lot of money _____

6. It's important _____

7. It takes a lot of time _____

8. It doesn't take long _____

EXERCISE 14 Complete each statement. Begin with an *it* phrase. Share your answers with a partner.

1. _____ It's impossible _____ to get every billionaire to sign the Giving Pledge.

2. _____ It isn't hard _____ to get donations of materials.

3. _____ to help other people.

4. _____ to give away money.

5. _____ to die rich.

6. _____ to have a lot of money.

7. _____ not to have a good education.

8. _____ to live in the U.S.

EXERCISE 15 Change these statements to make them less formal by starting them with *it*.

1. To raise money for charity is a good thing.

   It's a good thing to raise money for charity.

2. To raise one million dollars is not easy.

   _____

3. To fight disease takes a lot of money.

   _____

4. To help poor people is everyone's responsibility.

   _____

5. To produce high-quality education takes a lot of money.

   _____

6. To build libraries was Carnegie's dream.

   _____

7. To raise money for sick children is Joyce's goal.

   _____

8. To fight disease in poor countries will take time.

   _____

8.7 Infinitives to Show Purpose

Examples	Explanation
Joyce sells cards **in order to raise** money.	*In order to* shows purpose. It answers the question *Why?* or *What for?*
Joyce sells cards **to raise** money.	*In order to* can be shortened. We can simply use *to*.
In order to raise money, Joyce sells cards.	The purpose phrase can come before the main clause. If so, we use a comma after the purpose phrase.

EXERCISE 16   Fill in the blanks to complete the sentences. Answers may vary.

1. In order to _____ learn _____ more about volunteering, you can use the Internet.

2. Carnegie donated his money to _____ libraries.

3. You can volunteer in order to _____ job experience.

4. To _____ a job, you need experience. To _____ experience, you need a job.

5. You can volunteer your time in order to _____ people. There are many people who need help.

6. Joyce started making and selling cards in order to _____ money to send kids to camp.

7. Leslie Natzke went to Africa in order _____ in the Peace Corps.

8. She brings girls from Niger to Chicago _____ them a better education.

8.8 Infinitives with *Too* and *Enough*

Examples	Explanation
This card is **too** big to fit in that envelope. I have **enough** time to make a card.	*Too* shows excess for a specific purpose. *Enough* shows sufficiency for a specific purpose.
You are never **too young to help** others. I worked **too slowly to finish** the card.	*too* + adjective/adverb + infinitive
I have **too much work to do**, so I have no time to volunteer. There are **too many problems** in the world **to solve** in one day.	*too much* + noncount noun + infinitive *too many* + plural count noun + infinitive
Am I **talented enough to design** a card? Joyce sells cards **easily enough to raise** money.	Adjective/adverb + *enough* + infinitive
I have **enough time to volunteer** this summer.	*enough* + noun + infinitive
Making cards is not too hard **for me to do**.	The infinitive phrase can be preceded by *for* + object.
I can't volunteer this summer because I'm **too busy**. Carnegie could build libraries because he had **enough money**.	Sometimes the infinitive phrase can be omitted. It is understood from the context: too busy = too busy to volunteer enough money = enough money to build libraries

EXERCISE 17 Fill in the blanks with the words given. Put the words in the correct order. Add *to* where necessary.

A: I heard about your card project, and I'd like to help you. But I don't have ___enough talent___ .

1. talent/enough

I'm _____ something new.

2. old/too/learn

B: It's so _____ cards. Anyone can do it.

3. easy/make

A: I think it takes _____ a card. I don't have _____

4. long/too/make   **5.** time/enough

and I'm not _____ .

6. talented/enough

B: It only takes about 15 minutes _____ a card.

7. make

A: I'd really like to help but I'm _____ you at this time. I have

8. busy/too/help

_____ at my job.

9. work/too much/do

B: That's not a problem. When people have _____ , they help. If not, that's okay too.

10. time/enough/help

A: But I'd really like to help. Is there anything else I can do?

B: You can make a donation. You can buy just one card for $2.

A: Really? They're so inexpensive. I have _____ five cards now.

11. money/enough/buy

B: Great! Every dollar helps.

EXERCISE 18 Fill in the blanks with *too, too much, too many,* or *enough* and any other words necessary to complete the conversation. Answers may vary.

A: I heard about a volunteer project at the park. Some friends and I are going to pick up garbage.

B: Why would you want to do that? I don't have ___enough time___ to pick up garbage. I have

1.

_____ things to do.

2.

A: You always say you want to volunteer. About 50 volunteers are coming. It won't take

_____ to finish the job.

3.

B: But it's _____ to spend the whole day in the sun. It's almost 90 degrees today.

4.

A: We can go swimming afterwards. The park has a big swimming pool. You swim, right?

B: Yes, but I don't swim _____ to swim in deep water.

5.

A: Don't worry. There's a shallow end and a deep end. You can stay in the shallow end.

B: The shallow end has a lot of kids. And the kids make _____ noise.

6.

A: I guess you're just not interested in helping out.

3. A: Do you think it's hard for Bill Gates to give away money?

B: I don't think so. He's been doing it for a long time. So I think he _____
$\underset{\text{give}}{}$

away a lot of money.

4. A: Don't you think the story about Dawson is strange?

B: Why?

A: He had a lot of money but he continued to drive his old car.

B: Well, he _____ his old car. So it wasn't a problem for him.
$\underset{\text{drive}}{}$

5. A: Patty Stonesifer had a high-paying job, but now she works with people in need. It must be hard.

B: She loves it. She learned from her parents to help others. So she _____
$\underset{\text{help}}{}$

other people.

6. A: I have a volunteer job on the weekends.

B: Do you like it?

A: I like the job, but I _____ on the weekend. I always used to relax
$\underset{\text{work}}{}$

and watch sports on TV on the weekend.

7. A: Joyce invites people to her house to make cards.

B: I'm glad she's not inviting me. I _____ anything artistic.
$\underset{\text{a. do}}{}$

A: Everyone tells her the same thing. She _____ that. But she always explains that
$\underset{\text{b. hear}}{}$

no artistic talent is necessary.

8. A: I want to do an AIDS bike ride. I have a lot of experience riding a bike.

B: Why don't you do it, then?

A: There's just one problem. I'm from Thailand, where we always ride on the left side of the street.

I _____ on the right side. I'm afraid I'll have an accident.
$\underset{\text{ride}}{}$

EXERCISE 33 Here is a story of a San Francisco man who did the Alaska AIDS ride. Circle the correct words to complete the story.

In 2001, I went on the AIDS bike ride in Alaska. My friends told me about it and asked me to join them.

At first I was afraid. My friends are good bikers. They (*used to ride*/*are used to riding*) long distances
1.

because they do it all the time. They persuaded me to try it because it was for such a good cause. To get

ready for the ride, I had to make some lifestyle changes. (*I'm*/*I*) used to be a little overweight, so I had to
2.

slim down and get in shape. First, I went on a diet. (*I*/*I was*) used to eating a lot of meat, but now I eat
3.

mostly vegetables and fish. Also, I decided to get more exercise. I used to (*take*/*taking*) the bus to work every
4.

day, but I decided to start riding my bike to work. I work ten miles from home, so it was hard for me at first.

But little by little, I (*got used to*/*used to*) it. On the weekends, I started to take longer rides. Eventually I got
5.

used to (*ride*/*riding*) about 45–50 miles a day. When the time came for the AIDS ride, I thought I was
6.

prepared. I live in San Francisco, which is hilly, so I was used to (*ride*/*riding*) up and down hills. But it's not
7.

cold in San Francisco. On some days the temperature in Alaska was only 25 degrees Fahrenheit, with strong

winds. At first I (*wasn't*/*couldn't*) get used to the cold. It was especially hard to (*used*/*get used*) to the strong
8.   **9.**

winds. But eventually, I got (*use*/*used*) to it. I am proud to say I was one of the 1,600 riders who finished the
10.

ride. I didn't (*use*/*used*) to think that one person could make a difference, but I raised close to $4,000. As a
11.

group we raised $4 million. And I've become a much healthier person because of this experience.

Cyclists during an AIDS Day Bike Ride in Davis, California

8.18 Sense-Perception Verbs

After sense-perception verbs, we can use either the *-ing* form or the base form with only a slight difference in meaning.

Examples	Explanation
I **heard** you **talk** about the Giving Pledge a few days ago. Dan Pallotta **saw** many people around him **die** of AIDS.	When the base form is used after a sense-perception verb (*saw*, *heard*, etc.), it indicates completion.
I **heard** you **talking** about a charity project. I **saw** some teenagers **volunteering** in the park last week.	When the *-ing* form is used after a sense-perception verb, it shows that something is sensed while it is in progress. I heard you **while you were talking** about a charity project. I saw teenagers **who were volunteering** in the park.

Language Note:

The sense-perception verbs are: *hear, listen, feel, smell, see, watch, observe.*

EXERCISE 34 Fill in the blanks with the base form or *-ing* form of the verb given. In some cases, both forms are possible.

By their example, my parents always taught me to help others. One time, when I was a child on the way

to a birthday party with my father, we saw a small boy _____walking_____ alone on the street. As we
1. walk

approached him, we heard him _____. My father went up to him and asked him what was
2. cry

wrong. The boy said that he was lost. I saw my father _____ his hand and heard him
3. take

_____ the boy that he would help him find his parents. My father called the police. Even
4. tell

though we were in a hurry to go to the party, my father insisted on staying with the boy until the police

arrived. I really wanted to go to the party and started to cry. I felt my father _____ my hand
5. take

and talk to me softly. He said, "We can't enjoy the party while this little boy is alone and helpless." Before

the police arrived, I saw a woman _____ in our direction. It was the boy's mother. She was
6. run

so grateful to my father for helping her son that she offered to give him money. I heard my father

_____ her, "I can't take money from you. I'm happy to be of help to your son."
7. tell

I hear so many children today _____, "I want" or "Buy me" or "Give me." I think it's
8. say

important to teach children to think of others before they think of themselves. If they see their parents

_____ others, they will probably grow up to be charitable people.
9. help

SUMMARY OF LESSON 8

Infinitives and Base Forms

Examples	Explanation
Matel Dawson *wanted* **to help** others.	An infinitive is used after certain verbs.
His mother wanted *him* **to help** others.	An infinitive can follow an object noun or pronoun.
He was *happy* **to give** away his money.	An infinitive can follow certain adjectives.
We sell cards (**in order**) **to raise** money.	An infinitive is used to show purpose.
It's important **to help** others. **To help** others is our moral obligation.	INFORMAL: *It* introduces a delayed infinitive subject. FORMAL: The infinitive can be in the subject position.
It's good *for people* **to help** others. It's fun *for me* **to volunteer.**	*For* + noun or object pronoun is used to give the infinitive a subject.
I have *enough* time **to volunteer.** Dawson was *too* poor **to finish** school.	An infinitive can be used after a phrase with *too* and *enough.*
He often *heard* his mother **talk** about helping.	After sense perception verbs, a base form is used for a completed action.
It is important **to be loved.**	An infinitive can be used in the passive voice.
She *let* me **work.** She *made* me **work.** She *had* me **work.** She *got* me **to work.** She *convinced* me **to work.** She *persuaded* me **to work.**	After causative verbs *let, make,* and *have,* we use the base form. After causative verbs *get, convince,* and *persuade,* we use the infinitive.
He *helped* students **to get** an education. He *helped* them **pay** their tuition.	After *help,* either the infinitive or the base form can be used.

Gerunds

Examples	Explanation
Going to college is expensive in the U.S.	A gerund can be the subject of the sentence.
Dawson *enjoyed* **giving** money away.	A gerund follows certain verbs.
He learned *about* **giving** from his parents.	A gerund can be used after a preposition.
He had a hard *time* **supporting** his family.	A gerund is used after certain nouns.
Those teenagers over there are volunteers. You can *see* them **cleaning** the park.	An *–ing* form is used after sense perception verbs to describe an action in progress.
He doesn't like to **go shopping.**	A gerund is used in many expressions with *go.*
I appreciate **being given** an education.	A gerund can be used in the passive voice.

Gerund or Infinitive—Differences in Meaning

Examples	Explanation
I **used to spend** all my extra money. Now I save it.	Discontinued past habit
Patty **is used to working** in a poor neighborhood.	Present custom
Mimi always rode her bike on flat land. It was hard for her to **get used to riding** in the mountains.	Change of custom
Bicyclists can **stop to rest** when they get tired.	Stop one activity in order to do something else
When I was younger, I did the AIDS ride. I **stopped doing** it because it's too hard for me now.	Stop something completely
I **try to give** a little money to charity each year.	Make an attempt or effort
My old bike wasn't good enough for the ride. I **tried using** a mountain bike, and it was much better.	Experiment with a different method
Remember to help other people.	Remember and then do
Do you **remember reading** about Patty Stonesifer?	Remember something about the past

TEST/REVIEW

Fill in the blanks with the correct form of the verb given. Add prepositions, if necessary. In some cases, more than one answer is possible.

It's difficult for a college student ___to have___ time for anything else but studying. But when Charity
1. have

Bell was a student at Harvard, she made time in her busy schedule _____ babies in need.
2. help

When Bell was 23, she became interested _____ needy babies. She was volunteering at a
3. help

children's hospital. The volunteer organization wanted her _____ to the kids and
4. read

_____ games with them. The parents of these very sick children were there too, but they were
5. play

often too tired _____ or _____ with their kids. They were grateful to her
6. read   **7.** play

_____ them. One day she went to the hospital and heard a baby _____ loudly in
8. help   **9.** cry

the next room. She went into that room and picked up the baby; the baby immediately stopped

_____. She stayed with the baby for a few hours. When she began _____, the
10. cry   **11.** leave

baby started _____ again. Bell asked the nurse about this baby, and the nurse told her that the
12. cry

baby was taken away from her parents and they couldn't find a temporary home for her.

The next day, Bell started _____ about how to be a foster parent. She made herself
13. learn

available to help on nights and weekends. Her phone started _____ immediately. She got used
14. ring

to _____ up the phone in the middle of the night. She became accustomed _____
15. pick   **16.** take

in children all the time. Before she started taking care of babies, she used to _____ seven or
17. sleep

eight hours a night. Then she had to get used to _____ only three or four hours a night.
18. sleep

By the time she was 28 years old and in graduate school, Bell had been a foster mother to 50 children.

_____ her studies, she had to take "her" babies to class with her. Her professors let her
19. complete

_____ this. They understood that it was necessary for her _____ and
20. do   **21.** study

_____ care of the babies at the same time. And her classmates didn't complain about
22. take

_____ a baby in the back of the class. Everyone understood how important it was for her
23. have

_____ these babies.
24. help

Even though Bell is sometimes tired, she is never too tired _____ in a child that needs her.
25. take

She gets very little money for _____ care of these children. However, she gets great satisfaction
26. take

_____ a baby _____. _____ her babies _____ is always
27. watch   **28.** grow   **29.** see   **30.** leave

a bit sad for her, but there are more babies who need her. _____ love to a child is her greatest joy.
31. bring

WRITING

PART 1 Editing Advice

1. Don't forget *to* when introducing an infinitive.

   He wants ∧ help other people. *to*

   It's important ∧ be a charitable person. *to*

2. Don't omit *it* when introducing a delayed infinitive.

   I̶s̶ important for rich people to help others. *It's*

3. After *want, need*, and *expect*, use the object pronoun, not the subject pronoun, before the infinitive.

   My parents want t̶h̶a̶t̶ ̶I̶ donate money to charity. *me to*

4. Don't use *to* between *cost* or *take* and the indirect object.

   It costs t̶o̶ Leslie five thousand dollars to bring a girl to the U.S. from Niger.

   It took t̶o̶ him twenty hours to finish the bike ride.

5. Use *for*, not *to*, when you give a subject to the infinitive.

   It is easy t̶o̶ me to ride my bike on flat land. *for*

6. Use *to* + base form, not *for*, to show purpose.

   Carnegie worked hard f̶o̶r̶ build libraries. *to*

7. Use a gerund or an infinitive, not a base form, as a subject.

   Help ∧ others makes me feel good. OR It makes me feel good to help others. *ing*

8. Don't confuse *used to* and *be used* to.

   I a̶m̶ used to drive to school. Now I ride my bike.

   I've lived in Alaska all my life and I love it. I ∧ used to l̶i̶v̶e̶ in Alaska. *'m* *living*

9. Be careful to use the correct form after *stop*.

   The story about Dawson was so interesting. I can't stop t̶o̶ think ∧ about it. *ing*

10. Use a gerund, not an infinitive, after a preposition.

    Have you ever thought about t̶o̶ volunteer ∧ with children? *ing*

11. Make sure to choose a gerund after certain verbs and an infinitive after others.

    I enjoy t̶o̶ help ∧ other people. *ing*

    He decided v̶o̶l̶u̶n̶t̶e̶e̶r̶i̶n̶g̶ in the public library. *to volunteer*

12. Use a base form after a sense-perception verb that shows completion.

I saw Mimi ~~to~~ finish her bike ride.

13. Use the base form, not the infinitive, after causative verbs *let*, *make*, and *have*.

Bill Gates has billionaires ~~to~~ sign the Giving Pledge.

PART 2 Editing Practice

Some of the shaded words and phrases have mistakes. Find the mistakes and correct them. If the shaded words are correct, write C.

It's important for everyone do something for others. I often thought about to help other people.
1. (C) **2.** (to) **3.**

My parents wanted that I help in their business, but I saw my parents to work too hard, and they
4. **5.**

had very little satisfaction from it or time for our family. I decided become a nurse instead. It took
6.

to me three years to complete the nursing program, and I'm happy I did it. First, find a job was easy
7. **8.** **9.**

because nurses are always in demand. Second, I enjoy working with sick people and make them
10. **11.**

to feel better. Some of my friends think is depressing to work with sick people all day, but it's easy for
12. **13.** **14.** **15.**

me to do it because I love helping people.
16. **17.**

There's one thing I don't like about my job: I have to work nights, from 11 p.m. to 7 a.m. At
18.

first, I couldn't get used to sleep in the day. My kids are home on Saturday and Sunday, and when
19.

I was trying sleeping, they sometimes wouldn't stop to make noise. When they were younger,
20. **21.**

they're used to make a lot of noise, but now that they're older, they understand. My wife made them
22.

understand that their dad needed his sleep and she needed them be quiet in the morning. My
23. **24.**

daughter is now thinking about become a nurse too.
25.

People work for make money, but it's important for everyone finding a job that they love.
26. **27.** **28.**

Working as a nurse has been wonderful for me. I get a lot of satisfaction helping other people.
29. **30.**

PART 3 Write About It

1. Andrew Carnegie wrote: "It is not good to have money if your spirit is poor." Describe what it means to have a rich spirit or a poor spirit. Give examples using people you know or have read about.

2. How does volunteering enrich the life of the volunteer?

PART 4 Edit Your Writing

Reread the Summary of Lesson 8 and the editing advice. Edit your writing from Part 3.

Adverbial Clauses and Phrases
Sentence Connectors (Conjunctive Adverbs)
So/Such That **for Result**

COMING TO
AMERICA

The sun sets behind the Statue of Liberty,
an American symbol of freedom.

Everywhere immigrants have enriched and strengthened the fabric of American life.

— John F. Kennedy

A NATION of IMMIGRANTS

🎧
CD 2
TR 12
Read the following article. Pay special attention to the words in bold.

Ever since the United States became a country, it has been a nation of immigrants. The United States takes in more foreigners than the rest of the world combined, almost one million a year.

It is not uncommon for Americans to ask each other about their family background. Except for Native Americans, Americans have their roots in one or more countries. **Even though they are proud to be Americans**, many people often use two or more words to describe their national identity: "I'm Greek American," or "I'm an African American," or "I'm one-fourth English, one-fourth Irish, and one-half Polish."

Why have so many people chosen to leave everything behind to come to a new land **in spite of the hardships**[1] **they face**? The answer to that question is as diverse as the people who have come to the United States. In the 1600s, the first group of immigrants were the Pilgrims, who left England **to seek** religious freedom in America. Many other groups followed **to escape** hardship or **to find** opportunity.

In the 1800s, Germans came **because of political unrest and economic problems in Germany**. Irish and Chinese people came **because of famine in their countries**. At the beginning of the twentieth century, many Jews came from Eastern Europe **in order to escape** religious persecution.[2] Many Italians came **for** work.

By 1910, almost 15 percent of the population was foreign born. Some people thought: **if immigration continues at this pace**, the United States will lose its "American" identity. In 1924, Congress passed a law limiting the number of immigrants. By 1970, less than 5 percent of the population was foreign born, an all-time low.

In 1965, Congress passed a bill allowing more immigrants to come, and the foreign-born population started to rise quickly. In the 1970s, Vietnamese and Cambodians came **because of war**. Immigration from Asian countries quadrupled. Many others, such as Bosnians and Iraqis, came **because their countries were at war**. And, as always, people came **so that they could be reunited with family members who had come before**.

According to the 2010 census, 12.9 percent of the population was foreign born, with most of the immigrants from Asia and Latin America. In addition to legal immigration, about 11.7 million immigrants are living in the United States illegally. **Since the U.S. Census cannot count these people**, this number is only an estimate.

The United States is and has always been perceived as the land of freedom and opportunity.

Foreign-Born Population and Percentage of Total Population, for the United States: 1850 to 2010

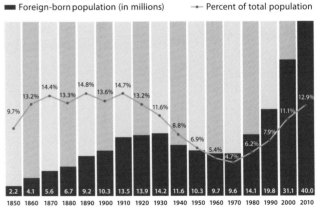

Source: U.S. Census Bureau, Census of Population, 1850 to 2000 and the American Community Survey, 2010.

---

[1] *hardship:* difficulty
[2] *persecution:* unjust or cruel treatment because of differences in belief

COMPREHENSION CHECK Based on the reading, tell if the statement is true (**T**) or false (**F**).

1. The highest percentage of foreign-born Americans was in 1910.

2. Americans often identify themselves with the nationality of their ancestors.

3. Most of the immigrants coming to America today are from Europe.

9.1 Adverbial Clauses and Phrases—Introduction

Some sentences have an adverbial clause or phrase and a main clause.

Examples	Explanation
Before the 1960s, more than half of immigrants came from Europe.	An adverbial clause or phrase can show **time**.
Germans came to the U.S. **because of economic problems in Germany**.	An adverbial clause or phrase can show **reason**.
Many immigrants come **so that they can be reunited with family members**.	An adverbial clause or phrase can show **purpose**.
Even though it's hard to be an immigrant, many people make that choice.	An adverbial clause or phrase can show **contrast**.
If there is a war in a country, many people leave that country.	An adverbial clause or phrase can show **condition**.

Language Note:

The adverbial clause or phrase can come before or after the main clause. If it comes before, it is usually separated from the main clause with a comma.

I went to Canada before I came to the United States. (NO COMMA)
Before I came to the United States, I went to Canada. (COMMA)

EXERCISE 1 Listen to the following story about the author's family. Fill in the blanks with the words you hear.

CD 2
TR 13

I'm a Jewish American. My maternal grandfather came to the United States from Poland in 1911

___because___ he wanted a better life for his wife and children. Life was hard for them in Poland,
     1.

and they had heard stories of how you could better yourself in America _____ you were
     2.

poor. _____ my grandfather was working as a tailor in Chicago, he saved money
     3.

_____ he could bring his family to join him. _____ ten years of hard work,
     4.   **5.**

he had finally saved up enough money. _____ he had been in the United States for
     6.

ten years, he didn't learn much English _____ he had to go to work immediately.
     7.

continued

_____ my grandmother and her four children started their journey in 1921, they had
                    8.

never left their village before. They arrived in New York _____ that was the entry point for
                                                                              9.

most immigrants at that time. They were tired and scared _____ they didn't speak one word
                                                                        10.

of English. They were afraid of what to do next, _____ finally, they saw my grandfather
                                                                 11.

waiting for them. The immigration officials detained them in New York _____ my mother's
                                                                                        12.

youngest sister was sick. At that time, you couldn't enter the country _____ your health was
                                                                                     13.

good. She was taken to a hospital. _____ she was in the hospital for one week, she was
                                                        14.

released and the family was ready to start their new life. From New York, they took a train to Chicago.

_____ they arrived in Chicago, my mother, the oldest, was sixteen years old. She went to
          15.

work in a factory _____ she could help her younger brother and sisters get an education.
                            16.

EXERCISE 2 In Exercise 1, tell if the filled in words express time (T), reason (R), purpose (P),
contrast (Ct), or condition (Cd).

1. __R__	5. _____	9. _____	13. _____
2. _____	6. _____	10. _____	14. _____
3. _____	7. _____	11. _____	15. _____
4. _____	8. _____	12. _____	16. _____

**Immigrants arrive at Ellis Island
in the early 1900s.**

9.2 Reason and Purpose

Examples	Explanation
My family left Poland **because they wanted to improve their lives**.	*Because* introduces a clause of reason.
My grandfather didn't have time to go to school **because of his job**.	*Because of* introduces a noun or noun phrase.
Since the U.S. Census cannot count illegal immigrants, their number is only an estimate.	*Since* means *because*. It is used to introduce a fact. The main clause is the result of this fact.
The Pilgrims came **in order to seek religious freedom**. Vietnamese people came **to escape war**.	*In order to* shows purpose. The short form is *to*. We follow *to* with the base form of the verb.
My grandmother came **so that the family could be reunited**. He wants his wife to come next year **so they can be together again**.	*So that* shows purpose. The short form is *so*. The purpose clause usually contains a modal: *can, will,* or *may* for future; *could, would,* or *might* for past.
She came to the U.S. **for a better life**.	*For* shows purpose. *For* is followed by a noun (phrase).

Language Notes:

1. Remember: *Since* can also be used to show time. The context tells you the meaning of *since*.

    He has been in the U.S. **since** 2003. (time)

    Since my grandfather had to work hard, he didn't have time to study English. (reason)

2. *So* is also used to show result. The context tells you the meaning of *so*.

    I came to the U.S. alone, **so** I miss my family. (result)

    I came to the U.S. **so (that)** I could get an education. (purpose)

    Notice that a comma is used for result but not for purpose.

EXERCISE 3 Fill in the blanks with *because, because of, since, for, (in order) to,* or *so (that)*.

1. Many immigrants came to the U.S. ___(in order) to___ escape famine.

2. Many immigrants came _____ they didn't have enough to eat.

3. _____ they could give their children a good education, many immigrants came to the U.S.

4. _____ the political situation, many people left their countries.

5. Many immigrants came _____ they could escape war.

6. Many immigrants came _____ the poor economy in their countries.

7. Many immigrants came _____ be reunited with their relatives.

8. _____ war destroyed their homes, many people left their countries.

9. _____ escape poverty, many immigrants came to the U.S.

continued

10. Often immigrants come _____ they want a better future for their children.

11. Immigrants come to the U.S. _____ a better life.

EXERCISE 4 Complete the conversation using *because, because of, for, since, so (that),* or *(in order) to*. Answers may vary.

A: I heard you moved.

B: Yes. We moved last month. We bought a bigger house ____*so that*____ we would have room for my
1.
parents. They're coming to the U.S. next month _____ they want to be near us.
2.

A: Don't you mind having your parents live with you?

B: Not at all. It'll be good for them and good for us. _____ our jobs, we don't get home until
3.
after 6 p.m., and we don't want the kids to come home to an empty house.

A: Are your parents going to work?

B: No. They're not coming here _____ jobs. They're in their late 60s and are both retired.
4.
They're coming here _____ they can help out. But they're not just coming
5.
_____ babysit. We want the kids to spend time with my parents _____ they
6.   7.
won't forget our language. Also, we want them to learn about our culture _____ they've
8.
never been to our country. Our son is starting to speak more English than Spanish. He prefers English
_____ all his friends speak English.
9.

A: That's how many kids are in America. They prefer to speak English _____ they can be just
10.
like their friends. Do your parents speak English?

B: Just a little. What about your parents? Where do they live?

A: They live a few blocks away from me, but we almost never see each other _____ our
11.
different schedules. _____ they work in the day and I work in the evening, it's hard for us to
12.
get together.

EXERCISE 5 About You Fill in the blank with a reason or purpose. Discuss your answer with a partner.

1. I (or My family) decided to come to the U.S. _____.

2. I (or We) chose this city _____.

3. I (or We) plan/don't plan to go back _____.

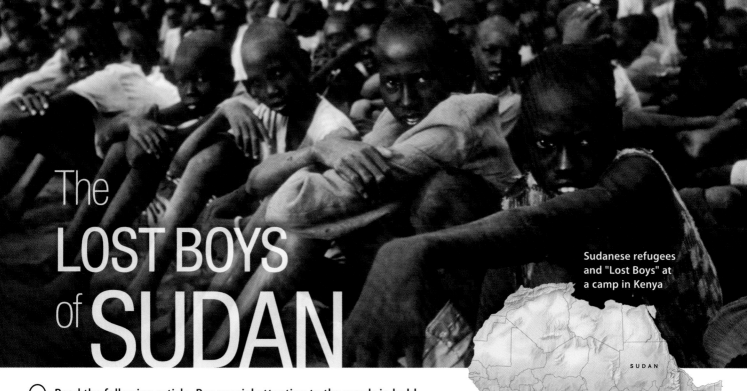

The LOST BOYS of SUDAN

Sudanese refugees and "Lost Boys" at a camp in Kenya

SUDAN

SOUTH SUDAN ETHIOPIA

KENYA

🎧 **Read the following article. Pay special attention to the words in bold.**

CD 2
TR 14

Besides immigrants, the United States takes in thousands of refugees a year. The Lost Boys of Sudan were children, living in southern Sudan in the late 1980s, when their long and difficult journey to the United States began. **While** these young boys were in the field taking care of their cattle,[3] their villages were attacked. These children, mostly boys between the ages of 4 and 12, ran for their lives. **For** three months, they walked hundreds of miles **until** they reached Ethiopia. They survived by eating leaves, roots, and wild fruit.

During that time, many died of starvation[4] and disease or were eaten by wild animals. Those who reached Ethiopia stayed in refugee camps **until** 1991, when a war started in Ethiopia and the camps were closed. They ran again, back to Sudan and then to Kenya, where they stayed in refugee camps **for** almost ten years. Of the approximately 27,000 boys who fled Sudan, only 11,000 survived.

During their time in the refugee camp, they got some schooling and learned basic English. In 1999, the United Nations and the U.S. government agreed to resettle 3,800 Lost Boys in the United States.

When they arrived in the United States, many challenges awaited them. They had to learn a completely new way of life. Many things were new for them: apartment living in a big city, strange foods, new technologies, and much more. **When** they saw an American supermarket for the first time, they were amazed by the amount of food. One boy was so surprised by the quantity of food in a supermarket that he asked if it was the palace of the king.

Agencies helped the Lost Boys with money for food and rent for a short time **until** they found jobs. **While** they were working, most of them enrolled in ESL classes. Now men, many have graduated from college and have started projects to help their villages back home. Peter Magai Bul, of Chicago, helped establish a school in his hometown. **While** he was studying for his college degree, Peter helped to raise funds for this school, which is currently educating over five hundred South Sudan students.

Although their future in the United States looks bright, **whenever** they think about their homeland, they are sad because so many of their family members and friends have died.

---

[3] *cattle:* cows, bulls, and oxen as a group
[4] *starvation:* the state of having no food, being extremely hungry

COMPREHENSION CHECK Based on the reading, tell if the statement is true (**T**) or false (**F**).

1. The Lost Boys were in a refugee camp in Ethiopia until they came to the U.S.

2. When their villages were attacked, the Lost Boys ran back home.

3. Some of the Lost Boys are helping their people in South Sudan.

9.3 Time Clauses and Phrases

Examples	Explanation
When their villages were attacked, the Lost Boys ran. Some young men will help their people back home **when** they finish college.	*When* means "at that time" or "immediately after that time." In a future sentence, we use the present in the time clause.
Whenever they think about their country, they are sad. **Whenever** they tell their story, Americans are amazed.	*Whenever* means "any time" or "every time."
They walked **until** they reached Ethiopia. They received money for a short time **until** they got jobs.	*Until* means "up to that time."
Peter has been a student **since** he came to the U.S. He has been working **(ever) since** he arrived in the U.S.	*Since* or *ever since* means "from that time in the past to the present." We use the present perfect or present perfect continuous in the main clause.
While they were taking care of their cattle, their villages were bombed. **As** they were coming to the U.S., they were thinking about their new life ahead.	We use *while* or *as* with a continuous action.
They walked **for** three months. They stayed in a refugee camp **for** many years.	We use *for* with an amount of time.
During the day, they walked. **During** their time in the refugee camp, they studied English.	We use *during* with a time such as *the day* or *summer*, or with a specific time period (*their time in Ethiopia, the month of August*) or an event (*the flight to the U.S.*).

EXERCISE 6 Fill in the blanks with *since, until, while, when, as, during, for,* or *whenever*. In some cases, more than one answer is possible.

1. The Lost Boys were very young _____*when*_____ they left Sudan.

2. The Lost Boys walked _____ many months.

3. _____ their march to Ethiopia, many of them died.

4. They lived in Ethiopia _____ about four years.

5. They crossed the river _____ the rainy season.

6. Some died _____ they were walking to Ethiopia.

7. They studied English _____ they were living in Kenya.

8. _____ they were traveling to the U.S., they were wondering about their future.

9. They had never seen a gas stove _____ they came to the U.S.

10. _____ they came to the U.S., they have had to learn many new things.

11. _____ they came to the U.S., they saw modern appliances for the first time.

12. They enrolled in ESL classes _____ they came to the U.S.

13. In the U.S. many of them worked _____ they were going to school.

14. Peter has been working on his project back home _____ 2004.

15. _____ they think about their terrible journey, they feel sad.

EXERCISE 7 Fill in the blanks with an appropriate time word. In some cases, more than one answer is possible.

_____When_____ I was a child, I heard many stories about life in America. _____
        1.   **2.**

I saw American movies, I dreamed about coming to the U.S. My uncle had lived in the U.S.

_____ many years, and he often came back to visit. _____ he came back, he
        3.   **4.**

used to tell me stories and show me pictures of the U.S. _____ I was a teenager, I asked my
                                                                                    5.

mother if she would let me visit my uncle _____ my summer vacation, but she said I was too
                                                                    6.

young and the trip was too expensive. _____ I was 20, I finally decided to come to the U.S.
                                                                7.

_____ I was traveling to the U.S., I thought about all the stories my uncle had told me.
        8.

But I really knew nothing about the U.S. _____ I came here. _____
                                                                    9.   **10.**

I came to the U.S., I've been working hard and trying to learn English. I haven't had time to meet Americans

or have much fun _____ I started my job. I've been here _____ five months
                                11.   **12.**

now, and I just work and go to school. _____ I'm at school, I talk to my classmates
                                                                13.

_____ our break, but on the weekends I'm alone most of the time. I won't be able to make
        14.

American friends _____ I learn more English.
                                15.

EXERCISE 8 About You Write sentences about leaving your country and traveling to the U.S. or another country using the words given. Share your answers with a partner.

1. for

   <u>For many years I wanted to leave my country. But my parents thought I was too young, so they wouldn't let me.</u>

2. whenever

   _____

   _____

3. before

   _____

   _____

4. since

   _____

   _____

5. while

   _____

   _____

6. until

   _____

   _____

7. during

   _____

   _____

8. for

   _____

   _____

9. after

   _____

   _____

9.4 Using the –*ing* Form after Time Words

    Subject   **Subject**

The Lost Boys went to Ethiopia after **they left** Sudan.

The Lost Boys went to Ethiopia after **leaving** Sudan.

       Subject   **Subject**

While **they were crossing** a river, some of the Lost Boys drowned.

While **crossing** a river, some of the Lost Boys drowned.

Explanation

If the subject of the main clause and the subject of the time clause are the same, the sentence can be shortened by deleting the subject of the time clause and changing the verb to a present participle (-*ing*). Instead of a verb phrase, a participial phrase is used.

EXERCISE 9 Change the time clause to a participial phrase.

1. While they were running from their homes, they saw many dangerous animals.

   <u>While running from their homes, they saw many dangerous animals.</u>

2. The Lost Boys went to Kenya before they came to the U.S.

   _____

3. While they were living in Kenya, they studied English.

   _____

4. Before they came to the U.S., the Lost Boys had never used electricity.

   _____

5. Peter Bul learned how to use a computer after he came to the U.S.

   _____

6. Before he found a job, Peter got help from the U.S. government.

   _____

7. Peter went to visit South Sudan after he graduated from college.

   _____

8. While he was studying for his degree, Peter raised money for a school in South Sudan.

   _____

SLAVERY— An AMERICAN PARADOX[5]

A slave family picking cotton near Savannah, Georgia

Read the following article. Pay special attention to the words in bold.

Even though most immigrants have come to the United States with great hopes and dreams, one group of people came unwillingly. They were taken as slaves from Africa. Almost half a million Africans were brought to work in the agricultural South. African families were torn apart as slaves were treated like property to be bought and sold.

In 1776, when the thirteen American colonies declared their independence from England, Thomas Jefferson, one of the founding fathers of the United States, wrote, "All men are created equal" and that every person has a right to "life, liberty, and the pursuit of happiness." **In spite of** these great words, Jefferson owned two hundred slaves. The newly formed U.S. Constitution considered each slave to be three-fifths of a person. In order to keep slaves divided from each other and dependent on their masters, they were prohibited from learning to read and write.

Since the main southern crop, tobacco, was exhausting the land at the end of the eighteenth century, it seemed that the need for slavery would come to an end. However, there was suddenly a big demand for cotton. Previously, the production of cotton had been very slow because it was very time-consuming to remove the seeds. But a new invention made the production of cotton much faster. Suddenly, southern farmers found a new area of wealth— and a new reason to keep slaves. **Even though** the African slave trade ended in 1808, domestic slave trade continued. The slave population continued to grow as children were born to slave mothers. By 1860, there were four million slaves in the United States.

The country became divided over the issue of slavery, and the Civil War, between the North and the South, was fought from 1861 to 1865. **In spite of the fact that** the North won and African Americans were freed, it took another hundred years for Congress to pass a law prohibiting discrimination because of race, color, religion, sex, or national origin. **In spite of** this law, discrimination still exists today.

Although many new arrivals see the United States as the land of equality, it is important to remember this dark period of American history.

---

[5] *paradox:* a situation that has contradictory aspects

COMPREHENSION CHECK Based on the reading, tell if the statement is true (**T**) or false (**F**).

1. The U.S. Constitution did not count slaves as part of the population.

2. Thomas Jefferson owned slaves.

3. When the slaves were freed, they gained equality.

9.5 Contrast

Examples	Explanation
Even though African slave trade ended, domestic slave trade continued. **Although** the U.S. Constitution guaranteed freedom, many African Americans weren't free. **In spite of the fact that** Jefferson wrote about equality, he owned slaves.	For an unexpected result or contrast of ideas, we use a clause beginning with *even though, although,* or *in spite of the fact that.*
In spite of the difficulties, the Lost Boys started a new life in the U.S.	We use *in spite of* + a noun (phrase) to show contrast.
Although the Lost Boys are happy in the U.S., they **still** miss their country. **Even though** it's hard to start a new life in a different country, many immigrants do it **anyway**.	In speech and informal writing, *still* and *anyway* can be used in the main clause to emphasize the contrast.

Language Note:

1. Informally, *even though* and *although* can be shortened to *though.*

   Though it was difficult, I adjusted to life in a new country.

2. In speech, *though* is often used at the end of a statement to show contrast with the preceding statement. (We don't use *even though* and *although* at the end of a statement.)

   I adjusted to life in a new country. It was difficult, **though**.

3. *While* is also used to show contrast. (Remember: *While* can also be a time word. The context tells you whether it shows time or contrast.)

   While it's not hard to understand slavery from an economic perspective, it's difficult for me to comprehend how people could have been so cruel to others.

EXERCISE 10 Circle the correct words to complete the conversation. If both choices are possible, circle both of them.

A: Are you surprised by slavery in the U.S.?

B: (*Even though*/In spite of) I've read about it and seen movies about it, it's hard for me to understand. I've
   _1._

   always thought of the U.S. as a land of freedom and opportunity, (*although/in spite of*) I know it's not
   _2._

   perfect. But slavery was so terrible. How could that have happened in the U.S.?

A: I rented a movie recently about an African American man in the North who was kidnapped in the 1800s

   and taken to the South. (*In spite of the fact that/Even though*) he was a free man, he was sold into slavery.
   _3._

The name of the movie is *12 Years a Slave*.

B: (*Although/In spite of*) I saw it a few years ago, I remember it well. (*In spite of/In spite of the fact that*) it
    4.   5.
was a wonderful movie, it was very hard to watch the cruel way slaves were treated.

A: Do you think it was a realistic movie?

B: Unfortunately, it was. In fact, the reality was probably even worse than what we saw in the movie.

EXERCISE 11 Fill in the blanks with *in spite of* or *in spite of the fact that*.

1. ___In spite of the fact that___ the law says everyone has equal rights, some people are still suffering.

2. _____In spite of_____ Thomas Jefferson's declaration of equality for all, he owned slaves.

3. _____ slavery ended in 1865, African Americans did not receive equal

    treatment under the law until 1964.

4. The slave population continued to grow _____ Americans stopped

    importing slaves from Africa.

5. Many immigrants come to America _____ the difficulty of starting a new life.

6. The Lost Boys did not lose hope for a bright future _____ the challenges they faced.

7. _____ his busy schedule, Peter always tries to help his village in South Sudan.

8. _____ everything in America was new for them, the Lost Boys have adapted

    well to life in the U.S.

9. Many people still believe in the American dream _____ life is not perfect in the U.S.

EXERCISE 12 Circle the correct words to complete the paragraph. If both choices are possible,
circle both of them.

When I was 16 years old, I wanted to come to the U.S. (*Even*/*Even though*) I was very young, my parents
                                                                                                              1.
gave me permission to leave home and live with my uncle in New Jersey. (*In spite of the fact that/In spite of*)
                                                                                                                              2.
I was only in high school, I worked part-time and saved money for college. (*Although/In spite of*) it was
                                                                                                              3.
hard, I managed to finish high school and start college. My uncle always encouraged me to go to college

(*in spite of/even though*) he is not an educated man. A lot of my friends from high school didn't go to college
      4.
(*even though/in spite of*) the opportunities they had. I decided to become an English teacher
      5.
(*even though/although*) I still have a bit of an accent.
      6.

The Changing Face of the
UNITED STATES

🎧 **Read the following article. Pay special attention to the words in bold.**

CD 2
TR 16

As of 2014, the U.S. population was over 319 million. This number is expected to rise to more than 438 million by 2050. Most of the population growth will be from immigrants and their descendants. **Unless** there are changes in immigration patterns, nearly one in five people will be an immigrant in 2050. This is even higher than the top figures between 1890 and 1910, when about 15 percent were foreign born. Of course, these numbers assume that the immigration policy in the U.S. will remain the way it is now.

For most of the nineteenth and twentieth centuries, the majority of immigrants to the U.S. were Europeans. However, since 1970, this trend has changed dramatically. More than 50 percent of the immigrants who have arrived since 1970 are Spanish speakers.

In 2003, Hispanics passed African Americans as the largest minority. The Hispanic population increased more than 50 percent between 1990 and 2000. **If** current patterns of immigration continue and **if** the birth rate remains the same, Hispanics, who are now 17 percent of the total population, will be 29 percent of the population by 2050. Hispanics are already about 38 percent of the population of California and Texas.

Because of their increasing numbers, Hispanic voters are gaining political power. In 2008, President Obama received 67 percent of the Hispanic vote. In 2012, when Hispanics made up 10 percent of the voting population, Obama received 71 percent of their vote. It is clear that Hispanics have the power to determine elections.

Even if immigration policy changes, Hispanics, who have a higher birth rate than other Americans, will continue to see their numbers—and influence—grow.

There are many questions about the future of America. One thing is certain: the face of America is changing.

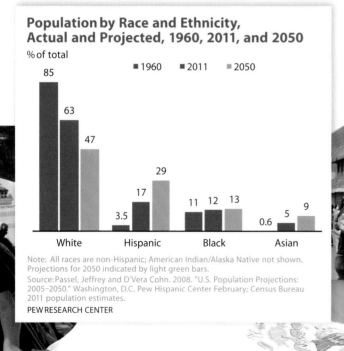

Population by Race and Ethnicity, Actual and Projected, 1960, 2011, and 2050

% of total

■ 1960 ■ 2011 ■ 2050

White: 85, 63, 47
Hispanic: 3.5, 17, 29
Black: 11, 12, 13
Asian: 0.6, 5, 9

Note: All races are non-Hispanic; American Indian/Alaska Native not shown. Projections for 2050 indicated by light green bars.
Source: Passel, Jeffrey and D'Vera Cohn. 2008. "U.S. Population Projections: 2005–2050." Washington, D.C. Pew Hispanic Center February; Census Bureau 2011 population estimates.
PEW RESEARCH CENTER

A Cinco de Mayo celebration in Detroit

COMPREHENSION CHECK Based on the reading, tell if the statement is true (**T**) or false (**F**).

1. African Americans are the largest minority in the U.S. today.

2. By the middle of this century, 50 percent of the population will be Hispanic.

3. Hispanics helped determine the presidential elections of 2008 and 2012.

9.6 Condition

Examples	Explanation
If Hispanics **vote** together, they **will have** a lot of political power.	We use *if* to show that the condition affects the result.
Even if the immigration of Hispanics **slows** down, their number **will** probably **increase**.	We use *even if* to show that the condition doesn't affect the result.
You don't have political power **unless** you vote.	We use *unless* to mean *if not. You don't have political power if you don't vote.*

Language Note:

If, *even if*, and *unless* can be used with present, past, and future sentences. In a future sentence, we use the simple present in the condition clause.

EXERCISE 13 Fill in the blanks with the correct form of the verb given.

1. If the Hispanic population _____continues_____ to grow, 29 percent of the U.S. population
   a. continue

   _____will be_____ Hispanic by the year 2050.
   b. be

2. Even if the number of immigrants _____ down, the general population _____ .
   a. go   b. increase

3. If more children _____ born in the next 50 years, more schools _____ .
   a. be   b. passive: need

4. School classes _____ bigger if the number of school-age children _____ .
   a. get   b. increase

5. The U.S. population _____ almost 440 million by 2050 if immigration _____
   a. be   b. continue

   at the same rate.

6. Children of immigrants _____ their native language unless their parents
   a. forget

   _____ them to speak it.
   b. encourage

EXERCISE 14 Change the *if* clause in the sentences below to an *unless* clause.

1. Immigrants can't become American citizens if they don't pass a test.

   Immigrants can't become American citizens unless they pass a test.

2. Visitors can't enter the U.S. if they don't have a passport.

_____

3. Immigrants will continue to come to the U.S. if conditions in their native countries don't improve.

_____

4. In the 1800s, Southern farmers couldn't prosper if they didn't find a new crop to grow.

_____

5. Cotton production was going to be slow if they didn't have a machine to help.

_____

6. Foreigners cannot work in the U.S. if they don't have permission.

_____

EXERCISE 15 Fill in the blanks in this conversation. Use _if_ or _unless._

A: My youngest daughter is seven years old, and she doesn't speak Spanish anymore. ____If____ I say
                                                                                            1.
something to her in Spanish, she understands, but she answers in English.

B: _____ all her friends speak English, of course she's going to speak English.
         2.

A: My mother lives with us. She doesn't speak English. She can't understand what my daughter is saying

_____ I translate it for her.
  3.

B: I have the same problem. My son is 14 and he won't speak Spanish _____ he has to.
                                                                             4.
Last month my parents came to visit from Guatemala. My parents had a hard time understanding my

son because he mixes Spanish and English. There are a lot of Spanish words he doesn't remember

_____ I remind him.
  5.

A: Maybe we should put our kids in a bilingual program at school. _____ they're in the
                                                                           6.
bilingual program, they'll have to speak Spanish.

B: I don't think the school will put them in a bilingual program _____ they're already fluent
                                                                         7.
in English.

A: We can't fight it. Our kids won't speak Spanish well _____ we go back to live in our
                                                               8.
native countries.

EXERCISE 16 About You Fill in the blanks and discuss your answers with a partner.

1. My English won't improve quickly unless _____

2. People understand my English even if _____

3. If _____, people don't understand me well.

EXERCISE 17 Fill in the blanks to complete this conversation between a Colombian woman who's going to immigrate to the U.S. and her friend. Use context clues to help you. Answers may vary.

A: I'm planning to go to Boston. I'm worried about the weather. They say it's very cold in the winter.

B: I'm sure people go out even if ___the weather is cold___.
                                        1.

A: What if people won't understand me? My accent isn't perfect.

B: Even if _____, people will probably understand you.
              2.

A: But I make so many grammar mistakes.

B: Don't worry. People will understand you even if _____. Are you
                                                          3.
planning to get a job there?

A: I don't think I'm going to need one. I'm going to live with my relatives and they said I can live

there for free.

B: Even if _____, you'll need money for other things, like books,
              4.
clothes, and transportation.

A: I know college is going to be expensive for me because I'm going to be an international student. I think

college is free for American residents, isn't it?

B: No. Even if _____, you have to pay for college, but it's cheaper
                 5.
for residents.

An American woman holds her adoptive daughter.

ADOPTING a BABY from ABROAD

Read the following article. Pay special attention to the words in bold.

CD 2
TR 17

Many American couples want to adopt children. **However**, the adoption of an American child is a long and complicated process. There are so few babies available for adoption in the United States that parents who want an American baby often have to wait years. **As a result**, many Americans turn to foreign countries for adoption. In 2009, 13,000 foreign babies were adopted from 106 countries by American families. Americans bring home babies from many countries, with the majority coming from China, Ethiopia, Ukraine, and South Korea.

The process of foreign adoption takes time and patience. **First**, the United States Citizenship and Immigration Services (USCIS) must determine if a family can provide a loving, stable home for the child. Social workers do a home study on each family. They give the USCIS a family's personal, financial, and medical information. **Also**, there are many forms to fill out and documents to produce to complete the process. **For example**, the family has to show proof of health insurance.

In addition, foreign adoption is not cheap. **In fact**, the average cost of an international adoption in 2009 was $44,000. **Furthermore**, parents have the expense of traveling to the country and staying there for many weeks while the process is being completed.

In spite of all these difficulties, these tiny immigrants bring joy to many American families.

COMPREHENSION CHECK Based on the reading, tell if the statement is true (**T**) or false (**F**).

1. Adopting a baby from abroad is very expensive.

2. When the family returns with the child, a home study is done.

3. If a family adopts a baby from abroad, they have to go to the foreign country to pick up the baby.

9.7 Sentence Connectors

Sentence connectors[6] show the relationship between ideas.

Examples	Explanation
Some couples want to adopt American children. **However**, there are very few babies available in the U.S. Some couples want to adopt a baby from abroad. **Nevertheless**, the process isn't cheap or easy.	Sentence connectors that show contrast are *however* and *nevertheless*. These words are similar in meaning to *but*.
Foreign adoption is not for everyone. It can be expensive. **In addition**, it can take a long time. Adopting a baby from abroad is expensive. Parents have to pay the adoption agencies. **Furthermore**, they have the expense of traveling to pick up the baby.	Sentence connectors that add more information to the same idea are *in addition, furthermore, also*, and *moreover*. These words are similar in meaning to *and*.
Adoptive parents have many things to do. **First**, they have to fill out an application. **Next**, they have to produce many documents. **Furthermore**, they need to have a home study done.	Ideas can be ordered using *first, second, third, next, then*, etc. We can begin with *first* and continue with *furthermore, moreover, also, in addition*.
It takes a long time to adopt an American baby. **As a result**, many Americans go to foreign countries to adopt. Many couples in China prefer sons. **Therefore**, the majority of adoptions from China are girls.	Sentence connectors that show result or conclusion are *therefore, as a result*, and *for this reason*. These words are similar in meaning to *so*.
Adoptive families have to produce many documents. **For example**, they have to show proof of health insurance. Foreign adoption is not cheap. **In fact**, the average cost was $44,000 in 2009.	Other connectors are *for example* and *in fact*. *In fact* emphasizes the preceding statement. Sometimes it introduces something that might surprise the reader or listener.

Punctuation Notes:

1. We use either a period or a semicolon (;) before a sentence connector if it comes at the beginning of a sentence. We use a comma after a sentence connector.

   My friends couldn't adopt a baby here. **Therefore**, they went to another country to adopt.

   My friends couldn't adopt a baby here; **therefore**, they went to another country to adopt.

2. Some sentence connectors can come in the middle of a sentence. We separate these from the sentence by putting a comma before and after the connector.

   Many people want to adopt a baby. The process, **however**, is not cheap or easy.

---

[6] The grammatical name for these connectors is conjunctive adverbs.

EXERCISE 18 Choose the correct sentence connectors to fill in the blanks. In some cases both choices are possible, so circle both options.

1. The Lost Boys were happy living with their families in Sudan. (*However*/*In addition*), a war forced them to leave.

2. The Lost Boys faced many problems when they left Sudan. They didn't know where to go. (*Furthermore*/*Moreover*), they didn't have enough to eat.

3. Some of them couldn't swim. (*As a result*/*However*), some drowned when they had to cross a river in their escape.

4. Finally they found safety in a refugee camp in Kenya. (*However*/*In fact*), conditions in the camp were very poor.

5. Many of the Lost Boys had never seen modern appliances before. (*Also*/*For example*), they had never used a gas stove.

6. They faced problems in the U.S. They had to find jobs quickly. (*For example*/*In addition*), they had to go to school to improve their English.

7. They are happy that they came to the U.S. (*In fact*/*Nevertheless*), they still miss their family and friends back home.

8. Jews had a hard life in Eastern Europe. Many lived in poor conditions. (*Moreover*/*However*), they suffered religious persecution.

9. My grandfather immigrated to the U.S. for several reasons. (*First*/*In addition*), he needed to find a job to make more money. (*In fact*/*Furthermore*), he wanted to be reunited with his relatives who had come before him.

10. There was a big famine in Ireland. (*As a result*/*For this reason*), many Irish people left and came to the U.S.

11. Many people wanted to escape political problems in their countries. (*However*/*For example*), some of them couldn't get permission to come to the U.S.

12. A war broke out in Yugoslavia in 1992. (*As a result*/*For example*), many people died or lost their homes.

13. Most immigrants have come to the U.S. because they wanted to. (*However*/*Furthermore*), Africans were brought to America against their will to work as slaves.

14. In 1776, Thomas Jefferson wrote, "All men are created equal." (*Nevertheless*/*Therefore*), Jefferson had 200 slaves at that time.

15. Members of the same African family were sent to different areas to work as slaves. (*Therefore*/*As a result*), families were torn apart.

16. Slavery officially ended in 1865. (*However*/*Consequently*), many African American families continued to suffer.

17. African Americans had been the largest minority for many years. (*In fact*/*However*), this changed in 2003 when the Hispanic population became the largest minority.

18. Adopting a foreign baby is complicated. People have to pay a lot of money. (*Moreover*/*Furthermore*), they have to travel to the foreign country to fill out forms and pick up the baby.

19. The U.S. started to have serious economic problems in 2008. (*However*/*Consequently*), some foreigners were afraid to immigrate because they thought they wouldn't find jobs.

20. The U.S. attracts more immigrants than any other country. (*In fact*/*For example*), one in five of the world's immigrants lives in the U.S.

EXERCISE 20 Fill in the blanks with *so, so much, so many, so few, so little,* or *such (a/an).*

1. We had _____ so many _____ problems in our country that we decided to leave.

2. I waited _____ long time that I thought I would never get permission.

3. When I got to the airport, the security lines were _____ long that I had to wait for 2 hours.

4. There were _____ people arriving at the same time that the process took a long time.

5. I was _____ happy when I got my Green Card that I started to cry.

6. The U.S. offers _____ freedom that people from all over the world want to come here.

7. Before I got my visa, I had to fill out _____ papers and give _____

   information that I thought I would never be able to do it.

8. We have been in the U.S. for _____ long time that we hardly speak our

   native language anymore.

9. My neighbor's daughter was _____ young when she arrived from China that she doesn't

   remember anything about China at all.

10. There are _____ American babies to adopt that many families adopt babies from abroad.

11. I spoke _____ English when I arrived in the U.S. that I always had to take my dictionary

   with me everywhere.

EXERCISE 21 Fill in the blanks with *so, so much, so many, so little, so few,* or *such a.*
Then complete each statement with a result. Answers will vary.

1. I was _____ happy when I got permission to come to the U.S. that _____

   _____ .

2. Most adopted children are _____ young when they come to the U.S. that _____

   _____ .

3. Some people have _____ hard time learning English in the U.S. that _____

   _____ .

4. Some people had _____ hard life in their native countries that _____

   _____ .

5. In 1910, there were _____ foreign-born Americans that _____

   _____ .

6. I had _____ time to prepare for that trip that _____ .

SUMMARY OF LESSON 9

1. Words that connect a dependent clause or phrase to an independent clause: *(Abbreviations: C = Clause; NP = Noun Phrase; VP = Verb Phrase; PP = Participial Phrase)*

Function	Connectors	Examples
Reason	*because* + C	**Because** he studies hard, his English is improving.
	since + C	**Since** he studies hard, his English is improving.
	because of + NP	**Because of** his effort, his English is improving.
Time	*when* + C	They decided to adopt a Korean baby **when** they couldn't get an American baby.
	whenever + C	**Whenever** they have a chance, they visit Korea.
	until + C or NP	The baby lived in an orphanage **until** she was adopted. The baby lived in Korea **until** May.
	while + C or PP	**While** they were traveling to the U.S., they were thinking about the baby's future.
	for + NP	**While** traveling to the U.S., they were holding their new baby. They stayed in Korea **for** 3 weeks.
	during + NP	They went to Korea **during** the summer.
	since + NP or C	The baby has been living in the U.S. **since** June. The baby has been living in the U.S. **since** the family brought her here.
Purpose	*(in order) to* + VP	He came to the U.S. **(in order) to** have a better life.
	so (that) + C	He came to the U.S. **so (that)** he could improve his life.
	for + NP	He came to the U.S. **for** a better education.
Contrast	*even though* + C	**Even though** life was difficult for them, the Lost Boys didn't lose hope.
	although + C	**Although** life was difficult for them, the Lost Boys didn't lose hope.
	in spite of the fact that + C	**In spite of the fact that** life was difficult for them, the Lost Boys didn't lose hope.
	in spite of + NP	**In spite of** the difficulties, the Lost Boys didn't lose hope.
Condition	*if* + C	**If** population growth continues in the same way, the U.S. will have 438 million people by 2050.
	even if + C	**Even if** immigration slows, the population will increase.
	unless + C	**Unless** there are changes in population patterns, one in five people in the U.S. will be an immigrant by 2050.

WRITING

PART 1 Editing Advice

1. Use *to*, not *for*, with a verb when showing purpose.

   She came to the U.S. ~~for~~ _to_ get a better education.

2. Don't combine *so* with *because*, or *but* with *even though*.

   Because his country was at war, ~~so~~ he left his country.

   Even though he speaks English well, ~~but~~ he can't find a job.

3. Use *because of* when a noun phrase follows.

   People don't understand me well because _of_ my accent.

4. Don't use *even* without *though* or *if* to introduce a clause.

   Even _though_ Peter misses his family, he's happy in the U.S.

5. Use the *-ing* form, not the base form, after a time word if the subject is deleted.

   Before ~~come~~ _coming_ to the U.S., he studied English.

6. Don't confuse *so that* (purpose) with *so* (result).

   She wanted to have a better life, so ~~that~~ she came to the U.S.

7. After *so that*, use a modal before the verb.

   Farmers used slave labor so that they _could_ become rich.

8. In a future sentence, use the simple present in the *if* clause or time clause.

   If I ~~will~~ go back to my hometown, I will tell my family about life in the U.S.

9. *However* connects two sentences. *Although* connects two parts of the same sentence.

   I studied English in my country. ~~Although~~ _However,_ I didn't understand Americans when I arrived.

10. An adverbial clause or phrase must be attached to the main clause.

    She went to Canada because her parents were living there.
    ~~She went to Canada. Because her parents were living there.~~

11. Use *so* + adjective/adverb. Use *such* when you include a noun.

    It was ~~so~~ _such a_ long and boring trip to the U.S. that I slept most of the way.   *OR*
    The trip to the U.S. was so long and boring that I slept most of the way.

12. Use correct punctuation with sentence connectors.

    She likes living here _. H_ ~~, h~~owever, she misses her family back home.

PART 2 Editing Practice

Some of the shaded words and phrases have mistakes. Find the mistakes and correct them. If the shaded words are correct, write C.

      Life as an immigrant can be hard. I came to the U.S. five years ago ~~for~~ *to* study English. I chose

1.

to live in this city because my sister was living here. Even I had studied English in my country,

    C

2.   **3.**

I didn't have experience talking with native speakers. I wanted to prepare myself, therefore, I took

                                                     4.

private lessons with an American in my country for learn American expressions. In addition, before

                                   5.   **6.**

come here, I read a lot about life in the U.S. so that I was prepared. But I wasn't. There were many

7.   **8.**

surprises. For example, I was surprised by how cold it is in the winter in this city. Therefore, I

          9.   **10.**

couldn't believe that some students call their teachers by their first names. Back home, we always

call our teachers "Professor" for show respect. I also miss getting together with friends after class.

                        11.

Now I'm at a city college and most students have jobs and families. As a result, everyone leaves after

                                                      12.

class. Because they want to get home to their families. I gave my phone number to some classmates

13.

so that we get together on weekends, but no one ever calls me. I thought I wouldn't be lonely since I'd

14.   **15.**

be with my sister and her family. But I was wrong. Because my sister has a busy life, so she doesn't

                                                      16.

have much time for me either.

      I had so hard time when I arrived here that I wanted to go back. Even though, little by little I got

          17.   **18.**   **19.**

used to life here. I discovered that church is a good place to meet people, so that I joined a church.

                                                      20.

When I will save more money, I'm going to get an apartment with one of my new friends from

          21.

church. Even though life has become easier, but I still miss my family back home.

                                  22.

PART 3 Write About It

1. Describe the problems or challenges immigrants or refugees can face when they arrive in the U.S.

2. Describe the challenges international students can face when they become students in the U.S.

PART 4 Edit Your Writing

Reread the Summary of Lesson 9 and the editing advice. Edit your writing from Part 3.

10

Noun Clauses

CHILDREN

ldren peer out a window
ubljana, Slovenia

Children must be taught how to think, not what to think.

—Margaret Mead

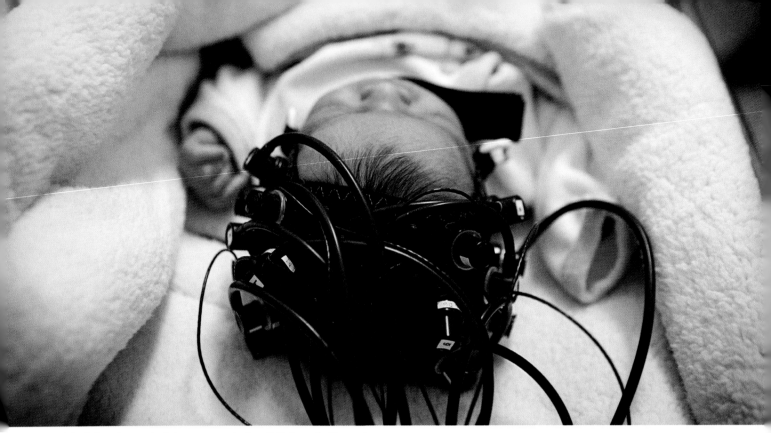

A brain imaging method that measures brain activity is applied to newborns to study early perception of speech and the ability to learn syntactically.

EARLY **CHILD** DEVELOPMENT

 Read the following article. Pay special attention to the words in bold.

CD 2
TR 18

Do you think **that babies can benefit from listening to classical music or seeing great works of art**? Some parents think **that these activities can increase a baby's intelligence**. While there is no scientific evidence to support this, research shows **that a baby's early experiences influence brain development**. The first three years of a baby's life affect his emotional development and learning abilities for the rest of his life. It is a well-known fact **that talking to infants increases their language ability** and **that reading to them is the most important thing parents can do to raise a good reader**. A recent study shows **that children from birth to eight years old are spending much more time with screens than books**.

Babies whose parents rarely talk to them or hold them can be damaged for life. One study shows **that kids who hardly play or who aren't touched very much develop brains 20 to 50 percent smaller than normal**.

A recent study at the University of North Carolina followed children from preschool to young adulthood. The results showed **that children who got high-quality preschool education from the time they were infants benefited in later life**. In this study, 23 percent of children who had high-quality preschool education graduated from college, compared with only 6 percent of children who did not have preschool education.

While it is important to give babies stimulating activities, experts warn **that parents shouldn't overstimulate them**.

COMPREHENSION CHECK Based on the reading, tell if the statement is true (**T**) or false (**F**).

1. If a baby listens to classical music, this will help develop his brain.

2. Reading to babies helps them become better readers.

3. The first three years of children's lives affect their learning for the rest their lives.

10.1 Noun Clauses

A noun clause has a subject and a verb. It functions as a noun in a sentence.

Examples	Explanation
Parents know **(that) kids need a lot of attention.** Studies show **(that) early childhood education is important.**	A noun clause can follow certain verbs. *That* introduces a noun clause. *That* is often omitted, especially in conversation.
I'm sure **(that) children need a lot of attention.** Some parents are worried **(that) they don't spend enough time with their kids.**	A noun clause can be the complement of the sentence after certain adjectives.
A: I hope **that our children will be successful.** **B:** I hope **so** too. **A:** Do you think **that the children are learning in pre-school?** **B:** Yes, I think **so.**	Noun clauses can be replaced by *so* after the verbs *think, hope, believe, suppose, expect,* and *know.*
I realize that the child is tired **and that** he hasn't eaten lunch. I know that you are a loving parent **but that** you can't spend much time with your child.	Connect two noun clauses in the same sentence with *and that* or *but that.*

Language Notes:

1. A noun clause often follows one of these verbs:

believe	find out	predict	suppose
complain	forget	pretend	think
decide	hope	realize	understand
dream	know	regret	
expect	learn	remember	
feel*	notice	show	

* *Feel* followed by a noun clause means "believe" or "think."

   I *feel* that early education is important. = I *believe/think* that early education is important.

2. A noun clause often follows *be* + the following adjectives:

afraid	clear	sure
amazed	disappointed	surprised
aware	glad	worried
certain	happy	

EXERCISE 1 Listen to the following conversation. Fill in the blanks with the words you hear.

CD 2
TR 19

A: _____Do you know that_____ it's good to read to children when they're very young?
   _{1.}

B: Yes, I do. But _____ playing music was important too.
   _{2.}

A: _____ that music is beneficial, but I suppose it can't hurt.
   _{3.}

B: _____ it's good to give kids as much education as possible before they go to
   _{4.}

school.

A: I'm sure that's a good idea. But _____ they're just kids. They need to play too.
   _{5.}

B: Of course they do. _____ my children will be successful one day.
   _{6.}

A: _____ they'll be very successful and happy.
   _{7.}

B: _____ .
   _{8.}

EXERCISE 2 Fill in the blanks to complete the noun clause based on the reading on page 282. Answers may vary.

1. Research shows that _____a baby's early experiences_____ influence his brain development.

2. A recent study shows that _____ reading books.

3. Some parents think that _____ classical music for babies.

4. We all know that _____ increases their language ability.

5. A study shows that _____ have smaller brains.

EXERCISE 3 Respond to each statistic[1] about American families by beginning with *I'm surprised that . . .* or *I'm not surprised that . . .* Discuss your reactions with a partner.

1. The number of children in the U.S. is increasing rapidly.

   _____I'm surprised that the number of children in the U.S. is increasing rapidly._____

2. About 7 million American children are home alone after school.

   _____

3. About 22 percent of American children live in poverty.

   _____

4. About 70 percent of married mothers work outside the home.

   _____

---

[1] Source: http://www.childstats.gov

5. Sixty-nine percent of children live with two parents.

_____

6. Twenty-three percent of American children live with at least one foreign-born parent.

_____

7. Twenty-two percent of children ages five to seventeen speak a language other than English at home.

_____

8. By 2050, 39 percent of U.S. children are projected to be Hispanic.

_____

EXERCISE 4 About You Fill in the blanks with a noun clause to talk about families or raising children in the U.S. or your country. Discuss your answers with a partner.

1. I'm surprised _____.

2. I think _____.

3. I know _____.

4. It's unfortunate _____.

5. I'm not surprised _____.

6. I've noticed _____.

EXERCISE 5 About You What's your opinion? Answer the questions using *I think* and a noun clause. Discuss your answers with a partner.

1. Should the government help families pay for childcare while the parents work?

2. Can children get the care and attention they need in day care?

3. Should fathers take a greater part in raising their kids?

4. Should grandparents help more in raising their grandchildren?

5. Should employers give new mothers maternity leave? For how long?

6. Should parents read books to babies before they learn to talk?

7. Should parents buy a lot of toys for their children?

The TEENAGE BRAIN

🎧 **Read the following article. Pay special attention to the words in bold.**

CD 2
TR 20

For many American teenagers, sixteen is the magic number—the age when they can get their driver's license. But this is also the time when parents worry the most about their kids.

In the United States, one in three teen deaths is from a car crash. Parents often wonder **if kids really understand the risks they are taking when they are behind the wheel.** They warn their kids **what to do and what not to do** while driving, but they really don't know **whether their kids will follow their advice or not**. They hand over the car keys—and hope for the best.

Studies show that when teens drive alone, they take risks at the same rate as adults. But when they drive with other teens, they take more risks.

Scientists have been using scans[2] to study the teenage brain. Even though the brain is almost full size by the time a child is six years old, scientists are finding that the brain makes great changes between the ages of twelve and twenty-five. During this time,

it is natural that young people seek thrills.[3] According to Laurence Steinberg, a developmental psychologist from Temple University, "The teenage brain is like a car with a good accelerator but a weak brake. . . . Adolescents are more impulsive,[4] thrill-seeking, drawn to the rewards of a risky decision than adults."

While new technologies can make driving more dangerous, there are other technologies that help parents keep track of their teenagers' driving habits. There are phone apps that let parents know **what their kids are doing behind the wheel**. Parents can know **if their child is texting or tweeting while driving** or **how fast their teenager is driving**.

Risky behavior is a normal stage of development in teenagers. "I can't stand riding on a roller-coaster now," said Professor Steinberg. "I liked it as a teenager. I can't stand driving fast now. I liked driving fast when I was a teenager. What has changed? I'm not as driven today by this thrill-seeking sensation."

---

2 *scans:* an examination of an inside part of the body done with a special machine
3 *thrill:* a feeling of strong excitement, or pleasure
4 *impulsive:* done with a sudden urge

A young driver practices driving.

COMPREHENSION CHECK Based on the reading, tell if the statement is true (**T**) or false (**F**).

1. When teenagers drive with other teenagers in the car, they take more risks.

2. The brain is fully developed by the age of twelve.

3. The majority of teen deaths are the result of car crashes.

10.2 Noun Clauses as Included Questions[5]

A noun clause is used to include a question in a statement or another question.

Direct Question	Included Question
Wh- questions with auxiliaries or **be**	We use statement word order. Put the subject before the verb.
How fast is my daughter driving? What app can I use?	I'd like to know **how fast she is driving**. Please tell me **what app I can use**.
Wh- questions with auxiliaries or **do/does/did**	We remove *do/does/did*. The verb shows *-s* ending for *he, she, or it*, or the past form.
Why does a teenager take risks? How did the car accident happen?	Scientists want to know **why a teenager takes risks**. I'd like to know **how the car accident happened**.
Wh- questions about the subject	There is no change in word order.
Who bought the app? What makes the teenage brain different?	I'd like to know **who bought the app**. Scientists want to know **what makes the teenage brain different**.
Yes/No questions with auxiliaries or **be**	We add the word *if* or *whether*. We use statement word order. We put the subject before the verb.
Is the teenager driving too fast? Will my teenage brother follow my advice?	The app can tell you **if the teenager is driving too fast**. I wonder **whether my teenage brother will follow my advice**.
Yes/No questions with auxiliaries or **be**	We remove *do/does/did*. We add *if* or *whether*. The verb shows the *-s* ending for *he, she,* or *it*, in the present or the past form.
Does my teenager follow my advice? Did you do the same thing when you were my age?	I want to know **if my teenager follows my advice**. My son wants to know **whether I did the same thing when I was his age**.

An included question can be used after phrases such as these:

I don't know	I'm not sure	Do you remember
Please tell me	Nobody knows	Can you tell me
I have no idea	I can't understand	Do you understand
I wonder	I'd like to know	Would you like to know
I don't remember	I can't tell you	Does anyone know
You need to decide	It's important to ask	Do you know

---

[5] Grammar books often refer to included questions as "embedded questions."

continued

EXERCISE 12 Fill in the blanks with one of the words from the box below. You may use a verb more than once.

to compare	to chat	to get	to begin	to write	to make	to do

A: I need to go to my friend Marek's house. Mom won't let me use the car. I don't know how

_____*to get*_____ there without a car. Can you drive me there?
1.

B: I'm busy studying for a test. Why do you have to go to his house?

A: We have to work on a project together. We can't decide what _____.
2.

B: What's your assignment?

A: We have to write about children in different countries. We can't decide what countries

_____. We don't even know where _____.
3.   4.

B: Well, since we're from Russia, why don't you compare Russia with your friend's country?

A: He's from Poland. I'm not sure that our countries are so different.

B: I'm sure there are lots of differences.

A: We don't know whether _____ about small children or teenagers.
5.

B: Since you're a teenager, you know a lot about that subject already.

A: You're right. That's a good place to begin. But we don't know what kind of comparisons

_____.
6.

B: You could compare education, number of children in a typical family, the kinds of games or electronics

they have, or whether the family lets them use the car or not. There are a lot of things.

A: I'd really like to get together with my friend so we can brainstorm these ideas.

B: Why don't you just use a video chat?

A: I forgot how _____ online. I haven't done it in a long time.
7.

B: Don't worry. I'll show you what _____.
8.

A: Thanks!

DR. BENJAMIN SPOCK

A father plays gently with his baby.

Read the following article. Pay special attention to the words in bold.

CD 2
TR 21

New parents worry that they might be making a mistake with their new baby. The baby cries, and they don't know if they should let him cry or pick him up. The baby is sick, and they don't know what to do. **"Trust yourself. You know more than you think you do,"** wrote Benjamin Spock in his famous book *Dr. Spock's Baby and Child Care,* which first appeared in 1946. This book has sold over 50 million copies, making it one of the biggest-selling books of all time. For many parents, this book is the parents' favorite guide for raising children.

Before Dr. Spock's book appeared, John Watson was the leading child-care expert in the 1920s and 1930s. He wrote, **"Never hug or kiss your children; never let them sit in your lap."** He continued, **"If you must, kiss them once on the forehead when they say good night. Shake hands with them in the morning."** Also, he told parents **that it was necessary to feed children on a rigid schedule.** Dr. Spock disagreed with this strict manner of raising children and decided **that he would write a book. "I wanted to be supportive of parents rather than scold**[6] **them,"** Dr. Spock said. **"Every baby needs to be smiled at, talked to, played with . . . gently and lovingly. Be natural and enjoy your baby."**

When Dr. Spock died in 1998 at the age of ninety-four, his book was in its seventh edition. He will be remembered for his common-sense advice. **"Respect children because they deserve respect, and they'll grow up to be better people."**

---

[6] *to scold:* to tell someone, in an angry way, that he or she did something wrong

COMPREHENSION CHECK Based on the reading, tell if the statement is true (**T**) or false (**F**).

1. Attitudes toward raising children have always been pretty much the same.

2. Dr. Spock had a gentle approach to taking care of babies.

3. People are still buying the 1946 edition of Dr. Spock's book.

10.4 Exact Quotes

Examples	Explanation
Dr. Spock said, **"Trust yourself."** John Watson said, **"Never hug or kiss your children."**	An exact quote is used when the exact words are worth repeating and are remembered because they have been recorded on video or audio or in print.
Dr. Spock said, "Every baby needs to be smiled at." "Every baby needs to be smiled at," **Dr. Spock said.** "Every baby needs to be smiled at," **said Dr. Spock.**	The *said* or *asked* clause can come at the beginning or the end of a quote. If it comes at the end, the subject and the verb can be inverted.
"More than anything else," **said Dr. Spock,** "children want to help. It makes them feel grown up."	An exact quote can be split, with the *said* or *asked* clause in the middle, separated from the quote by commas.

Punctuation Note:

Study the punctuation of sentences that contain an exact quote. Note that the first letter of an exact quote is a capital.

> Dr. Spock said, "Trust yourself."
> The mother asked, "Why is the baby crying?"
> "Why is he crying?" asked the father.
> "We need to feed him," said the mother.
> "More than anything else," said Dr. Spock, "children want love."

EXERCISE 13 Read these quotes. Add capital letters, quotation marks, and other punctuation.

1. Watson said, "Never ~~never~~ hug or kiss your children."

2. Watson said give your children a pat on the head if they have made an extraordinarily good job of a difficult task

3. Dr. Spock said you know more than you think you do

4. I wanted to be supportive of parents said Dr. Spock

5. Parents can dramatically influence systems in their child's brain wrote child psychologist Margot Sunderland

6. To reduce violence in our society said Dr. Spock we must eliminate violence in the home and on television

7. Adolescence is a period of significant changes in brain structure and function wrote Dr. Steinberg

8. Parents sometimes ask what is wrong with teenagers why do they take so many risks

9. This process of maturation once thought to be largely finished by elementary school continues throughout adolescence wrote David Dobbs in a *National Geographic* article

10.5 Exact Quotes vs. Reported Speech

Exact quote	Reported speech
Dr. Spock said, **"You know more than you think you do."**	Dr. Spock told parents **that they knew more than they thought they did.**
John Watson said, **"It is necessary to feed children on a rigid schedule."**	John Watson told parents **that it was necessary to feed children on a rigid schedule**.
Dr. Steinberg wrote, **"I liked driving fast."**	Dr. Steinberg said **that he had liked driving fast.**

Language Notes:

1. We use an exact quote when we want to write exactly what someone has said. Exact quotes are common in stories and news reports.
2. We use reported speech when we want to report what someone has said.

EXERCISE 14 In the paragraph below, underline the noun clauses that show reported speech. Circle the verbs in the noun clauses.

Last week my daughter's teacher called me at work and told me <u>that my daughter (had) a fever and</u> <u>(was resting) in the nurse's office</u>. I told my boss that I needed to leave work immediately. He said that it would be fine. As I was driving my car on the highway to the school, a police officer stopped me. She said that I was driving too fast. She said that I had been going ten miles per hour over the limit. I told her that I was in a hurry because my daughter was sick. I said I needed to get to her school quickly. I told the police officer that I was sorry, that I hadn't realized I had been driving so fast. She said she wouldn't give me a ticket that time, but that I should be more careful in the future, whether my daughter was sick or not.

6. The father said to his daughter, "Help me in the garage."

_____

7. The girl said to her parents, "Take me to the zoo."

_____

8. The dentist said to the boy, "Brush your teeth after every meal."

_____

9. I said to my parents, "Don't spoil your grandchildren."

_____

10. The girl said to her mother, "Comb my hair."

_____

11. The father said to his daughter, "Do your homework."

_____

12. The father said to his teenage daughter, "Don't come home late."

_____

13. The father said to his teenage son, "Drive safely."

_____

10.10 Using Reported Speech to Paraphrase

We often use reported speech when we want to paraphrase what someone has said. The exact words are not important or not remembered. The idea is more important than the exact words.

Exact quote	Reported speech
Dr. Spock said, **"You know more than you think you do."**	Dr. Spock told parents **that they knew enough to trust themselves.**
John Watson said, **"It is necessary to feed children on a rigid schedule."**	John Watson told parents **that they had to feed their children on a strict schedule.**
Dr. Steinberg wrote, **"Peer pressure declines as adolescents grow into adulthood."**	Dr. Steinberg said **that adults are not as influenced by their peers as teenagers.**

EXERCISE 20 Circle the correct words to complete this story. In some cases, both answers are possible, so circle both options.

Last month I babysat for a family that lives near me. It was my first babysitting job. They (*said*/told) that
1.

the children (*would/will*) sleep through the night and not cause any problems. But Danielle, the
2.

three-year-old girl, woke up at 9:00 and (*said/told*) that (*I/she*) (*can't/couldn't*) sleep. I (*said/told*) her that I
3.   **4.**   **5.**   **6.**

(*will/would*) read (*her/you*) a story. Every time I finished the story, she (*said/told*) me (*read/to read*) (*her/me*)
7.   **8.**   **9.**   **10.**   **11.**

another one. She finally fell asleep at 10:00. Then Estelle, the five-year-old, started crying. When I went to

her room, she told me that (*I/she*) (*has seen/had seen*) a monster in the closet. I tried to (*tell/say*) her that
12.   **13.**   **14.**

monsters (*don't/didn't*) exist, but she didn't stop crying. I tried to call the parents and tell them that Estelle
15.

(*is/was*) upset and that she (*is/was*) crying. They told me (*call/to call*) (*them/us*) in case of any problem, but
16.   **17.**   **18.**   **19.**

when I called, there was no answer. Later they told me that they (*must/had to*) turn off their cell phone
20.

because they were at a concert.

They said (*we/they*) (*would/will*) be home by 11:00 p.m. But they didn't come home till 1:00 a.m. They
21.   **22.**

called and told me that the concert (*has started/had started*) an hour late. I called my mother and told her
23.

that I (*couldn't/can't*) leave because the parents hadn't come home. She told me (*don't/not to*) worry. She
24.   **25.**

said that it (*is/was*) my responsibility to stay with the kids until the parents came home. When they finally
26.

got home, they told me that (*we/ they*) (*don't/didn't*) have any money to pay (*me/you*) because they
27.   **28.**   **29.**

(*had forgotten/have forgotten*) to stop at an ATM. They said that (*they/we*) (*would/will*) pay (*you/me*)
30.   **31.**   **32.**   **33.**

(*next/the following*) week.
34.

When I got home, my mother was waiting up for me. I told her that I (*don't/didn't*) ever want to have
35.

children. She laughed and told me that the children's behavior (*wasn't/isn't*) unusual. She told me that
36.

(*you/I*) (*will/would*) change (*my/your*) mind someday. I (*said/told*) her that I (*didn't/don't*) want to babysit
37.   **38.**   **39.**   **40.**   **41.**

ever again. She told me that I (*will/would*) get used to it.
42.

An Innovation in KIDS' TV

CD 2
TR 22

Read the following article. Pay special attention to the words in bold.

It is one of the most watched TV shows in the world. It is seen in 120 countries and is translated into a number of different languages. At the beginning, the producers were not sure if this program **was going** to be successful or not. They never imagined that more than forty-five years later it **would** still **be** here. Welcome to the world of Sesame Street.

In the 1960s, documentary television producer Joan Cooney realized that children **were watching** a lot of TV but **were learning** very little from it. Cooney wanted to investigate how television **could be used** to educate young children and entertain them at the same time. She thought that she **could help** prepare them better for school.

At first, TV producers didn't think that Sesame Street **would hold** the interest of young children. They thought that small children

Joan Cooney and some of the Sesame Street characters at the 10th Sesame Street Workshop Benefit Gala

didn't have the attention span[7] to watch an hour of educational TV. Cooney thought otherwise. "What if it went down more like ice cream than spinach?"

Cooney brought in puppeteer[8] Jim Henson. Henson created the Muppets, with such characters as Big Bird and Elmo. Henson wanted to create characters that kids **could relate** to. Cooney realized that without these characters, learning the alphabet and learning to count **wouldn't be** as much fun.

The show was always excellent at helping kids learn the basics of numbers and letters, but it became clear that children's emotions **needed** to be addressed too. After the events of September 11, 2001, the producers realized that kids **had become** fearful and that they **needed** a way to express how they **were feeling**. So the show started dealing with children's fears. In 2002, the producers of the South African version of the program, "Takalani Sesame," thought that it **would** be a good idea to deal with HIV.[9] They understood how frightening this disease **could be** for small children, so they brought in a five-year-old Muppet named Kami, who is HIV positive.

It is clear that Sesame Street has evolved over the years. But it is still a favorite TV show for pre-school kids around the world.

---

7 *attention span:* the time that a person can concentrate on something
8 *puppeteer:* an artist who makes puppets behave like actors
9 *HIV:* human immunodeficiency virus

COMPREHENSION CHECK Based on the reading, tell if the statement is true (**T**) or false (**F**).

1. Children don't have the attention span to watch an hour of educational TV.

2. Not only does Sesame Street teach numbers and letters, it also deals with children's fears.

3. The characters in Sesame Street are the same in all countries.

10.11 Noun Clauses after Past-Tense Verbs

Examples	Explanation
The producers thought that small children **could learn** from TV. They didn't imagine that Sesame Street **would last** over forty-five years.	If the verb in the main clause is past (for example: *thought, realized*), we follow the rule of sequence of tenses in Chart 10.6.

EXERCISE 21 Use the words under the blank to complete each statement.

1. No one imagined that _Sesame Street would be such a popular program._
   Sesame Street will be such a popular program.

2. Joan Cooney thought that _____
   Early education can be fun.

3. She realized that _____
   Small children are watching a lot of TV.

4. She thought that _____
   I can help kids prepare for school.

5. People believed that _____
   Kids don't have the attention span to watch a one-hour program.

6. The producers realized that _____
   Kids became fearful after September 11.

7. They thought that _____
   We should address kids' fears.

8. Parents were happy that _____
   Our kids can learn at home.

9. Dr. Spock decided that _____
   I will write a book about babies.

10. He thought that _____
    I can help parents feel more comfortable.

11. He knew that _____
    I want to help parents.

12. He told parents _____
    You can trust yourselves.

13. He never imagined that _____
    My book will become so popular.

14. I didn't know that _____
    I can use an app to check my son's driving habits.

10.12 Noun Clauses as Reported Questions

A noun clause can be used to report a question. If the main verb is in the past tense (*asked, wanted to know, tried to understand,* etc.), we follow the rule of sequence of tenses. (See Chart 10.8 for exceptions.)

Exact Quote	Reported Speech
Wh-* Questions with auxiliaries or *be	
"How old are your kids?" "What are you watching on TV?"	She asked *me* **how old my kids were.** I wanted to know **what she was watching on TV.**
Wh-* Questions with *do/does/did	
"How do kids learn?" "How did you get the idea for Sesame Street?"	She wanted to **know how kids learned.** Cooney was asked **how she had gotten** (*or* **got**) **the idea for Sesame Street.**
***Wh-* Questions about the subject**	
"Which kids watched the show?" "Who saw the September 11 episode?"	She asked me **which kids (had) watched the show.** I wanted to know **who had seen** (*or* **saw**) **the September 11 episode.**
Yes/No* Questions with auxiliaries or *be	
"Will young kids watch a one-hour program?" "Can kids learn the alphabet from TV?"	She wanted to know **if young kids would watch a one-hour program (or not).** They asked her **whether (or not) kids could learn the alphabet from TV.**
Yes/No* Questions with *do/does/did	
"Do small kids like Sesame Street?" "Did Jim Henson create the Muppets?"	She asked me **whether small kids liked** (*or* **like**) **Sesame Street.** I asked her **if Jim Henson (had) created the Muppets.**

Language Notes:

1. Remember: Reported speech is often a paraphrase of what someone has said.

    She asked me, "Do your kids spend a lot of time in front of the TV?"

    She asked me if **my kids watched a lot of TV.**

2. The most common changes that are made are:

    will → would   can → could

EXERCISE 22 Change these exact questions to reported questions. Follow the rule of sequence of tenses. In some cases, it's not necessary to follow the rule of sequence of tenses.

1. Did you see the September 11 episode on Sesame Street?

    She asked me _if (or whether) I had seen the September 11 episode._

2. How much TV do your kids watch?

    She asked me _____

3. Do they like Sesame Street?

   She wanted to know _____

4. Why is this show so popular?

   At first I didn't understand _____

5. Have you ever seen the show?

   I asked my brother _____

6. How long has Sesame Street been on TV?

   I wanted to know _____

7. Do you like Big Bird?

   I asked my sister _____

8. Is Jim Henson still alive?

   He asked me _____

9. How does Sesame Street handle scary situations?

   We wanted to know _____

10. Has Sesame Street made any changes in the past forty-five years?

    He asked me _____

11. Will the Muppets hold kids' attention?

    Cooney wanted to know _____

12. Was Sesame Street the first educational TV program for kids?

    I asked my teacher _____

13. How long will Sesame Street last?

    They had no idea _____

EXERCISE 23 Choose the correct option to complete this essay. In some cases, both choices are possible, so circle both options.

When I was eighteen years old and living in my native Estonia, I didn't know where (*I wanted/did I want*)
                                                                                                    1.
to go in my life. I couldn't decide (*I should/if I should*) get a job or go to college. I didn't even know what I
                                    2.
(*want/wanted*) to study. Then I read an article about an *au pair* program in the U.S. This is a program where
  3.
young people go to live with a family for a year to take care of their small children.

continued

WRITING

PART 1 Editing Advice

1. Use *that* or nothing to introduce an included statement. Don't use *what*.

          that
    I know ~~what~~ she is a good driver.

2. Use statement word order in an included question.

          he is
    I don't know how fast ~~is he~~ driving.

3. We *say* something. We *tell* someone something.

       told
    He ~~said~~ me that he wanted to go home.

       said
    He ~~told~~, "I want to go home."

4. Use *tell* or *ask*, not *say*, to report an imperative. Follow *tell* and *ask* with an object.

         told
    Dr. Spock ~~said~~ parents to trust themselves.

         me
    My son asked ∧ to give him the car keys.

5. Don't use *to* after *tell*.

    She told ~~to~~ me that she wanted to be a teacher.

6. Use *if* or *whether* to introduce an included *yes/no* question. Use statement word order.

          whether
    I don't know ∧ teenagers understand the risks while driving.

          if I should
    I can't decide ∧ ~~should I~~ let my daughter get her driver's license.

7. Follow the rule of sequence of tenses when the main verb is in the past.

          would
    Last year my father said that he ~~will~~ teach me how to drive, but he didn't.

8. Don't use *so* before a noun clause.

    I think ~~so~~ raising children is the best job.

9. Use an infinitive to report an imperative.

          to
    My parents told me ∧ drive carefully.

          not to
    My parents told me ∧ ~~don't~~ text while driving.

PART 2 Editing Practice

Some of the shaded words and phrases have mistakes. Find the mistakes and correct them. If the shaded words are correct, write C.

                                                            that

When I was fourteen years old, I told my parents ~~what~~ I wanted to work as a babysitter, but they
1.

C
told me that I was too young. At that time, they told me that they will pay me $1 an hour to help
2.   **3.**   **4.**

with my little brother. A few times they asked me could I watch him when they went out. They
5.

always told me call them immediately in case of a problem. They told me don't watch TV or text my
6.   **7.**

friends while I was working as a babysitter. They always told me that I have done a good job.
8.

    When I was fifteen, I got a few more responsibilities, like preparing small meals. They always

told that I should teach my brother about good nutrition. I asked them whether I could get more
9.   **10.**   **11.**

money because I had more responsibilities, and they agreed. I asked them if I can buy something
12.

new with my earnings. My parents said, "Of course."
13.

    When I turned eighteen, I started working for my neighbors, who have three children. The

neighbors asked me had I gotten my driver's license yet. When I said yes, they were pleased because
14.   **15.**

I could drive the kids to different places. I never realized how hard was it to take care of so many
16.

kids. As soon as we get in the car, they ask, "Are we there yet?" They think so we should arrive
17.   **18.**

immediately. When they're thirsty, they ask me to buy them soda, but I tell them what it is healthier
19.   **20.**   **21.**

to drink water. They always tell, "In our house we drink soda." I don't understand why do their
22.   **23.**

parents give them soda instead of water. I didn't know whether to follow the rules of my house or
24.

theirs. So I asked my parents what should I do. My parents told me not to say anything about their
25.   **26.**

parents' rules but that I should try to encourage healthy habits by example.
27.

    Little by little I'm learning how to take care of children. I hope that I will be as good a mom to
28.

my kids as my mom has been to me.

PART 3 Write About It

1. Write about some good advice your parents gave you when you were a child. Explain what the advice was and how this has helped you.

2. Write about how a teacher or another adult helped you or encouraged you when you were a child.

PART 4 Edit Your Writing

Reread the Summary of Lesson 10 and the editing advice. Edit your writing from Part 3.

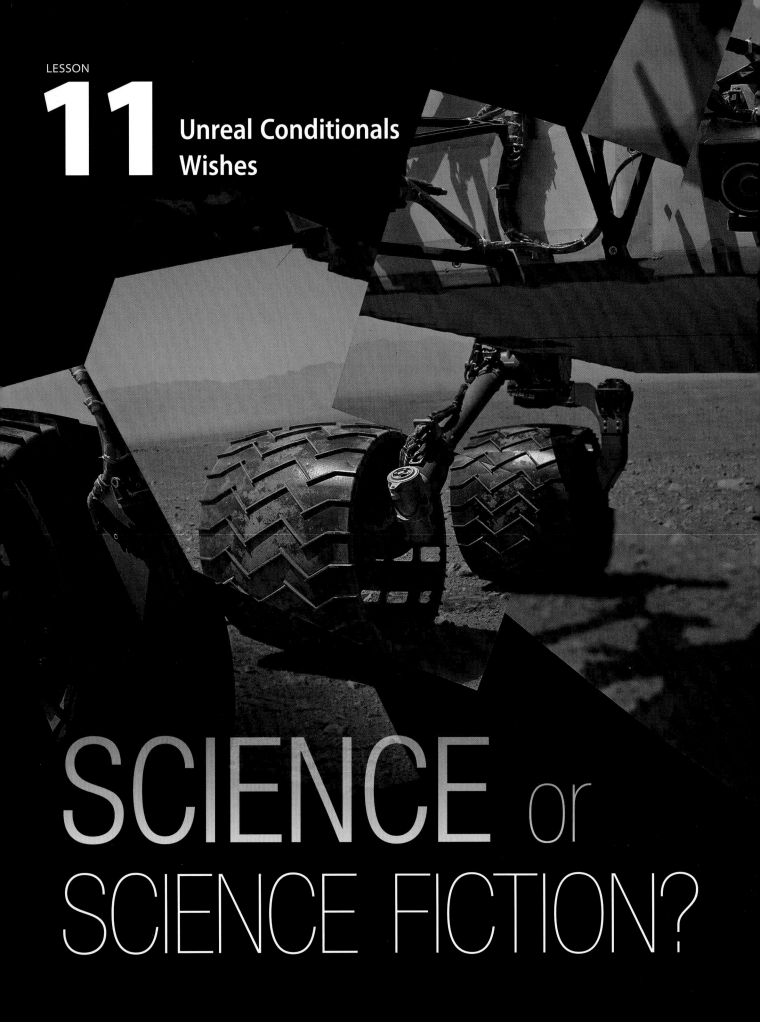

SCIENCE or SCIENCE FICTION?

Self-portrait taken by *Curiosity*
rover on the surface of Mars

Somewhere, something incredible
is waiting to be known.

— Carl Sagan

Time Travel

Wormhole

CD 2
TR 23

Read the following article. Pay special attention to the words in bold.

If you **could travel** to the past or the future, **would** you **do** it? If you **could travel** to the past, **would** you **want** to visit anyone? If you **could travel** to the future, **would** you **come** back to the present and warn people about possible disasters?

Time travel, first presented in a novel called *The Time Machine,* written by H.G. Wells over one hundred years ago, is the subject not only of fantasy but of serious scientific exploration.

About one hundred years ago, Albert Einstein proved that the universe has not three dimensions but four—three of space and one of time. He proved that time changes with motion. Einstein believed that, theoretically,[1] time travel is possible. The time on a clock in motion moves more slowly than the time on a stationary clock. If you **wanted** to visit the Earth in the future, you **would have to** get on a rocket ship going at almost the speed of light,[2] travel many light-years[3] away, turn around, and come back at that speed. While traveling, you **would age** more slowly.

Einstein came up with an example he called the "twin paradox." Suppose there is a set of 25-year-old twins, Nick and Rick. If Nick **decided** to travel fast and far on a rocket ship and Rick **decided** to stay at home, Nick **would be** younger than Rick when he returned. Specifically, if Nick **traveled** 25 light-years away and back, the trip **would take** 50 "Earth years." Rick **would be** 75 years old, but Nick **would be** 25 and a half years old. If Nick **had** a five-year-old daughter when he left, his daughter **would be** 55 years old. So Nick **would be visiting** the future.

Using today's technologies, time travel is still impossible. If you **wanted** to travel to the nearest star which is 4.3 light-years away, it **would take** eighty thousand years to arrive. (This assumes the speed of today's rockets, which is thirty-seven thousand miles per hour.) According to Einstein, you can't travel faster than the speed of light. While most physicists believe that travel to the future is possible, it is believed that travel to the past will never happen.

Although the idea of time travel seems the subject of science fiction, not science, many of today's discoveries and explorations, such as traveling to the moon, had their roots in science fiction novels and movies.

---

[1] *theoretically:* possible in theory, but not proven
[2] *speed of light:* 299,792,458 meters per second (or 186,000 miles per second)
[3] *light-year:* the distance that light travels in a year through a vacuum (6 trillion miles or 9.46 trillion kilometers)

COMPREHENSION CHECK Based on the reading, tell if the statement is true (**T**) or false (**F**).

1. Scientists sometimes get ideas from science fiction.

2. Scientists believe that travel to the past is possible.

3. Einstein showed that time is dependent on motion.

11.1 Unreal Conditionals—Present

An unreal conditional is used to talk about a hypothetical or imagined situation. An unreal conditional in the present describes a situation that is not real now.

Examples	Explanation
If we **had** a time machine, we **could travel** to the future. (Reality: We **don't have** a time machine.) I **would visit** my ancestors if I **could travel** to the past. (Reality: I **can't travel** to the past.)	We use a past form in the *if* clause and *would* or *could* + base form in the main clause. When the *if* clause precedes the main clause, a comma is used to separate the two clauses. When the main clause precedes the *if* clause, a comma is not used.
If we **could travel** at the speed of light, we**'d be able** to go to the future.	All pronouns except *it* can contract with *would*: *I'd, you'd, he'd, she'd, we'd, they'd.*
If time travel **were** possible, some people **would do** it. If Einstein **were** here today, what **would** he **think** of today's world?	*Were* is the correct form in an unreal conditional clause for all subjects, singular and plural. However, we often use *was* with *I, he, she, it,* and singular nouns.
If I **were** in a time machine, I**'d be traveling** at the speed of light.	For a continuous time, we use *would* + *be* + verb *-ing.*
I wouldn't travel to the past **unless** I could return to the present. **Even if** I could know my future, I wouldn't want to know it.	A conditional can begin with *unless* or *even if.*
If I were you, I**'d study** more science.	We often give advice with the expression *"If I were you . . ."*
What if you **could travel** to the future? *What if* you **had** the brain of Einstein?	We use *what if* to propose a hypothetical situation.
If you **had** Einstein's brain, what **would** you **do**? If you **could fly** to another planet, where **would** you **go**?	When we make a question with conditionals, the *if* clause uses statement word order. The main clause uses question word order.

EXERCISE 1 Listen to the following sentences. Fill in the blanks with the words you hear.

1. If dinosaurs _____were_____ alive today, the world _____would be_____ very different.
   a.   b.

2. Dinosaurs have been extinct for a long time. If dinosaur DNA[4] _____ not so old, scientists
   a.

   _____ possibly bring them back.
   b.

3. The world _____ unsafe for humans if scientists _____ back the dinosaurs.
   a.   b.

4. Some people say that if scientists _____ back extinct species, the world
   a.

   _____ interesting and exciting.
   b.

5. Other people say that scientists _____ the natural order of things if they
   a.

   _____ back an extinct species.
   b.

6. What do you think? _____ a good thing if scientists _____ to bring
   a.   b.

   back extinct species?

EXERCISE 2 Complete the conversation with the correct form of the verb given and any
other words you see. Use *would* + base form in the main clause. Use the past in the *if* clause. Use
contractions where possible.

A: If you _____could_____ clone any animal, which animal _____?
         1. can   **2.** you/clone

B: I _____ my dog.
         3. clone

A: Why?

B: Well, my dog is getting old, and I don't want to lose her. If I _____ make a copy of her,
                                                              4. can

   I _____ the same dog again for many more years. What about you?
      5. have

A: I just got a parrot, and they live about fifty years. I'm already forty years old. If I _____
                                                                              6. die

   sooner rather than later, my parrot _____ a home. Probably my parrot
                                          7. not/have

   _____ to clone me!
      8. want

B: I read about cloning sheep, but I don't understand why scientists would do that.

A: I read something about it too. If you _____ a cow that _____ high-quality
                                          9. have   **10.** produce

   milk or meat, it _____ good business if you _____ make many copies of
                      11. be   **12.** can

   this cow.

_____
[4] *DNA:* molecules that carry the genetic information in living organisms

B: I hadn't thought about that. How about cloning people? If you _____ clone a good cow or
13. can

sheep, why not clone a great person?

A: People have thought about cloning people. So far, it's never been done. Some people think that scientists

_____ with nature.
14. *continuous form of* interfere

B: But if you _____ clone a person, who _____?
15. can   **16.** you/clone

A: I think I _____ Albert Einstein. I read that his brain is preserved. If scientists
17. clone

_____ the DNA from his brain, they _____ make another
18. take   **19.** be able to

Einstein.

B: What if the "new" Einstein _____ any interest in science? What if he
20. not/ show

_____ to become a musician or a carpenter?
21. decide

A: Hmm. I never thought of that. Also, the "new" Einstein _____ in a different
22. *continuous form of* live

world. He _____ access to computers and other new technologies.
23. have

B: And he _____ the same parents or friends. If he
24. not/have

_____ born today, I think he _____ a completely different person.
25. be   **26.** be

A: Well, it's fun to imagine.

Cloning microinjection of
human stem cells into egg cell

EXERCISE 3 Complete the conversations with the correct form of the verb given and any other words you see. Use *would* + base form in the main clause. Use the past in the *if* clause. Use contractions where possible.

1. **A:** What __would you do__ if you _____ were _____ a scientist?
              a. you/do   **b.** be

   B: If I _____ a scientist, I _____ to find a cure for diseases.
             c. be   **d.** try

2. **A:** If you _____ make a copy of yourself, _____ it?
             a. can   **b.** you/do

   B: My mom says that one of me is enough. If she _____ two of me, it
                                               c. have

   _____ her crazy.
       d. drive

3. **A:** If you _____ come back to Earth in any form after you die, how
             a. can

   _____ back?
        b. you/come

   B: I _____ back as a dog. Dogs have such an easy life.
            c. come

   A: Not all dogs.

   B: I _____ as a dog in a good home.
           d. only/come back

4. **A:** If you _____ meet any person, dead or alive, who _____ to meet?
             a. can   **b.** you/want

   B: I _____ to meet Abraham Lincoln.
          c. want

5. **A:** If I _____ find a way to teach a person a foreign language in a week,
             a. can

   I _____ a million dollars.
        b. make

   B: You _____ a billion dollars. And I _____ your first customer.
            c. probably/make   **d.** be

6. **A:** If you _____ be invisible for a day, what _____ ?
             a. can   **b.** you/do

   B: I _____ to my teacher's house the day she writes the final exam.
           c. go

7. **A:** What _____ if you _____ to the past or future?
             a. you/do   **b.** can/travel

   B: I _____ to the past.
          c. go

   A: How far back _____ ?
                     d. you/go

   B: I _____ back millions of years.
          e. go

   A: Why?

   B: I _____ see dinosaurs.
            f. be able to

8. A: It _____ nice if people _____ live forever.
   a. be   b. can

B: If people _____, the world _____ overpopulated. There
        c. not/die   d. be

_____ enough resources for everybody.
        e. not/be

A: I didn't think of that. If the world _____ overpopulated, I _____
                                    f. be   g. never/find

a parking space!

EXERCISE 4 About You Answer the following questions. Discuss your answers with your partner.

1. If you could have the brain of another person, whose brain would you want?

   If I could have the brain of another person, I'd want Einstein's brain.

2. If you could travel to the past or the future, which direction would you go?

   _____

3. If you could make a clone of yourself, would you do it? Why or why not?

   _____

4. If you could travel to another planet, would you want to go?

   _____

5. If you could change one thing about today's world, what would it be?

   _____

6. If you could know the day of your death, would you want to know it?

   _____

7. If you could be a child again, what age would you be?

   _____

8. If you could change one thing about yourself, what would it be?

   _____

9. If you could meet any person from the past, who would it be?

   _____

10. If you could be any animal, what animal would you be?

   _____

EXERCISE 5 Fill in the blanks to tell what the following people are thinking. Use the correct unreal conditional and any other words you see.

1. One-year-old: If I _____*could*_____ walk, I ____*would walk*____ into the kitchen and take a cookie
                   a. can   **b. walk**

   out of the cookie jar.

2. Two-year-old: If I _____ talk, I _____ my mother that I hate peas.
                     a. can   **b. tell**

3. Fourteen-year-old: I _____ happier if I _____ drive.
                      a. be   **b. can**

4. Sixteen-year-old: If I _____ a car, my friends and I _____ out every night.
                     a. have   **b. go**

5. Nineteen-year-old: I _____ a private university if I _____ a lot of money.
                    a. attend   **b. have**

6. Twenty-five-year-old: If I _____ married, my parents _____ about
                   a. be   **b. not/worry**

   me so much.

7. Thirty-five-year-old mother: I _____ more time for myself if my kids
                      a. have

   _____ older.
   b. be

8. Sixty-year-old grandmother: If I _____ grandchildren, my life
                    a. not/have

   _____ so interesting.
   b. not/be

9. Ninety-year-old: If I _____ young today, I _____ learn all about
                 a. be   **b. have to**

   computers and other high-tech devices.

10. One hundred-year-old: If I _____ you the story of my life, you
                     a. tell

   _____ it.
   b. not/believe

EXERCISE 6 [About You] Give your opinion. Discuss your answers with a partner. Do you think the world would be better or worse if . . .

1. we could live to be 150 years old?
2. people didn't have to work?
3. every job paid the same salary?
4. there were no computers?
5. everyone spoke the same language?
6. we could predict the future?

11.2 Implied Conditionals

Examples	Explanation
I'**d love** to meet my great-grandparents. I **could** ask them about their lives. **Would** you **like** to see a living dinosaur? I **wouldn't want** to know the future. **Would** you?	Sometimes the conditional (the *if* clause) is implied, not stated. In the examples, the implication is "if you had the opportunity" or "if the possibility presented itself."

EXERCISE 7 Fill in the blanks with the missing words to complete the conversations. Use context clues. Use contractions where possible. Answers may vary.

1. **A:** _____Would_____ you want to travel to the future?
      a.

   B: Not really. _____ you?
                          b.

   A: Yes. It would _____ very interesting.
                        c.

   B: I _____ happy.
             d.

   A: Why not?

   B: I _____ miss my family and friends.
             e.

   A: But you could come back and tell them about the future. You _____ them about future
                                                                      f.

   disasters.

   B: Then I _____ changing the future. And it takes a long time to come back. By the time
                   g.
   I came back, everyone I know _____ much older.
                                      h.

2. **A:** I _____ love to know more about the past.
             a.

   B: Then you should study more history.

   A: But I wouldn't learn about my ancestors. I _____ only _____ about famous people.
                                                    b.   c.

3. **A:** _____ you want to live more than one hundred years?
             a.

   B: Yes. But I _____ to be healthy. What about you?
                      b.

   A: I _____ want to see my great-great-grandchildren.
             c.

4. **A:** I _____ love to meet a famous person from the past.
             a.

   B: Who _____ you want to meet and why?
               b.

   A: Maybe Michelangelo. I _____ to watch him paint the Sistine Chapel.
                                c.

5. **A:** _____ you _____ to see a living dinosaur?
             a.   b.

   B: No, I _____ .
                   c.

   A: I think it _____ interesting.
                       d.

   B: I _____ afraid.
             e.

6. **A:** I _____ to travel into space.
             a.

   B: I wouldn't want to. Why would you?

   A: I _____ what the Earth looks like from afar.
             b.

EXPLORING MARS

Read the following article. Pay special attention to the words in bold.

Mars, our closest planetary neighbor, has always fascinated people on Earth. **If** you **watch** a lot of science fiction movies, you **see** people from Earth meeting strange-looking "Martians." But, of course, this is just fantasy.

In 2004, *Spirit* rover[5] landed on Mars to study the climate and geology of the planet, and to prepare for human exploration. In 2012, *Curiosity* rover landed on Mars. Its mission is to find out if there was ever life on that planet. One of the jobs of *Curiosity* is to figure out where a future mission should look for life. **If** enough information is gathered, astronauts **will** probably **arrive** on Mars by the 2030s.

Travel to Mars will be much more difficult than landing on the moon. When people landed on the moon, they carried with them all the supplies they needed. But sending a spaceship with people and all the supplies they need for their time on Mars would make the spaceship too heavy. So **if** astronauts **go** to Mars, scientists **will send** supplies first. Many other problems **will have to** be solved too.

Astronauts **will have** to return within a given time period. **If** they **don't come** back within this period of time, they **will miss** their chance of return. **If** astronauts **have** a problem with their equipment, they **will not be able** to rely on messages from Earth to help them. Because of the distance from Earth, it can take about forty minutes from the time a message goes out from Earth until it is received on Mars. Also, a visitor to Mars **will be** gone for at least three years because of the distance and time necessary to travel. But one of the biggest problems with traveling to Mars is the danger of radiation. Astronauts **will be** exposed to much more radiation than someone traveling to the moon.

If you **had** the chance to go to Mars, **would** you **go**?

---

5 *rover:* a strong vehicle used for extraterrestrial exploration

COMPREHENSION CHECK Based on the reading, tell if the statement is true (**T**) or false (**F**).

1. Scientists are looking for signs of life on Mars.

2. One problem with traveling to Mars is exposure to radiation.

3. Astronauts on Mars will have quick communication with scientists on Earth.

11.3 Real Conditionals vs. Unreal Conditionals

Examples	Explanation
If astronauts **go** to Mars, they **will have** to return within a given time period. They **won't be able to** rely on scientists on Earth if they **have** a problem. **If** you're interested in Mars, you **should read** this article.	We can use *if* to describe a **real** future possibility. We use the present in the *if* clause and the future or a modal in the main clause.
If you **were** on Mars, you **would weigh** about one-third of what you weigh on Earth. If you **could** go to Mars, **would** you **go**?	We can use *if* to describe an **unreal** situation in the present. These examples are about hypothetical or imaginary situations. They are not plans for the future.

EXERCISE 8 Fill in the blanks with the correct form of the verb and other words given. Make real conditionals about the future. Use contractions where possible.

1. **A:** You're such a good science student.

   B: Thanks. If I _____*get*_____ a good grade point average in high school, I __*'ll apply*__ to the best
   a. get   b. apply
   universities. I want to major in chemistry.

2. **A:** I'm thinking about seeing the new science fiction movie this weekend.

   B: I love science fiction! If you _____, I _____ with you. What day?
   a. go   b. go

   A: I _____ on Saturday if I _____ work that day.
   c. go   d. not/have to

3. **A:** I've just finished reading a great science fiction book. You can borrow it. But if you _____
   a. start

   it, you _____ it down. It's so good. Let me tell you about it.
   b. not/be able to put

   B: If you _____ me about it, it _____ it for me. So please don't tell me.
   c. tell   d. ruin

4. **A:** I was going to rent the movie *Jurassic Park*. I heard it's about bringing back dinosaurs.

   B: I have it. I don't remember where it is, but if I _____ it, you _____ it.
   a. find   b. can/borrow

   A: That's OK. My library has a lot of DVDs. If I _____ in my library catalog,
   c. look

   I _____ it.
   d. probably/find

continued

5. A: I need to write a paper about cloning. I don't know much about it.

    B: If you _____ "cloning," you _____ a lot of information.
                           a. google   b. find

    A: If I _____ information about cloning humans, I _____ about that.
                           c. find   d. write

EXERCISE 9 Fill in the blanks with the correct form of the verb given. Use both real conditionals and unreal conditionals.

    A: Do you think that astronauts will travel to Mars soon?

    B: Not so soon. I read that there's too much radiation. If a person _____*is*_____ exposed to too much
                                                            1. be

radiation, it can be harmful. It could damage the bones or even cause cancer. Scientists are trying to

build a spacecraft that can minimize radiation to the astronauts. If they _____ the radiation
                                                                   2. solve

problem, probably travel to Mars _____ in our lifetime, possibly by the 2030s.
                                                    3. happen

    B: What about radiation at the airport security point? My cousin travels for business all the time. If she

_____ through radiation at the airport frequently, _____ cancer?
                4. pass   5. she/get

    A: I don't think so. But if she _____ worried about it, she _____ for a pat
                                 6. be   7. can/ask

down. I love to travel. If I _____ anywhere, I _____ into space.
                                  8. can/go   9. go

    A: Me too. If I _____ to Mars today, I _____ back a rock as a souvenir.
                          10. go   11. bring

    B: If you _____ for Mars today, you _____ back for at least three
                      12. leave   13. not/come

years.

    A: Oh. I _____ my friends and family if I _____ them for three years. So
                  14. miss   15. can/not/see

maybe I'll take a more normal vacation. I'm thinking about going to Canada this summer. If I

_____ there, I _____ the Rocky Mountains.
            16. go   17. visit

    B: If you _____, you can bring me back a souvenir rock from there. By the way, there's
                  18. go

going to be a program on TV tonight about Mars. Are you going to watch it?

    A: I don't know. If I _____ time, I _____ it. If not, I _____ it.
                  19. have   20. watch   21. record

LIFE One Hundred Years Ago

🎧 **Read the following article. Pay special attention to the words in bold.**

CD 2
TR 26

Most of us are amazed by the rapid pace of technology at the beginning of the twenty-first century. We often wonder what life will be like twenty or fifty or one hundred years from now. But do you ever wonder what your life **would have been** like if you **had been** alive one hundred years ago?

If you **had lived** around 1900 in the United States, you probably **wouldn't have graduated** from high school. Only six percent of Americans had a high school diploma at that time. If you **had been** a child living in a city, you **might have had** to work in a factory for twelve to sixteen hours a day, six days a week. In 1900, six percent of American workers were between the ages of ten and fifteen. If you **had worked** at a manufacturing job, you **would have had to work** about 53 hours a week and you **would have earned** about 20 cents an hour. (This is equivalent to about $5.00 an hour today.) Many of you **would have worked** on farms. Thirty-eight percent of laborers were farm workers.

If you **had been** a woman in 1900, you probably **wouldn't have been** part of the labor force. Only nineteen percent of women worked outside the home. If you **had gone** to a doctor, he probably **would not have had** a college education. And he **wouldn't have had** practical training before becoming a doctor. At that time, medical students learned only from textbooks.

If you **had had** a baby in 1900, it **would have been** born at home. If you **had gotten** an infection at that time, you **might have died**, because antibiotics had not yet been discovered. The leading causes of death at that time were pneumonia, influenza, and tuberculosis.

What about your home? If you **had been living** one hundred years ago, you probably **wouldn't have had** a bathtub or a telephone or electricity. You **would have been** living with a large number of people. Twenty percent of homes had seven or more people.

Do you think you **would have been** happy with life one hundred years ago?

Two young children with a street vendor in Alton, IL, circa 1912

COMPREHENSION CHECK   Based on the reading, tell if the statement is true (**T**) or false (**F**).

1. One hundred years ago, most children in the U.S. had to work.

2. One hundred years ago, most doctors in the U.S. had a college education.

3. One hundred years ago, most babies in the U.S. were born at home.

11.4 Unreal Conditionals—Past

Examples	Explanation
If you **had lived** one hundred years ago, you probably **wouldn't have graduated** from high school. (Reality: You didn't live one hundred years ago.)	An unreal conditional can describe a situation that was not real in the past.
You probably **would have been** born at home if you **had lived** in the U.S. around 1900. If you **had gotten** an infection, you **might have died**.	We use the past perfect in the *if* clause and *would/could/might* + *have* + past participle in the main clause.
If my great-grandparents **had been able to** come to the U.S. one hundred years ago, I **would have been** born here and my life **would have been** different. (Reality: They couldn't come to the U.S. one hundred years ago.)	In the *if* clause, we use *had been able to* to express the past perfect of *could*.
(a) If you **were** born one hundred years ago, your life **would have been** different. OR (b) If you **had been** born one hundred years ago, your life **would have been** different.	Sometimes we don't use the past perfect, especially with the verb *be*, if it is clear that the action is past. It is clear that you *were* born in the past. Sentences (a) and (b) have the same meaning.

Language Notes:

1. In relaxed speech, *have* after *could*, *would*, or *might* is pronounced /ə/.

2. In very informal conversational English, we often hear *would have* in both clauses.

    If I **would have known** about the movie, I **would have told** you. (Informal)

    If I **had known** about the movie, I **would have told** you. (Formal)

3. Sometimes we mix a past conditional with a present result.

    If my mother **had** never **met** my father, I **wouldn't be** here today.

4. Sometimes we mix a present conditional with a past result.

    If I **were** an astronaut, I **would have gone to the moon**.

5. We can use a continuous tense with unreal conditionals.

    If you **had been living** one hundred years ago, you probably wouldn't have had a bathtub.

EXERCISE 10   Fill in the blanks with the correct form of the verb to complete this conversation about life in the U.S. one hundred years ago. Answers may vary.

1. If you ___had worked___ in a factory, you ___would have earned___ about 20 cents an hour.
    a. work   b. earn

2. If you _____ a baby one hundred years ago, it probably _____
    a. have   b. be/born

    at home.

3. If you _____ a child in a big city, you _____ all day in a factory.
a. be   b. work

4. If you _____ around 1900, you probably _____ high school.
a. live   b. not/finish

5. You _____ a car if you _____ at the beginning
a. not/have   b. live

of the last century.

6. Your president _____ Theodore Roosevelt if you _____
a. be   b. live

in the U.S. at the beginning of the last century.

7. If you _____ to travel to another city, you _____ by train.
a. need   b. travel

EXERCISE 11 A middle-aged woman is telling her daughter how the young lady's life would have been different if she had grown up in the late 1950s. Fill in the blanks with the correct form of the verb given to complete the story.

It's great that you're thinking about becoming a doctor or astronaut. When I was your age, I didn't have

the opportunities you have today. You can be anything you want, but if you ___*had been*___ a woman
1. be

growing up in the fifties, your opportunities _____ limited. If you
2. be

_____ to college, you probably _____ in nursing or
3. go   4. major

education, or you _____ a secretarial course. You probably
5. take

_____ married in your early twenties. If you _____
6. get   7. get

pregnant, you probably _____ your job. You probably _____
8. quit   9. have

two or more children. Your husband _____ to support you and the children.
10. work

Also your house _____ one TV and one phone. Because we had only one TV, the
11. have

family spent more time together. You _____ a computer or a cell phone. If
12. not/have

you _____ up in the fifties, your life _____ completely different.
13. grow   14. be

EXERCISE 12 About You Complete each statement. Discuss your answers with a partner.

1. If I had been born 200 years ago, _____

2. If I had known _____ , I _____

3. I wouldn't have learned about time travel if _____

The SCIENCE of AGING

Read the following article. Pay special attention to the words in bold.

CD 2
TR 27

Do you **wish** you **could live** to be one hundred years old or more? The answer to that question probably depends on how healthy you are at an advanced age, both physically and mentally. Does an elderly person **wish** she **had** the memory of a young person? Probably. As we age, the memory of most people diminishes.[6]

How much of longevity[7] and health is determined by genetics?[8] How much by environment? To analyze why some people live a much longer, healthier life than others, scientists have been traveling to areas of the world where there are a number of centenarians.[9] They have found certain groups in Japan, Italy, New York, and California who outlive others around them.

Women are more likely than men to live to be one hundred by a ratio of four or five to one. However, scientists no longer think that this is genetic. Women take better advantage of diet and medical care than men do.

For years, scientists **wished** they **could find** the genes for diseases. But now they have changed their focus. They are looking for genes that can protect us from disease and aging. Scientists are looking at the genes of the "wellderly" (well + elderly). These are people over eighty who have no chronic[10] diseases, such as high blood pressure or diabetes. They have found that, besides genetics, there are many factors that influence longevity—diet, education, response to stress, and even luck.

Salvatore Caruso, a centenarian from Italy, broke his leg when he was a young man. As a result, he was unfit to serve in the Italian Army when his entire unit was called up[11] during World War II. He **wished** he **could have served** with his unit.[12] "They were all sent to the Russian front,"[13] he said, "and not a single one of them came back." Whatever factors contribute to long life, a little luck doesn't hurt either.

---

[6] *to diminish:* to lessen, reduce, or become limited

[7] *longevity:* the length of life

[8] *genetics:* the passing of physical characteristics from parents to children

[9] *centenarian:* a person who is one hundred years old or older

[10] *chronic:* long lasting, persistent

[11] *to call up:* to ask someone to report for military service

[12] *unit:* group of soldiers

[13] *front:* the area where two enemy forces meet in battle

COMPREHENSION CHECK Based on the reading, tell if the statement is true (**T**) or false (**F**).

1. Some areas of the world have more centenarians than others.

2. One factor that determines how long you will live is luck.

3. Salvatore Caruso was wounded in World War II.

11.5 Wishes

PART A

Examples	Explanation
Reality: We **have** to get old. **Wish:** I wish (that) we **didn't have** to get old. **Reality:** We **are learning** about Mars. **Wish:** I wish (that) we **were learning** about other planets too. **Reality:** I **can't live** 150 years. **Wish:** I wish (that) I **could live** 150 years.	We can wish that a present or future situation were different. We use a **past** verb for a wish about the **present or future**. After *wish*, we can use *that* to introduce the clause, but it is usually omitted.
I'm not young, but I wish (that) I **were**. I don't have a good memory, but I wish (that) I **did**.	We can use an auxiliary verb (*were, did, could,* etc.) to shorten the wish clause.
Reality: You don't want to study science. **Wish:** I wish (that) you **would study** more science. **Reality:** Scientists haven't found a cure for diabetes. **Wish:** I wish (that) scientists **would find** a cure for diabetes.	Putting *would* after a wish shows that one person wants a change in another person or situation. Using *would* sometimes conveys a complaint.

Language Note:

With *be*, the correct form is *were* for all subjects. In conversation, however, we often hear *was* with *I, he, she,* and *it*.

> I wish I **were** younger. (Formal)
> I wish I **was** younger. (Informal)

PART B

Examples	Explanation
Reality: I **didn't know** my grandparents. **Wish:** I wish (that) I **had known** them. **Reality:** Salvatore Caruso **couldn't serve** in the military. **Wish:** He wished (that) he **could have served**.	We can wish that a past situation were different. We use a past perfect verb for a wish about the past. If the real situation uses *could*, we use *could have* + past participle after *wish*.
I never knew my great-grandparents, but I wish I **had**.	We can use the auxiliary verb *had* to shorten the *wish* clause.

Usage Note:

In conversation, you sometimes hear *would have* + past participle for past wishes.

> I wish I *would have known* my great-grandparents.

SUMMARY OF LESSON 11

1. Unreal Conditionals—Present

Verb → Past	Verb → *Would/Could/Might* + Base Form
If I **were** an astronaut,	I **would go** to Mars.
If I **could** live to be 150 years old,	I **would know** my great-great-grandchildren.
If you **could** travel to the past,	you **could meet** your ancestors.
If we **didn't have** advanced technology,	we **wouldn't be** able to explore space.
If you **took** better care of yourself,	you **might live** to be one hundred years old.

2. Unreal Conditionals—Past

Verb → Past Perfect	Verb → *Would/Could/Might* + Have + Past Participle
If you **had lived** one hundred years ago,	you **wouldn't have had** a computer.
If you **had been** a doctor one hundred years ago,	you **could have practiced** medicine without a college degree.
If my father **had** not **met** my mother,	I **wouldn't have been** born.
If you **had gotten** an infection one hundred years ago,	you **might have died**.

3. Real Possibilities—Future

Conditional	Result
If we **explore** Mars,	we **will learn** a lot.
If you **eat** a healthy diet,	you**'ll live** longer.

4. Wishes

Examples	Explanation
I wish my grandparents **were** here. I wish I **could go** to Mars. I wish we **were learning** about dinosaurs.	Wish about the present
I wish I **could live to be** one hundred.	Wish about the future
I wish my grandpa **would tell** me more about his childhood. My mother wishes my father **would take** better care of his health.	Wish for a change in another person or situation
I wish I **had studied** more science when I was younger.	Wish about the past

TEST/REVIEW

Circle the letter of the correct word(s) to fill in the blanks.

1. I _____ help you with your science project if I had more time.

   a. were   (c.) would

   b. will   d. would be

2. I might become a scientist. If I _____ one, I'll try to find a cure for diseases.

   a. will become   c. would become

   b. became   d. become

3. If I _____ you, I'd spend more time on science and less on science fiction.

   a. were   c. will be

   b. am   d. would be

4. I can't help you with your project. I would help you if I _____.

   a. can   c. would

   b. could   d. had

5. We can't travel at the speed of light. If we could travel at the speed of light, we _____ able to visit far away stars.

   a. would be   c. would have been

   b. will be   d. were

6. We would know more about Mars if it _____ so far away.

   a. weren't   c. wouldn't have been

   b. won't be   d. wouldn't be

7. Some people don't take good care of their health. If they _____ better care of their health, they would probably live longer.

   a. take   c. had taken

   b. would take   d. took

8. I wouldn't go to Mars even if you _____ me a million dollars.

   a. pay   c. will pay

   b. paid   d. would pay

continued

9. If I could visit any planet, I _____ Jupiter.

    a. will visit   c. would be visit

    b. would visit   d. would have visited

10. I don't know much about science. I wish I _____ more about it.

    a. knew   c. have known

    b. will know   d. know

11. We can't travel to the past. I wish we _____ travel to the past.

    a. could   c. can

    b. would   d. will

12. If I had known my great-grandparents, I _____ them about their childhood.

    a. would ask   c. could ask

    b. will ask   d. would have asked

13. My uncle never exercised and was overweight. He had a heart attack and died when he was fifty years old.

If he _____ better care of himself, he might have lived much longer.

    a. would take   c. took

    b. had taken   d. will take

14. Salvatore Caruso broke his leg and couldn't serve in World War II. If he _____ in

World War II, he might have been killed.

    a. were served   c. would serve

    b. has served   d. had served

15. My favorite dog died ten years ago. I wish I _____ her.

    a. clone   c. had cloned

    b. will clone   d. would clone

16. I wish scientists _____ a cure for AIDS.

    a. find   c. would find

    b. found   d. will find

17. I didn't study physics in high school, but I wish I _____.

    a. have   c. were

    b. had   d. would

18. I don't know much about dinosaurs, but I wish I _____.

    a. had   c. would

    b. were   d. did

19. If you _____ the movie *Jurassic Park*, you would have been very scared.

    a. had seen   c. would have seen

    b. would see   d. will see

20. If scientists brought back dinosaurs back from extinction today, the world _____ very

dangerous for humans.

    a. will be   c. would be

    b. would have been   d. were

WRITING

PART 1 Editing Advice

1. Don't use *will* with an unreal conditional.

   were
   If I ~~will be~~ on Mars, I would look for life forms.

2. Always use the base form after a modal.

   have
   The teacher would ~~has~~ helped you with your science project if you had asked her.

3. Use the past perfect, not the present perfect, for unreal conditionals and wishes.

   had
   If you ~~have~~ seen the movie, you would have understood more about dinosaurs.

   had
   I wish you ~~have~~ seen the movie.

4. For a real conditional about the future, use the simple present in the *if* clause.

   If I ~~will~~ have time tomorrow, I will help you with your science project.

5. In formal writing, use *were*, not *was*, in an unreal conditional.

   were
   I wish I ~~was~~ a better student in science.

PART 2 Editing Practice

Some of the shaded words and phrases have mistakes. Find the mistakes and correct them. If the shaded words are correct, write *C*.

There are a few things in my life that I wish **were** different. First, I wish I **have** a better job and
        C 1.   *had* 2.

made more money. Unfortunately, I don't have the skills for a better job. When I was in high school,
 3.

I wasn't interested in college. My parents always said, "We wish you **would continued** your
                                                                    4.

education," but I was foolish and didn't listen to them. If I **have** gone to college, I **will** be making
                                                             5.   6.

much more money now. And if I **had** more money, I **could** help my family back home. And, if
                              7.   8.

I **will be** better educated, my parents **would** be very proud of me. I wish I **can** convince my younger
   9.   10.   11.

brothers and sister about the importance of an education, but they'll have to make their own

decisions.

Another thing I'm not happy about is my living situation. I have a roommate because I can't

afford to pay the rent alone. I wish I **don't have** a roommate. My roommate always watches TV, and
                                      12.

the TV is too loud. I wish he **would** turn off the TV at night and let me sleep. My parents have told
                               13.

me, "If I **were** you, I **will** get a better roommate." But we signed a one-year lease together and I can't
          14.   15.

do anything about it until next May. If I had known that he was going to be so inconsiderate, I never
16.

would had roomed with him. I wish it was May already! I prefer to live alone rather than live with
17.   18.

a stranger. I'm saving my money now. If I will have enough money, I'll get my own apartment next
19.

May. Another possibility is to room with my cousin, who's planning to come here soon. If he comes
20.

to the U.S. by May, I share an apartment with him. He's very responsible. I wish he has come to the
21.   22.

U.S. with me last year, but he didn't get his visa at that time.

I realize that we all make mistakes in life, but we learn from them. If I could give advice to every
23.

young person in the world, I'd say, "Look before you leap." And I will say, "Listen to your parents.
24.   25.

They've lived longer than you, and you can learn from their experience."

PART 3 Write About It

1. What do you think would be the advantages or disadvantages of cloning human beings?

2. Write about an important decision you made in the past. What would your life be like if you hadn't made this decision?

PART 4 Edit Your Writing

Reread the Summary of Lesson 11 and the editing advice. Edit your writing from Part 3.

Vowel and Consonant Pronunciation Charts

Vowels

Symbol	Examples
ʌ	love, cup
a	father, box
æ	class, black
ə	alone, atom
ɜ	ever, well
i	eat, feet
ɪ	miss, bit
ɔ	talk, corn
ʊ	would, book
oʊ	cone, boat
u	tooth, through
eɪ	able, day
aɪ	mine, try
aʊ	about, cow
ɔɪ	join, boy

Consonants

Symbol	Examples
b	bread, cab
d	door, dude
f	form, if
g	go, flag
h	hello, behind
j	use, yellow
k	cook, hike
l	leg, little
m	month, time
n	never, nine
ŋ	singer, walking
p	put, map
r	river, try
s	saw, parks
ʃ	show, action
ɾ	atom, lady
t	take, tent
tʃ	check, church
θ	thing, both
ð	the, either
v	voice, of
w	would, reward
z	zoo, mazes
ʒ	usual, vision
dʒ	just, edge

Noncount Nouns

There are several types of noncount nouns.

Group A: Nouns that have no distinct, separate parts. We look at the whole.			
milk	yogurt	paper	cholesterol
oil	poultry	rain	blood
water	bread	air	
coffee	meat	electricity	
tea	soup	lightning	
juice	butter	thunder	

Group B: Nouns that have parts that are too small or insignificant to count.			
rice	hair	sand	
sugar	popcorn	corn	
salt	snow	grass	

Group C: Nouns that are classes or categories of things. The members of the category are not the same.	
money or cash (nickels, dimes, dollars)	mail (letters, packages, postcards, flyers)
furniture (chairs, tables, beds)	homework (compositions, exercises, readings)
clothing (sweaters, pants, dresses)	jewelry (necklaces, bracelets, rings)

Group D: Nouns that are abstractions.					
love	happiness	nutrition	patience	work	nature
truth	education	intelligence	poverty	health	help
beauty	advice	unemployment	music	fun	energy
luck/fortune	knowledge	pollution	art	information	friendship

Group E: Subjects of study.		
history	grammar	biology
chemistry	geometry	math (mathematics*)

*Note: Even though *mathematics* ends with *s*, it is not plural.

continued

Notice the quantity words used with count and noncount nouns.

Singular Count	Plural Count	Noncount
a tomato	tomatoes	coffee
one tomato	**two** tomatoes	**two cups of** coffee
	some tomatoes	**some** coffee
no tomato	**no** tomatoes	**no** coffee
	any tomatoes (with questions and negatives)	**any** coffee (with questions and negatives)
	a lot of tomatoes	**a lot of** coffee
	many tomatoes	**much** coffee (with questions and negatives)
	a few tomatoes	**a little** coffee
	several tomatoes	**several** cups of coffee
	How many tomatoes?	**How much** coffee?

The following words can be used as either count nouns or noncount nouns. However, the meaning changes according to the way the nouns are used.

Count	Noncount
Oranges and grapefruit are **fruits** that contain a lot of vitamin C.	I bought some **fruit** at the fruit store.
Ice cream and butter are **foods** that contain cholesterol.	We don't need to go shopping today. We have a lot of **food** at home.
He wrote a **paper** about hypnosis.	I need some **paper** to write my composition.
He committed three **crimes** last year.	There is a lot of **crime** in a big city.
I have two hundred **chickens** on my farm.	We ate some **chicken** for dinner.
I don't want to bore you with all my **troubles.**	I have some **trouble** with my car.
She went to Puerto Rico three **times.**	She spent a lot of **time** on her project.
She drank three **glasses** of water.	The window is made of bulletproof **glass.**
I had a bad **experience** during my trip to Paris.	She has some **experience** with computer programming.
I don't know much about the **lives** of my grandparents.	**Life** is sometimes happy, sometimes sad.
I heard a **noise** outside my window.	Those children are making a lot of **noise.**

E. To make a formal generalization

Examples	Explanation
The shark is the oldest and most primitive fish.	To say that something is true of all members of a group, use *the* with singular count nouns.
The computer has changed the way people deal with information.	To talk about a class of inventions, use *the*.
The ear has three parts: outer, middle, and inner.	To talk about an organ of the body in a general sense, use *the*.

Language Note:
For informal generalizations, use *a* + a singular noun or no article with a plural noun.
    The computer has changed the way we deal with information. (Formal)
    A computer is expensive. (Informal)
    Computers are expensive. (Informal)	

PART 3 Special Uses of Articles

No Article	Article

Personal names:
    John Kennedy
	The whole family:
	    the Kennedys

Title and name:
    Queen Elizabeth
	Title without name:
	    the Queen

Cities, states, countries, continents:
    Cleveland
    Ohio
    Mexico
    South America
	Places that are considered a union:
	    the United States
	Place names: the _____ of _____
	    the District of Columbia

Mountains:
    Mount Everest
	Mountain ranges:
	    the Rocky Mountains

Islands:
    Staten Island
	Collectives of islands:
	    the Hawaiian Islands

Lakes:
    Lake Superior
	Collectives of lakes:
	    the Great Lakes

Beaches:
    Palm Beach
    Pebble Beach
	Rivers, oceans, seas:
	    the Mississippi River
	    the Atlantic Ocean
	    the Dead Sea

Streets and avenues:
    Madison Avenue
    Wall Street
	Well-known buildings:
	    the Willis Tower
	    the Empire State Building

Parks:
    Central Park
	Zoos:
	    the San Diego Zoo

continued

No Article	Article

Seasons:
    summer   fall   spring   winter
    Summer is my favorite season.
 	
Note: After a preposition, *the* may be used.
In (the) winter, my car runs badly.
	Deserts:
	    the Mojave Desert
	    the Sahara Desert

Directions:
    north   south   east   west
	Sections of a piece of land:
	    the West Side (of New York)

School subjects:
    history   math
	Unique geographical points:
	    the North Pole the Vatican

Name + *college* or *university*:
    Northwestern University
	The University/College of _____
	    the University of Michigan

Magazines:
    Time   *Sports Illustrated*
	Newspapers:
	    the *Tribune* the *Wall Street Journal*

Months and days:
    September   Monday
	Ships:
	    the *Titanic* the *Queen Elizabeth II*

Holidays and dates:
    Mother's Day
    July 4 (month + day)
	The day of month:
	    the fifth of May
	    the Fourth of July

Diseases:
    cancer   AIDS
    polio   malaria
	Ailments:
	    a cold a toothache
	    a headache the flu

Games and sports:
    poker
    soccer
	Musical instruments, after *play*:
	    the drums the piano
	Note: Sometimes *the* is omitted.
	    She plays (the) drums.

Languages:
    English
	The _____ language:
	    the English language

Last month, year, week, etc. = the one
before this one:
    I forgot to pay my rent last month.
    The teacher gave us a test last week.
	The last month, the last year, the last
	week, etc. = the last in a series:
	    December is the last month of the year.
	    Vacation begins the last week in May.

In office = in an elected position:
    The president is in office for four years.
	In the office = in a specific room:
	    The teacher is in the office.

In back/in front:
    She's in back
    of the car.
	In the back/in the front:
	    He's in the back of the bus.

Verbs and Adjectives Followed by a Preposition

Many verbs and adjectives are followed by a preposition.

accuse someone of	(be) familiar with	(be) prepared for/to
(be) accustomed to	(be) famous for	prevent (someone) from
adjust to	(be) fond of	prohibit (someone) from
(be) afraid of	forget about	protect (someone) from
agree with	forgive someone for	(be) proud of
(be) amazed at/by	(be) glad about	recover from
(be) angry about	(be) good at	(be) related to
(be) angry at/with	(be) grateful to someone for	rely on/upon
apologize for	(be) guilty of	(be) responsible for
approve of	(be) happy about	(be) sad about
argue about	hear about	(be) satisfied with
argue with	hear of	(be) scared of
(be) ashamed of	hope for	(be) sick of
(be) aware of	(be) incapable of	(be) sorry about
believe in	insist on/upon	(be) sorry for
blame someone for	(be) interested in	speak about
(be) bored with/by	(be) involved in	speak to/with
(be) capable of	(be) jealous of	succeed in
care about	(be) known for	(be) sure of/about
care for	(be) lazy about	(be) surprised at
compare to/with	listen to	take care of
complain about	look at	talk about
concentrate on	look for	talk to/with
(be) concerned about	look forward to	thank (someone) for
consist of	(be) mad about	(be) thankful (to someone) for
count on	(be) mad at	think about/of
deal with	(be) made from/of	(be) tired of
decide on	(be) married to	(be) upset about
depend on/upon	object to	(be) upset with
(be) different from	(be) opposed to	(be) used to
disapprove of	participate in	wait for
(be) divorced from	plan on	warn (someone) about
dream about/of	pray to	(be) worried about
(be) engaged to	pray for	worry about
(be) excited about		

Direct and Indirect Objects

The order of direct and indirect objects depends on the verb we use. It also can depend on whether we use a noun or a pronoun as the object.					
Group 1	Pronouns affect word order. The preposition used is *to*.				
Patterns:	He gave a present to his wife. (DO to IO)				
	He gave his wife a present. (IO/DO)				
	He gave it to his wife. (DO to IO)				
	He gave her a present. (IO/DO)				
	He gave it to her. (DO to IO)				
Verbs:	bring	lend	pass	sell	show	teach
	give	offer	pay	send	sing	tell
	hand	owe	read	serve	take	write
Group 2	Pronouns affect word order. The preposition used is *for*.				
Patterns:	He bought a car for his daughter. (DO for IO)				
	He bought his daughter a car. (IO/DO)				
	He bought it for his daughter. (DO for IO)				
	He bought her a car. (IO/DO)				
	He bought it for her. (DO for IO)				
Verbs:	bake	buy	draw	get	make
	build	do	find	knit	reserve
Group 3	Pronouns don't affect word order. The preposition used is *to*.				
Patterns:	He explained the problem to his friend. (DO to IO)				
	He explained it to her. (DO to IO)				
Verbs:	admit	explain	prove	report	say
	announce	introduce	recommend	speak	
	describe	mention	repeat	suggest	
Group 4	Pronouns don't affect word order. The preposition used is *for*.				
Patterns:	He cashed a check for his friend. (DO for IO)				
	He cashed it for her. (DO for IO)				
Verbs:	answer	change	design	open	prescribe
	cash	close	fix	prepare	pronounce
Group 5	Pronouns don't affect word order. No preposition is used.				
Patterns:	She asked the teacher a question. (IO/DO)				
	She asked him a question. (IO/DO)				
Verbs:	ask	charge	cost	wish	take (with time)

Plural Forms of Nouns

Irregular Noun Plurals		
Singular	**Plural**	**Explanation**
man woman tooth foot goose	men women teeth feet geese	Vowel change (**Note:** The first vowel in *women* is pronounced /ɪ/.)
sheep fish deer	sheep fish deer	No change
child person mouse	children people (OR persons) mice	Different word form
alumnus cactus radius stimulus syllabus	alumni cacti (OR cactuses) radii stimuli syllabi (OR syllabuses)	*us → i*
analysis crisis hypothesis oasis parenthesis thesis	analyses crises hypotheses oases parentheses theses	*is → es*
appendix index	appendices (OR appendixes) indices (OR indexes)	*ix → ices* OR *→ ixes* *ex → ices* OR *→ exes*
bacterium curriculum datum medium memorandum criterion phenomenon	bacteria curricula data media memoranda criteria phenomena	*um → a* *ion → a* *on → a*
alga formula vertebra	algae formulae (OR formulas) vertebrae	*a → ae*

Metric Conversion Chart

Length

When You Know	Multiply by	To Find
inches (in)	2.54	centimeters (cm)
feet (ft)	30.5	centimeters (cm)
feet (ft)	0.3	meters (m)
miles (mi)	1.6	kilometers (km)
Metric:		
centimeters (cm)	0.39	inches (in)
centimeters (cm)	0.03	feet (ft)
meters (m)	3.28	feet (ft)
kilometers (km)	0.62	miles (mi)
Note: 12 inches = 1 foot 3 feet = 36 inches = 1 yard		

Weight (Mass)

When You Know	Multiply by	To Find
ounces (oz)	28.35	grams (g)
pounds (lb)	0.45	kilograms (kg)
Metric:		
grams (g)	0.04	ounces (oz)
kilograms (kg)	2.2	pounds (lb)
Note: 1 pound = 16 ounces		

continued

Volume

When You Know	Multiply by	To Find
fluid ounces (fl oz)	30.0	milliliters (mL)
pints (pt)	0.47	liters (L)
quarts (qt)	0.95	liters (L)
gallons (gal)	3.8	liters (L)
Metric:		
milliliters (mL)	0.03	fluid ounces (fl oz)
liters (L)	2.11	pints (pt)
liters (L)	1.05	quarts (qt)
liters (L)	0.26	gallons (gal)
Note:		
1 pint = 2 cups		
1 quart = 2 pints = 4 cups		
1 gallon = 4 quarts = 8 pints = 16 cups		

Temperature

When You Know	Do this	To Find
degrees Fahrenheit (°F)	Subtract 32, then multiply by $\frac{5}{9}$	degrees Celsius (°C)
Metric:		
degrees Celsius (°C)	Multiply by $\frac{9}{5}$, then add 32	degrees Fahrenheit (°F)
Note:		
32°F = 0°C		
212°F = 100°C		

Irregular Verb Forms

Base Form	Past Form	Past Participle	Base Form	Past Form	Past Participle
be	was/were	been	find	found	found
bear	bore	born/borne	fit	fit	fit
beat	beat	beaten	flee	fled	fled
become	became	become	fly	flew	flown
begin	began	begun	forbid	forbade	forbidden
bend	bent	bent	forget	forgot	forgotten
bet	bet	bet	forgive	forgave	forgiven
bid	bid	bid	freeze	froze	frozen
bind	bound	bound	get	got	gotten
bite	bit	bitten	give	gave	given
bleed	bled	bled	go	went	gone
blow	blew	blown	grind	ground	ground
break	broke	broken	grow	grew	grown
breed	bred	bred	hang	hung	hung
bring	brought	brought	have	had	had
broadcast	broadcast	broadcast	hear	heard	heard
build	built	built	hide	hid	hidden
burst	burst	burst	hit	hit	hit
buy	bought	bought	hold	held	held
cast	cast	cast	hurt	hurt	hurt
catch	caught	caught	keep	kept	kept
choose	chose	chosen	know	knew	known
cling	clung	clung	lay	laid	laid
come	came	come	lead	led	led
cost	cost	cost	leave	left	left
creep	crept	crept	lend	lent	lent
cut	cut	cut	let	let	let
deal	dealt	dealt	lie	lay	lain
dig	dug	dug	light	lit/lighted	lit/lighted
dive	dove/dived	dove/dived	lose	lost	lost
do	did	done	make	made	made
draw	drew	drawn	mean	meant	meant
drink	drank	drunk	meet	met	met
drive	drove	driven	mistake	mistook	mistaken
eat	ate	eaten	overcome	overcame	overcome
fall	fell	fallen	overdo	overdid	overdone
feed	fed	fed	overtake	overtook	overtaken
feel	felt	felt	overthrow	overthrew	overthrown
fight	fought	fought	pay	paid	paid

continued

Base Form	Past Form	Past Participle	Base Form	Past Form	Past Participle
plead	pled/pleaded	pled/pleaded	sting	stung	stung
prove	proved	proven/proved	stink	stank	stunk
put	put	put	strike	struck	struck/stricken
quit	quit	quit	strive	strove	striven
read	read	read	swear	swore	sworn
ride	rode	ridden	sweep	swept	swept
ring	rang	rung	swell	swelled	swelled/swollen
rise	rose	risen	swim	swam	swum
run	ran	run	swing	swung	swung
say	said	said	take	took	taken
see	saw	seen	teach	taught	taught
seek	sought	sought	tear	tore	torn
sell	sold	sold	tell	told	told
send	sent	sent	think	thought	thought
set	set	set	throw	threw	thrown
sew	sewed	sewn/sewed	understand	understood	understood
shake	shook	shaken	uphold	upheld	upheld
shed	shed	shed	upset	upset	upset
shine	shone/shined	shone/shined	wake	woke	woken
shoot	shot	shot	wear	wore	worn
show	showed	shown/showed	weave	wove	woven
shrink	shrank/shrunk	shrunk/shrunken	wed	wedded/wed	wedded/wed
shut	shut	shut	weep	wept	wept
sing	sang	sung	win	won	won
sink	sank	sunk	wind	wound	wound
sit	sat	sat	withdraw	withdrew	withdrawn
sleep	slept	slept	withhold	withheld	withheld
slide	slid	slid	withstand	withstood	withstood
slit	slit	slit	wring	wrung	wrung
speak	spoke	spoken	write	wrote	written
speed	sped	sped			
spend	spent	spent			
spin	spun	spun			
spit	spit/spat	spit/spat			
split	split	split			
spread	spread	spread			
spring	sprang	sprung			
stand	stood	stood			
steal	stole	stolen			
stick	stuck	stuck			

Note:

The past and past participle of some verbs can end in *-ed* or *-t*.

burn	burned or burnt
dream	dreamed or dreamt
kneel	kneeled or knelt
learn	learned or learnt
leap	leaped or leapt
spill	spilled or spilt
spoil	spoiled or spoilt

Map of the United States of America

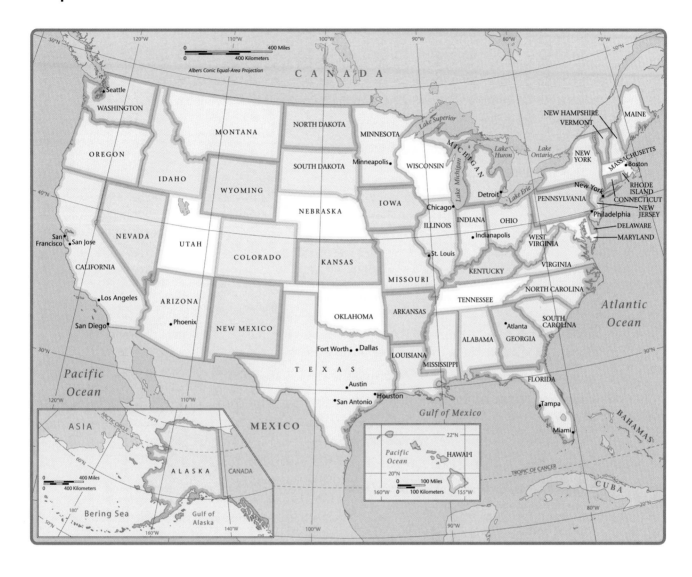

- **Adjective** An adjective gives a description of a noun.

  It's a *tall* tree.   He's an *old* man.   My neighbors are *nice*.

- **Adverb** An adverb describes the action of a sentence or an adjective or another adverb.

  She speaks English *fluently*.   I drive *carefully*.

  She speaks English *extremely* well.   She is *very* intelligent.

- **Adverb of Frequency** An adverb of frequency tells how often an action happens.

  I *never* drink coffee.   They *usually* take the bus.

- **Affirmative** *Affirmative* means "yes."

  They *live* in Miami.

- **Apostrophe** ' We use the apostrophe for possession and contractions.

  My *sister's* friend is beautiful. (possession)

  Today *isn't* Sunday. (contraction)

- **Article** An article comes before a noun. It tells if the noun is definite or indefinite. The definite article is *the*. The indefinite articles are *a* and *an*.

  I have *a* cat.   I ate *an* apple.   *The* teacher came late.

- **Auxiliary Verb** An auxiliary verb is used in forming tense, mood, or aspect of the verb that follows it. Some verbs have two parts: an auxiliary verb and a main verb.

  You *didn't* eat lunch.   He *can't* study.   We *will* return.

- **Base Form** The base form of the verb has no tense. It has no ending (*-s* or *-ed*): *be, go, eat, take, write*.

  I didn't *go*.   We don't *know* you.   He can't *drive*.

- **Capital Letter** A B C D E F G . . .

- **Clause** A clause is a group of words that has a subject and a verb. Some sentences have only one clause.

  She speaks Spanish.

  Some sentences have a **main clause** and a **dependent clause**.

MAIN CLAUSE	DEPENDENT CLAUSE (**reason clause**)
She found a good job	because she has computer skills.

MAIN CLAUSE	DEPENDENT CLAUSE (**time clause**)
She'll turn off the light	before she goes to bed.

MAIN CLAUSE	DEPENDENT CLAUSE (***if* clause**)
I'll take you to the doctor	if you don't have your car on Saturday.

- **Colon** :

- **Comma** ,

- **Comparative** The comparative form of an adjective or adverb is used to compare two things.

    My house is *bigger* than your house.

    Her husband drives *faster* than she does.

    My children speak English *more fluently* than I do.

- **Consonant** The following letters are consonants: *b, c, d, f, g, h, j, k, l, m, n, p, q, r, s, t, v, w, x, y, z.*

    NOTE: *Y* is sometimes considered a vowel, as in the world *syllable*.

- **Contraction** A contraction is two words joined with an apostrophe.

    He's my brother.   *You're* late.   They *won't* talk to me.

    (*He's = he is*)   (*You're = you are*)   (*won't = will not*)

- **Count Noun** Count nouns are nouns that we can count. They have a singular and a plural form.

    1 pen–3 pens   1 table–4 tables

- **Dependent Clause** See **Clause**.

- **Direct Object** A direct object is a noun (phrase) or pronoun that receives the action of the verb.

    We saw *the movie*.   You have *a nice car*.   I love *you*.

- **Exclamation Mark** !

- **Frequency Word** Frequency words (*always, usually, generally, often, sometimes, rarely, seldom, hardly ever, never.*) tell how often an action happens.

    I *never* drink coffee.   We *always* do our homework.

- **Hyphen** -

- **Imperative** An imperative sentence gives a command or instructions. An imperative sentence omits the subject pronoun *you*.

    Come here.   *Don't be* late.   Please *help* me.

- **Infinitive** An infinitive is *to* + the base form.

    I want to *leave*.   You need *to be* here on time.

- **Linking Verb** A linking verb is a verb that links the subject to the noun, adjective, or adverb after it. Linking verbs include *be, seem, feel, smell, sound, look, appear,* and *taste*.

    She *is* a doctor.   She *looks* tired.   You *are* late.

- **Main Clause** See **Clause**.

- **Modal** The modal verbs are *can, could, shall, should, will, would, may, might,* and *must.*

    They *should* leave.   I *must* go.

- **Negative** *Negative* means "no."

- **Nonaction Verb** A nonaction verb has no action. We do not use a continuous tense (*be +* verb -*ing*) with a nonaction verb. The nonaction verbs are: *believe, cost, care, have, hear, know, like, love, matter, mean, need, own, prefer, remember, see, seem, think, understand, want,* and sense-perception verbs.

    She *has* a laptop.   We *love* our mother.   You *look* great.

- **Noncount Noun** A noncount noun is a noun that we don't count. It has no plural form.

    She drank some *water.*   He prepared some *rice.*

    Do you need any *money?*   We had a lot of *homework.*

- **Noun** A noun is a person, a place, or a thing. Nouns can be either count or noncount.

    My *brother* lives in California.   My *sisters* live in New York.

    I get *advice* from them.   I drink *coffee* every day.

- **Noun Modifier** A noun modifier makes a noun more specific.

    fire department   *Independence* Day   *can* opener

- **Noun Phrase** A noun phrase is a group of words that form the subject or object of the sentence.

    A very nice woman helped me.   I bought *a big box of cereal.*

- **Object** The object of the sentence follows the verb. It receives the action of the verb.

    He bought *a car.*   I saw *a movie.*   I met *your brother.*

- **Object Pronoun** We use object pronouns (*me, you, him, her, it, us, them*) after the verb or preposition.

    He likes *her.*   I saw the movie. Let's talk about *it.*

- **Parentheses** ( )

- **Paragraph** A paragraph is a group of sentences about one topic.

- **Past Participle** The past participle of a verb is the third form of the verb.

    You have *written* a good essay.   I was *told* about the concert.

- **Period** .

- **Phrasal Modal** Phrasal modals, such as *ought to, be able to,* are made up of two or more words.

    You *ought to* study more.   We *have to* take a test.

- **Phrase** A group of words that go together.

    Last month my sister came to visit.   There is a strange car *in front of my house.*

- **Plural** *Plural* means "more than one." A plural noun usually ends with -*s.*

    She has beautiful *eyes.*   My *feet* are big.

- **Possessive Form** Possessive forms show ownership or relationship.

    Mary's coat is in the closet.   *My* brother lives in Miami.

- **Preposition** A preposition is a short connecting word. Some common prepositions include *about, above, across, after, around, as, at, away, back, before, behind, below, by, down, for, from, in, into, like, of, off, on, out, over, to, under, up,* and *with.*

    The book is *on* the table.   She studies *with* her friends.

- **Present Participle** The present participle of a verb is the base form + *-ing.*

    She is *sleeping.*   They were *laughing.*

- **Pronoun** A pronoun takes the place of a noun.

    I have a new car. I bought *it* last week.

    John likes Mary, but *she* doesn't like *him.*

- **Punctuation** The use of specific marks, such as commas and periods, to make ideas within writing clear.

- **Question Mark** ?

- **Quotation Marks** " "

- **Regular Verb** A regular verb forms its past tense with *-ed.*

    He *worked* yesterday.   I *laughed* at the joke.

- **-s Form** A present tense verb that ends in *-s* or *-es.*

    He *lives* in New York.   She *watches* TV a lot.

- **Sense-Perception Verb** A sense-perception verb has no action. It describes a sense. The sense-perception verbs are: *look, feel, taste, sound,* and *smell.*

    She *feels* fine.   The coffee *smells* fresh.   The milk *tastes* sour.

- **Sentence** A sentence is a group of words that contains a subject and a verb and gives a complete thought.

    SENTENCE: She came home.

    NOT A SENTENCE: When she came home

- **Singular** *Singular* means "one."

    She ate a *sandwich.*   I have one *television.*

- **Subject** The subject of the sentence tells who or what the sentence is about.

    My sister got married last April. *The wedding* was beautiful.

- **Subject Pronoun** We use a subject pronoun (*I, you, he, she, it, we, you, they*) before a verb.

    They speak Japanese.   *We* speak Spanish.

- **Superlative** The superlative form of an adjective or adverb shows the number one item in a group of three or more.

    January is the *coldest* month of the year.

    My brother speaks English the *best* in my family.

- **Syllable** A syllable is a part of a word. Each syllable has only one vowel sound. (Some words have only one syllable.)

    change (one syllable)   after (af·ter = two syllables)

    look (one syllable)   responsible (re·spon·si·ble = four syllables)

- **Tag Question** A tag question is a short question at the end of a sentence. It is used in conversation.

    You speak Spanish, *don't you*?   He's not happy, *is he*?

- **Tense** Tense shows when the action of the sentence happened. Verbs have different tenses.

    SIMPLE PRESENT: She usually *works* hard.

    PRESENT CONTINUOUS: She *is working* now.

    SIMPLE PAST: She *worked* yesterday.

    FUTURE: She *will work* tomorrow.

- **Verb** A verb is the action of the sentence.

    He *runs* fast.   I *speak* English.

- **Vowel** The following letters are vowels: *a, e, i, o, u.*

    NOTE: *Y* is sometimes considered a vowel, as in the world *syllable*.

INDEX

of *used to/be used to/get used to*, 241

Negative statements
    with *be*, present, 5
    with *be*, simple past, 25
    with *be going to*, 19
    with irregular verb, 25
    with modals, 135
    with passive voice, 75
    with present continuous, 13
    with present perfect continuous, 62
    with regular verb, 25
    with *–s* form, 7
    with simple present, 7
    with *will*, 19
    with *yet*, 48

Never
    with present perfect, 65
    with present perfect vs. *ever*, 45
    with present perfect with indefinite past time, 43

Never . . . before, 112
Nevertheless, 270
Nonaction verbs, 16, 118
Noncount nouns, AP2–3
    after *too much*, 226
    with *so much/so little*, 273
Nonessential adjective clauses, 200–201, 203
Not . . . yet with past perfect, 112
Not have to, 146
Noun clauses, 283–312
    after adjectives, 283
    after verbs, 283, 305
    as exact quotes, 294–295
    as included questions, 287–288
    as reported questions, 306
    as reported speech, 306
    defined, 115, 283
    included questions shortened to infinitive, 291
    introduction, 283
    past perfect in, 115
    question words followed by infinitive, 291
    reporting an imperative, 301
    rule of sequence of tenses, 296, 300, 306
    say vs. *tell*, 298
    summary, 310
    using reported speech to paraphrase, 302

Nouns
    contraction with *has*, 37
    count and noncount
        with *so . . . that/so much . . . that*, 273
        after *too many/too much*, 226
    gerunds after, 231
    gerunds as, 229
    plural forms, 7, AP10
    possessive form *whose*, 195
    prepositions after, 233

O

Objects
    and transitive verbs, 84
    before infinitives, 216
    direct, 82, AP9
    indirect, 82, 298, AP9
    of prepositions, relative pronouns as, 190
    relative pronouns as, 187
    with verbs and prepositions, 232
Obligation, with *must, have to*, and *have got to*, 137
Opportunity not taken, with *could have*, 170
Ought to, 141

P

Paraphrasing, in reported speech, 302, 306
Participial phrases after time words, 261
Participles, 91–96
    summary, 96
    used as adjectives, 91, 94
Passive voice, 72–85, 96
    adverbs with, 75
    agents in, 75, 79
    compared to active voice, 75, 76, 79
    form, 75
    introduction, 75
    patterns with past, 75
    pronouns in, 75
    summary, 96
    transitive verbs and, 84–85
    use, 79
    verb tenses with, 76
    verbs with two objects, 82
    with gerunds, 229
    with get, 88
    with infinitives, 213

    with modals, 135, 163
    with past continuous, 76, 103
    with past perfect, 110
Past, 25
Past continuous, 103–108
    active vs. passive voices in, 76
    adverbs with, 103
    compared to other past tenses, 123
    form, 103
    present participle with, 103
    summary, 128
    use, 104
    vs. simple past, 106
    with passive voice, 103
    with simple past, 104
Past direction not taken, with *could have*, 170
Past participle, 38, AP13–14
    adverbs before, 94
    and placement of adverbs, 39
    be with, 94
    in descriptive phrases, 203
    of irregular verbs, 38
    of regular verbs, 38
    summary, 96
    used as adjectives, 91, 94
    with *get* vs. *be*, 95
    with passive voice, 75
    with past perfect, 110
    with present perfect, 37
    with unreal conditionals in the past, 328
Past perfect continuous, 117–121
    compared to other past tenses, 123
    form, 117
    present participle with, 117
    summary, 128
    use, 118
    vs. present perfect continuous, 120
    with adverbs, 117
Past perfect, 110–116
    compared to other past tenses, 123
    form, 110
    in adjective clauses, 115
    in noun clauses, 115
    or simple past, with *when*, 114
    summary, 128
    use, 112, 115
    vs. present perfect, 120